THIS BUSINESS OF

Artist
Management

Revised and Enlarged Third Edition

Xavier M. Frascogna, Jr. and H. Lee Hetherington

BILLBOARD BOOKS

AN IMPRINT OF WATSON-GUPTILL PUBLICATIONS

NEW YORK

For Fran, Bernadean, and Frank

This edition first published in 1997 in the United States by Billboard Books, an imprint of Watson-Guptill Publications, a division of BPI Communications, Inc., 1515 Broadway, New York, NY 10036-8986

Library of Congress Cataloging-in-Publication Data
Frascogna, Xavier M., 1946-
    This business of artist management / Xavier M. Frascogna, Jr. and
  H. Lee Hetherington.— Rev. and enl. ed.
        p.   cm.
    Includes index.
    ISBN 0-8230-7705-5
    1. Music trade—United States.   2. Music—Economic aspects.
  3. Performing arts—Vocational guidance.   I. Hetherington, H. Lee,
  1948-   .   II. Title.
  ML3790.F7   1997
  791'.0068—dc21   96-52598
                                                        CIP
                                                        MN
Manufactured in the United States of America

Senior editor: Bob Nirkind
Designers: Areta Buk, Jay Anning
Production manager: Hector Campbell

1 2 3 4 5 / 01 00 99 98 97

Contents

PART ONE

Establishing the Artist–Manager Relationship   1

1	OVERVIEW	2
2	LAUNCHING A CAREER: THE FIRST STEP	13
3	FINDING A MANAGER/FINDING AN ARTIST	20
4	ASKING THE RIGHT QUESTIONS	34
5	THE MANAGEMENT CONTRACT	45

PART TWO

Planning the Artist's Career   63

6	TAKING CARE OF BUSINESS	64
7	ATTORNEYS, ACCOUNTANTS, AND BUSINESS MANAGERS	77
8	TAKING CREATIVE INVENTORY	83
9	CREATING THE CAREER PLAN	97

PART THREE

Making the Plan Work   105

10	MAKING YOUR OWN BREAKS	106
11	THE ARTIST'S DEVELOPMENT TEAM	114
12	THE RECORD DEAL	122
13	MUSIC PUBLISHING	143
14	MUSIC VIDEOS, TV, RADIO, AND FILM	158
15	PERSONAL APPEARANCES	171
16	MERCHANDISING, COMMERCIALS, AND CORPORATE SPONSORSHIPS	183
17	THINKING GLOBALLY	194

PART FOUR

Career Maintenance and Control   203

18	THE MANAGER'S JUGGLING ACT	204
19	HELPING THE RECORD COMPANY HELP YOU	214
20	MANAGING THE ROAD	223
21	CAREER REVIEW AND EVALUATION	233

PART FIVE

Mastering Success   **241**

22 COPING WITH THE STRESS OF SUCCESS   242

23 HOLDING ON TO YOUR MONEY   251

24 STARDOM AND BEYOND   257

Appendices   **262**

1   AMERICAN FEDERATION OF MUSICIANS
    AGENT–MUSICIAN AGREEMENT   262

2   AF OF M PERFORMANCE CONTRACT
    (LOCAL ENGAGEMENTS)   265

3   AF OF M PERFORMANCE CONTRACT (TOURING)   266

4   BROADCAST MUSIC, INC. (BMI)
    WRITER AGREEMENT   267

5   SONGWRITERS GUILD OF AMERICA
    WRITER–PUBLISHER CONTRACT   271

6   POPULAR SONGWRITERS CONTRACT   276

7   EXCLUSIVE SONGWRITER CONTRACT   278

8   MANAGEMENT AGREEMENT   280

9   RECORDING CONTRACT (EXCERPTS)   287

10 ORGANIZATIONS, UNIONS, AND GUILDS   295

INDEX 296

Acknowledgments

This book is the product of the authors' nearly thirty years of experience as agents, managers, performers, lawyers, and law teachers. Since the first edition of this book was written and published under the title *Successful Artist Management,* in 1979, we have been extremely fortunate to have been assisted by many industry professionals who have freely and generously shared their knowledge and insights with us. To each of them we offer our thanks: Ed Benson, Gary Borman, Tom Carrico, Connie Bradley, Tim DuBois, Cecille Edwards, Henry Green, Scott Hendricks, Rush Hicks, Wade Jesson, Ken Kragen, Larry Latimer, Scott Mateer, Marc Oswald, David Ross, Bud Schaetzle, Evelyn Shriver, Bill Simmons, James Stroud, Steve Weaver, Dr. Larry Wacholtz, Doug Williams, Melvin Williams, and Walt Wilson.

Also, we thank once again the individuals who helped us with this and/or with earlier editions of this book: Paul Adler, Buddy Allen, Steve Allen, Robert Altshuler, Billy Arnell, Larry Baunach, Sid Bernstein, Marty Blackman, Lorraine Bobruk, Woody Bowles, Nat Burgess, Buzz Cason, Terry Cline, Mario Conti, Ezra Cook, Paul Corbin, Marilyn Craig, Mike Daniel, Stewart Fine, Jim Foglesong, Greg Frascogna, Steve Gatlin, Gina Gaylord, Mark Goldstein, Juanita Elefante Gordon, Cathy Gurley, Gail Hamilton, Mike Hightower, Frank Jones, C. W. Kendall, Barry Knittel, Al Kugler, Judy Libow, Steve Loeb, David Ludwick, Kathryn Lumpkin, David Maddox, Bill Martin, Brad McCuen, Jim Morey, Tom Noonan, Max Okun, Chip Peay, Ralph Peer II, Diane Petty, Judi Pfosky, Michael J. Pollack, Frances Preston, Bob Reno, Emma Sansing, Ed Shea, David Skepner, Debbie Smith, Doyle Smith, Roy Smith, Jimmy Walker, Josh Wattles, Larry Welch, Gerry Wood, and Rolland Yancey.

Additionally, we acknowledge the special contributioins of the following companies and firms: American Federation of Musicians, Arista Records, American Society of Composers, Authors & Publishers, *Billboard* magazine, Bridge Entertainment, Broadcast Music, Inc., Conference of Personal Managers, Harry Fox Agency, David L. Maddox & Associates PC, Peermusic, SESAC, the Songwriters Guild of America, and Warner Brothers Records.

Special thanks go to Bob Nirkind, Dale Ramsey, and Paul Lukas of Watson-Guptill Publications, in New York; Norm Rowland and Linda Schreiner, in Nashville; and Shawnassey Howell-Hotard, Carolyn Turner, Gladys Purser, and Patsy Hall, in Jackson. We are also grateful to Mississippi College School of Law, and especially to Richard Hurt, Dean of the Law School, Howell Todd, President of the College, and our colleagues on the law faculty, for their support.

And finally to our wives Judy and Michelle and all the many friends and family who have provided encouragement and support over the years, a sincere "thank you" for the many large and small contributions you have made along the way.

X. M. FRASCOGNA, JR.
H. LEE HETHERINGTON
June 1997

PART ONE

Establishing the Artist-Manager Relationship

Overview

Show business has been around for as long as there have been singers, dancers, musicians, and audiences willing to pay to see and hear them. But it was not until the 1950s, with the advent of rock and roll, along with modern technology and mass marketing techniques, that the music business began to evolve into the complex, multi-billion-dollar industry it is today. In those early days, the music business was first dominated by publishers who controlled the best songs and, later, by record companies who controlled the means of making, promoting, and distributing recordings to the public.

The profile of a recording artist in the early days of rock, country, or rhythm and blues was most often that of a young, starstruck, unsophisticated teenager, usually male, whose talent and ambition were his two primary assets. Almost without exception, these singers, performers, and sometime songwriters were without a clue about the business and legal matters that so vitally affected their careers. This absence of knowledge and experience made most artists the pawns of producers, publishers, and promoters—and of the contracts that bound artists to them. If the artist was talented, lucky, and hooked up with honest and capable people, they prospered. If not . . . well, we have all heard the horror stories.

Even if success came their way, too much fame and too much money too soon, coupled with the dangers of the road, made show business a high-risk calling. Hank Williams, Buddy Holly, Otis Redding, Janis Joplin, Jimi Hendrix, Sam Cook, Elvis Presley, and a hundred more sadly prove the point. And then there are those thousands of promising artists who briefly tasted the thrill of a hit record or a sold-out concert. How many have been the victim of a fickle change in public taste that turned their careers into memories and their dreams into what might have been?

But this obvious downside of being an artist is not enough to overcome the powerful lure of fame and fortune and the overwhelming artistic drive planted deep in the souls of the truly creative people who are called to the stage and studio. Year in and year out, the entertainment industry continues to draw aspiring singers, writers, and performers in numbers that far exceed the available opportunities for success. Despite the overwhelming odds, aspiring artists answer the creative call of their souls to seek their place in the complex, competitive, frustrating, yet exhilarating world called the entertainment industry. Chances are you are one of them. It is for you that this book has been written.

This book is also written for another class of people. Managers don't sing, write, or perform, yet they are oftentimes the critical difference between success and failure for those who do. It is also for the alter-egos, advisers, and friends who, by design or circumstance, will agree to take that roller-coaster ride called a career with their artist-clients that we have written this book.

As authors we have, over the years, collectively played the roles of both artist and manager. Unfortunately, we were forced to rely mostly on our instincts, common sense, and lessons learned by experience—usually painful—to find our way through the tough world of show biz. And we wouldn't have traded one minute of it. But it could have been easier, and our efforts more effective—which brings us back to you, the reader. Despite the promise of big money, heavy-duty ego gratification, extensive travel, and a job that allows you to sleep late and not wear a tie, music is first and foremost a *business*.

Now if you don't care how much you make and keep, you need not read any further. Go out, play and sing, and have fun. If you are fortunate enough to be independently wealthy, you won't need the money and can reap most of the other benefits, provided you are good enough to get work. But if you want to take a serious shot at earning a living in the music business, this book is for you. We have done our best to give you a blueprint for beating or at least improving the odds of making it in what is probably the most competitive industry this side of professional sports and national politics.

Drawing from our backgrounds and collective experiences, as well as the advice gleaned from over a hundred interviews with some of the most successful players in the music business, we seek to provide you with information and insights with which each one of you will be able to make better and more effective career decisions. Because very little happens by itself in the music business, this book is also a tool which incorporates goal-directed career-planning techniques essential to achieving and maintaining success in the industry. Finally, we offer approaches that we hope will help you recognize and make the most of any given opportunity. This book, when taken as a whole, will serve as both a catalyst and a guide for artists and managers, systematically showing them how to develop a career philosophy built on optimism, realism, self-discipline, hard work and good judgment.

GOOD NEWS, BAD NEWS

Before we get into specifics, we feel obligated to give you the good and bad news about your career choice. First the bad news: You have a better statistical chance of being struck by lightning than of having a number-one hit record. Because of the sheer numbers of aspiring recording artists, musicians, and songwriters attracted by the apparent glamour associated with the entertainment industry, show business is in reality a "no" business. No one in the executive offices of record companies located in Los Angeles, New York, or on Nashville's Music Row is holding their breath in anticipation of your arrival. And when you or your audition tape do arrive, their first inclination will be to tell you "no" to the career you so badly want.

So what's new? And while this is bad news, there is worse news. If your self-concept allows you to view yourself as merely a statistic, rather than a unique artist with something to say, or if you are the type who folds up your tent at the first hint of rejection, then there is a certified, one-hundred-percent certainty that you will not have that number-one hit record. So if you are serious, you had better toughen your hide. And that tape had better be good—no, it had better be great!

Now for the good news. There has never been a better time in the history of show business for an aspiring artist to make it into the select circle of stardom. Why? Several very logical reasons.

1. Worldwide demand for entertainment is growing at a frantic pace. This demand is driven by an improved standard of living almost everywhere in the industrialized world.

2. This greater worldwide affluence is coupled with a dazzling array of technology that has and will continue to revolutionize the marketing and distribution of all forms of entertainment while reducing production costs of entertainment products. Translation: There will be more and cheaper creative outlets for more artists.

3. These creative efforts will be financed by ever larger, more affluent, and receptive audiences around the globe. While other countries have taken the lead from America in producing steel, automobiles, and computer chips, no one even approaches the United States when it comes to producing compact disks, concerts, videos, movies, and television programs. In fact, entertainment products recently eclipsed aerospace as the leading U.S. export to the rest of the world. One need only look at the big-money jockeying of international media conglomerates—Time-Warner, Disney, Sony, and the rest—to confirm the bright financial potential for entertainment products.

4. As a consequence, a vast, integrated worldwide marketing and distribution system for entertainment is in place and growing. And the lifeblood of this industry is the creative individual artist.

So, while those music executives in Los Angeles, New York, and Nashville don't appear to be waiting for you to show up at their doors, in fact they desperately are. Their fat paychecks and perks depend on you and only you. No new hits and no new stars, and they'll be replaced. Believe us, if they could make hit records themselves, they would.

Another major portion of the good news relates to the emergence of the celebrity-artist as the focal point of this integrated industry. As James Stroud, one of the country's most successful record producers based in Nashville, puts it: "We are in the age of the multimedia artist." Just having a great voice is no longer enough. Today's recording artist is by necessity a video artist and is often an actor, writer, commercial spokesperson, and always a celebrity. Artists like Michael Jackson and Reba McEntire illustrate the point. In short, the public requires stars. That spells unlimited opportunity for the artist capable of giving the public what it wants. This rare and elusive ability also means unprecedented power for those artists talented, smart, and lucky enough to make it into the spotlight and stay there.

ARTIST MANAGEMENT: WHAT IS IT?

Artist management—everybody in the business tosses the term around, but what exactly does it encompass? Usually we think of a manager as the artist's personal representative. While this is generally true, it still doesn't tell us what managers do or how they do it. More importantly, it provides little information on how you can make better decisions on behalf of your clients if you are already a manager, or how you can make better decisions about your career if you are an artist trying to make it in the music business. That's what this book is all about.

THE ROLE OF THE MANAGER

Actually, artist management consists of anything that will help enhance or further an artist's career. This can range from comprehensive career planning or complex contract negotiation to suggesting a lyric change in a song or commenting on a new recording. The personal manager is the alter-ego of the artist, the part of the artist the audience never sees. An artist's manager is a planner, adviser, organizer, strategist, overseer, manipulator, coordinator, detail person, traveling companion, and friend. The manager's involvement in an artist's career is total in scope and crucial to its success. In fact, the manager is the only other individual, besides the artist, who gets to see and touch all the jigsaw puzzle pieces that fit together to create the artist's career.

Certain types of managers have narrowly defined duties. A business manager, for example, will ordinarily not be involved in creative decisions or day-to-day details. Rather, it's his or her function to take care of the books, make sure the bills are paid, and be responsible for making other business-related decisions. In other instances, the manager might be totally involved in every detail of the artist's career from both a business and creative standpoint.

In the final analysis, the role a manager plays is directly dependent on the needs of the artist, the capabilities of the manager, and what both of them are willing and able to bring to the relationship. Probably the closest analogy is that of a good marriage. To succeed, it takes a lot of hard work along with a willingness to communicate, compromise, and change as the relationship grows and new challenges are presented. Above all, a good marriage requires a strong sense of mutual trust and the ability to see things as they are.

"Why do I need a manager?" It's a question often posed by artists, especially those inexperienced in the realities of the music business who would prefer to avoid paying a management commission. The answer might indeed be: "Maybe you don't need a manager—but you sure need management." The two aren't necessarily interchangeable.

Granted, not every artist's career is complex enough to merit a full-time manager, especially at the outset. But if the artist is to have any chance of making it, his or her career demands at least as much management as there is talent and ambition. Much of this will be driven by the artist's goals. If you aspire to play local clubs on the weekends for fun and a little money, there is no reason to pay someone else to perform basic management functions. However, as your ambitions and the demands on your time grow, you will have little choice but to retain someone to handle these responsibilities.

MANAGEMENT AND RECORD DEALS

Because the record deal drives everything else, an artist or manager must do whatever is necessary to connect with that faceless record executive who holds the key to the artist's future. A "yes" from that label exec can mean a commitment by the record company of half a million dollars and more to cover recording costs, video production, tour support, promotion budget, and so on. Have no doubt that the executive who "green-lights" your deal expects to recoup all of that and a whole lot more. Covering costs and making a healthy profit is what allows a record company to meet its quarterly income targets and provide that label's executive with a nice bonus, not to mention job security. If he or she harbors any serious doubt about you and your ability to recoup the company's investment, the executive will look elsewhere. Getting the picture?

The high-stakes risks associated with breaking a new artist or keeping an established artist on top is precisely why talent alone is never enough. That record executive has a lot of talent to choose from, but never enough artists and managers capable of doing all the big and little things that spell success. Specifically, that record executive wants an artist who sets goals, who plans, who executes, who follows up. He or she wants someone capable of interacting effectively with a seemingly unending stream of producers, agents, publishers, promoters, publicists, program directors, roadies, lawyers, bankers, accountants, and fans—all competing for a few minutes of the artist's time. That record exec wants someone with enough drive and discipline to return phone calls, sign autographs, do interviews, and deal with the ongoing pressure of endless details that won't wait until next week and still have enough energy left to put on a killer concert or do as many studio takes as are necessary to get a recording right.

Making sure those things get done is the essence of management, or at least part of management. Lacking that, record executives will most likely respond with a terse "Pass." Can you blame them? Even if the response is positive, the record company will surely insist that the artist retain experienced management as a condition to signing a record deal.

The bottom line is this: If you, the artist, can effectively handle all management-related responsibilities, then by all means do so, and save the commission. There's no sense in paying someone else to do what you can do just as well for yourself. However, if you can't, then maybe you do need a manager. More on this in the next chapter.

QUALIFICATIONS OF A MANAGER

If you're starting to get a handle on the what and how of management, consider a few more essentials to fold into the equation. The best managers, just like the best business executives, are planners. They are also catalysts that make things happen; movers, motivators, and communicators who work with record companies, producers, agents, promoters, publicists, and anyone else with a stake in the artist's career. The objective is simple: To make sure everyone pulls together with effectiveness and enthusiasm to make the artist shine. If that sounds like a tough order, just know that the reality of doing it consistently is even tougher.

Jim Morey, who has guided the careers of such diverse artists as Neil Diamond, the Pointer Sisters, and Dolly Parton, summed it up best: "The artist is the corporation; the manager is the CEO." If you need any more parallels, take a look at successful corporations and their chief executives. The process is the same; only the product is different.

The next obvious question is, "Who can be a manager?" The answer is simple: "Anybody." There are no universities offering degrees in artist management, although there are several very good commercial-music programs in music centers such as Belmont University in Nashville. Aside from a few states, the most notable being California, there are few if any requirements or qualifications a manager must meet. On the whole, artist management is wide open to anyone who wants to get involved. Relatively easy access to the field, coupled with little or no regulation, can potentially open the door to well-meaning incompetents as well as unscrupulous con artists whose livelihood is victimizing unsuspecting artists. Chapters 3 and 4 discuss techniques for recognizing and avoiding both types of would-be managers.

Many people earn their livelihood exclusively from the personal or business management of artists. They may work as individuals or as part of a corporate team. Other successful and competent managers have dual professions as practicing attorneys, accountants, or financial consultants. Because of their special qualifications or skills, they may be able to offer an artist more versatility. By the same measure, the artist should be certain that these dual-role individuals are as capable as managers as they are in their primary professions.

One basic requirement is practical experience in entertainment management. Booking agents, record producers, and music publishers may also double as managers, though the artist should guard against possible conflict-of-interest problems. These issues will be discussed in more depth in later chapters.

In addition to these traditional categories, friends and relatives may also serve as managers by virtue of their close personal relationship to the artist. When selecting a manager, a new artist may tend to choose a friend or relative, rather than seeking a professional with whom he or she has had no prior relationship. This is natural and understandable, but it may not be the best career decision. Often a friend or relative, while being well-meaning, will not possess the knowledge, experience, or contacts necessary to further the artist's career beyond a limited point. There's also the danger that, because of this close personal relationship, a friend or relative will not stand up to the artist and say "no" when firmness and objectivity are required. A "yes-man" may be an asset to an artist's ego but is of no value to meaningful career development. This is not to say that a friend or relative may not prove to be the right manager for a particular artist. We're only suggesting that the artist should make a special effort to look objectively when assessing a friend's or relative's strengths and weaknesses. If you find your judgment beginning to cloud, just remember those record executives working overtime to hit the parent corporation's profit projections. It's business first for them; it should be for you, too.

WHAT A MANAGER ISN'T

While a manager seems to have more responsibilities than a dozen neurotic overachievers, there are things he or she should not be expected to do to earn a management fee, unless certain duties are specifically agreed to by the parties. For instance, a manager is not a booking or theatrical agent. In California, such a dual role is prohibited by statute. In states where there is no such law, it is traditionally not the manager's responsibility to seek employment for the artist. This is the function of an agent specializing in this type of work who collects a fee that is separate and distinct from the manager's compensation.

It is, however, the manager's responsibility to locate agents willing to seek employment for the artist. It is also the manager's responsibility to accept or reject dates and coordinate the artist's schedule with those agents. This isn't to say that a manager may not be directly responsible, because of certain opportunities or contacts, for a booking now and then (subject to state law), but the artist should remember that the manager is generally under no obligation to do this.

Likewise, a manager is not normally a record producer. If a manager does fill this role by virtue of special expertise and experience, the artist and manager should work out provisions in the management contract for fair compensation for these additional duties.

A manager shouldn't be expected to promote, exploit, and administer copyrighted musical compositions written by the artist. This is the function of a music publisher. As in the case of dual arrangements for record production and management, there are usually separate forms of compensation to cover these added duties.

In certain situations, an attorney or accountant who also serves as a manager will command a higher percentage or fee because of the added dimension of expertise and additional services rendered. This doesn't mean that an artist's manager is required to also perform legal or accounting tasks because he or she possesses this special expertise. This is a matter to be resolved in the management contract under the section dealing with definition of duties and manager's compensation.

In addition to the foregoing major overlap areas, the personal manager should also be distinguished from a publicist, graphics specialist, choreographer, recording engineer, studio musician, side man, road manager, or songwriting partner.

The final substantive area of overlap and conflict involving artist's managers has to do with money. The manager is not a banker and should not be expected to make loans or gifts to the artists or to pay for business or personal expenses. However, there are exceptions. There have been and will continue to be wealthy and not-so-wealthy managers who sink a great deal of their own money into an artist's career. As with any investment, there are some dazzling success stories and probably a lot more tax writeoffs.

There is certainly nothing wrong with a manager investing more than just time in an artist, provided both parties go into such an arrangement with their eyes wide open. One potentially unfavorable consideration for the artist is the likelihood that he or she will be expected to give up a much greater percentage of future income in the form of a higher management commission when cash from the manager has been involved. One only need review some of the sad examples from professional boxing, where more than one heavyweight sold 150 percent of himself for some easy front money. The best advice here is for both parties to be represented by counsel and to spell out any such arrangement fully and completely in the management agreement. If there is a subsequent change in practice or policy, put it in writing.

Finally, artists tempted by generous offers of advances should remember that loans are just that. Those checks are easy to cash and a whole lot tougher to pay back.

THREE FUNDAMENTAL TRUTHS

Other than applying honesty, diligence, and time-tested principles of interpersonal relations, there is no single right or wrong way to manage a show-business career. This conclusion is supported by interviews we conducted with artists' managers and other music professionals in Los Angeles, New York, Nashville, and places in between. These music pros have collectively experienced all the highs and lows the music business has to offer, from the frustration of trying to get that first record deal to the challenge of turning an unknown artist into a national phenomenon or guiding the multifaceted careers of music legends. Besides providing valuable information, their insights and comments confirmed what we suspected would still be the case nineteen years after publication of the first edition of this book. We have distilled their wisdom into three fundamental truths that, in the final analysis, sum up the basics of effective career management:

1. Talk is much more plentiful and decidedly less effective than action.
2. You can never know enough people in the business, unless they have a negative opinion of you—then one is too many.
3. There is no substitute for hard work, imagination, and persistence.

Launching a Career:
The First Step

The first step for any artist who wants to launch a successful career in the music business is to evaluate and recognize his or her particular management needs. We have already established that every act needs some form of management. The next questions should be: What type? To what degree? What are the alternatives? The answers can only be supplied by the artist after careful examination of his or her goals, resources, and circumstances. Yet, all too often artists never get around to doing this, or if they do, the analysis is not as complete as it should be. The purpose of this chapter is to help artists take a good, hard look at what their management needs are.

The key to constructive self-appraisal is honesty. When you're looking at beating the tremendously long odds against financial success as an artist, your honesty needs to be brutal. For every solo artist or group who makes it to the charts, there are a lot more who end up doing their tour of duty in Los Angeles, New York, or Nashville before finally giving up and moving on to something that will do more than pay the rent on a dream that will never be realized.

We must say at the outset that there is absolutely nothing wrong with deciding not to bet all your marbles on something as elusive and potentially unrewarding as a career in show business. Any number of talented individuals lead extremely interesting and rewarding lives after having made an honest acknowledgment that singing, dancing, acting, or playing a musical instrument is better pursued as an avocation or hobby. We are two of them. If this is the case, you need not read beyond this page. However, there is no penalty for changing your mind.

One of the benefits of reading this book may be a decision not to bet the farm on being an artist. There are a number of paths to happiness and fullfillment. The only thing that is indisputable is that each of us must decide what to do with our lives. The more information you have, the better your decisions will be.

Whether or not an individual or group is really serious about a career in show business is a difficult question to answer honestly. The gut reaction of most 19-year-olds who can sing and play guitar is likely to be, "What do you mean, am I serious?" That's certainly understandable. The dream of wealth and fame and doing what you enjoy touches us all. But before we accept rock and roll as a ready-made ticket out of the nine-to-five world of adult reality and into the dream world of money and fame, it is essential for any would-be artist and his or her manager to ask three questions:

1. Do I have the talent?
2. Do I have the desire?
3. Do I have the belief in myself and my abilities?

TALENT

The best way we've heard it expressed came from David Skepner, a longtime manager in Nashville, who for many years guided the career of Loretta Lynn. He described the talent necessary to make a career happen as simply being "It": You can't describe "it," but you sure know it when you hear or see it. Don't confuse talent with perfect pitch or technical vocal mastery.

Bob Dylan, Rod Stewart, or Mick Jagger could never win an award from the local college music department for technical vocal proficiency, yet each of them possess the intangible "it" needed to make and sell great records. Finding, developing, and exploiting "it" is the life blood of the music industry, and while most record company A&R people can tell you what clearly is and is not talent, their collective track record over the years just proves that nobody knows anything for sure. Consider all those U.S. record companies that passed on the Beatles before the Liverpool four were eventually signed by Capitol Records back in the mid-1960s. Consider the Grand Ole Opry, who told Elvis in the mid-1950s to go back to driving trucks, and never to bother them again. So much for the experts, huh?

The only practical advice we're willing to give on the subject of talent is this:

1. Be yourself, and be original. If you sound too much like, say, Bob Dylan, Rod Stewart, Mick Jagger, or anybody else on the radio, chances are that no record company will be interested.
2. Your competition is whoever is currently on the charts. You had better be a little bit better and more original than they are.
3. CDs and concert tickets are expensive. You had better give potential fans some very good reasons to lay down their hard cash to see and hear you.

Everything else is just an opinion.

DESIRE

We have already alluded to the personal sacrifice, the thankless long hours of hard work, and the years of rejection and frustration that go into making it to the top and staying there. Every record company in (New York, L.A., Nashville—choose at least one) passed on _____ (fill in the name and you'll probably be right.) But even assuming that an artist is willing to give the effort, make the sacrifices, and put up with the rejection, there's no guarantee that years of dues-paying will finally pay off. Thousands of extremely talented never-weres have struggled for a lifetime, only to live permanently in the shadow of obscurity. Imagine a contemporary music-business version of Vincent van Gogh. He's out there right now, beating his brains out to make it. In fact, he might be you. This is the reality of show business.

Even for the few who do make it, how long does it last and at what cost? Decades of the *Billboard* Hot 100 bear witness to more forgotten one-hit acts than is humane to recall. Beyond that are the ever-present dangers associated with fast living and constant travel. If you are considering a music business career, you should balance your dream against the downside of fleeting fame, elusive financial reward, and the personal toll the road can extract from even the most driven and creative artist. The desire to take all this and more had better be burning in your soul. Otherwise, you are on a collision course with some serious disappointments, and worse.

BELIEF

You think you (or your potential artist-client) have the talent to make it. You say you have the desire and persistence to go the distance. Belief is the intangible quality that separates stars from talents. It draws the line between wanting and getting. Belief transcends desire and goes beyond persistence. It is the intangible, inner quality that every act with staying power shares. Without it, an artist and manager may achieve a measure of success but will never sustain it at the highest levels. There isn't enough talent in the world to make that happen. You've got to want it that badly.

WHAT ABOUT YOUR CAREER COMMITMENT?

The degree of commitment to a show-business career is a factor that can be controlled only by the artist. Some are willing and able to throw themselves totally into a full-time career. But many more artists are unable financially to support themselves solely with their entertainment-oriented income, especially at the outset. As a result, they often hold part-time jobs or pursue dual careers while working toward their career development goals. The management principles contained in this book are equally applicable to both types of artists and may be applied regardless of financial resources. What's important is not a person's financial status, but rather his or her talent and desire and belief in these to make it. Without this, management principles are worthless.

Once an artist has decided to pursue entertainment seriously as a career, he or she need only make a determination of the type and degree of management suitable to the particular circumstances. Regardless of the talent or specific goals, the artist will need to employ management principles to fully develop that talent and to realize those goals. For those not yet convinced of the need for some form of management, let's consider the alternative of no management.

"No management" means no planning, no organization, and no attention to the day-to-day details of the artist's career. The result of this "let's see what happens" approach is an aimless drift of one's career from one haphazard encounter to the next. The upside of no management is that it's cheap and anybody can do it. Unfortunately, no artist can have a realistic chance at success by taking this approach unless, of course, the lead singer's rich uncle owns controlling interest in a record label or booking agency. It's not at all probable, but we imagine it's happened.

MANAGEMENT ALTERNATIVES

What are the management alternatives available to an artist? Basically, there are three: Self-Management, Limited Management, and Total Management. The particular needs of the artist, coupled with his or her financial and creative goals and circumstances, will answer the question of which alternative should be adopted.

A word of caution: Whichever of these three options, discussed below, prove most appropriate to your circumstances, *you the artist should personally ensure that there is follow-through every day.* Very little of value just happens by itself. Nobody is going to care about your career more than you. That means you can't wait for someone else to do what you should be taking care of yourself. Let's take a look at your options when it comes to launching and maintaining your career.

SELF-MANAGEMENT

Self-management simply means that the artist will manage his or her own career rather than retain the services of a separate individual or firm. Every artist who doesn't intend to seek outside help should practice self-management.

Self-management may often be the most suitable alternative to a new artist who is in the "break-in" phase of a career. Often, his or her management needs are not sufficiently demanding to require a full-time manager. This is also a very attractive alternative for the artist who is financially unable to pursue a career on a full-time basis. Another obvious advantage of self-management is that it's less expensive than hiring someone else. It also provides the artist with a decision-making freedom that might not otherwise be present. Self-management avoids the need for interplay and communication between artist and manager, thus closing the gap between planning and execution.

Probably the greatest disadvantage of self-management is that many artists simply don't have the experience and expertise needed to manage their own careers effectively. This is especially true of new artists in the break-in phase, who need an experienced hand to organize and develop their careers. Many costly mistakes can be avoided and a great deal of time saved by taking the advice of a seasoned manager who has faced the same problems before and probably has some innovative solutions to offer.

Another problem is time. It takes a great deal of time to properly organize and map out long- and short-term career strategy, as well as to attend to day-to-day activities. When the artist is already spending a great deal of time in rehearsal or making personal appearances, his or her management needs often suffer.

A third problem of self-management arises if the artist lacks meaningful contacts in the business. A significant part of a manager's value is the ability to obtain exposure for the artist, which is often done through contacts with others in the industry. The new artist usually doesn't have these contacts.

Even though self-management isn't always the best approach, it's always preferable to no management. The principles contained in this book provide the self-manager with a basis for developing a personalized program. With the development of a career, he or she may eventually abandon or modify the self-management approach by utilizing a form of limited management or securing the services of a full-time personal manager.

LIMITED MANAGEMENT

A second alternative available to the artist is that of limited management. This approach involves retention of a person other than the artist to provide certain specific management services. The artist performs all other management functions not delegated to the manager.

The most prevalent example of limited management is the business manager. This person, or firm, is usually concerned only with business- or finance-oriented matters. The business manager, in most instances, has no input into creative decisions or day-to-day operations, but is restricted to the role of financial adviser and consultant. Usually he or she is responsible for payment of salaries, insurance, and other expenses, for banking relations, and for other business functions—in short, for the handling of the income generated by the artist. In some cases, depending on the business manager's qualifications and relationship to the artist, he or she will also advise the artist on tax planning and personal investments. Since the business manager's activities are more restricted than those of a personal manager, he or she will be paid less: Compensation is normally based on a percentage of earnings, or is a flat hourly, monthly, or annual fee.

There are other applications of limited management that can prove beneficial to the artist while stopping short of total career involvement. An example is a consultation arrangement with an established manager at a fixed hourly rate. This permits the artist to benefit from the manager's knowledge and experience through periodic consultation sessions, but without having to pay a percentage of earnings as a fee. Because of the limited nature of the relationship, the manager would not be involved in the day-to-day details of the artist's career but would serve as an adviser and counselor, much like an attorney rendering advice to a client.

Limited management relationships can be structured to fit the particular needs of artist and manager. This approach is often an effective bridge between the two extremes of self-management and total management. It should be considered as a potential solution to the artist's individual management needs, especially in the early stages of career development.

TOTAL MANAGEMENT

The third major category is the total management concept. This approach to artist management usually involves an individual or management firm that is completely involved in the creative and business development and maintenance of an artist's career. This type of manager, often referred to as the artist's personal manager, is concerned with the total picture. The personal manager's responsibilities usually invest him or her with the ultimate decision-making authority with regard to every aspect of the artist's professional life. The personal manager is in charge of day-to-day operations ranging from major policy decisions to seemingly trivial details.

Obviously, total management is preferable to the other management options, provided that the artist's career requires this full-time attention and the artist can pay for it. Clearly, the established artist is the type of performer most in need of total management; however, anyone whose career is sufficiently complex can benefit from the total-management approach.

TAKING CHARGE OF YOUR CAREER

Regardless of your particular circumstances, we reiterate the need for you to take responsibility for and control of your career. The key to success in any endeavor is to *make* things happen rather than just letting things happen. In the final analysis, planning and follow-up will spell the difference between realizing your goals and just dreaming about them. That is the essence of artist management. Make sure you are not just a dreamer, but a dreamer *and* a doer.

3

Finding a Manager/Finding an Artist

David Ross, editor-in-chief and publisher of *Music Row,* a respected and influential Nashville trade publication, got his start in the business as a musician in the Boston area. After several years of playing local clubs but not seeming to make a great deal of progress in his career, it dawned on him that something was wrong. As he tells it: "All those years I thought I was a musician working in the music business. In reality, I was a musician working in the alcohol business."

This illustrates a fundamental problem confronting artists who, despite a great deal of effort, fail to take the critical step to get their careers moving with some form of pro-active management program that stresses setting goals, assessment of progress toward these goals, and the like. The sad fact is, many otherwise gifted artists and musicians never make use of even the most basic management principles. Instead, they somehow hope that talent and luck alone will mysteriously get them to the top of the record charts and into packed concert arenas as headliners. A quick survey of any major- to medium-sized city's music scene will reveal a lot of talented artists spinning their wheels in small clubs or rehearsal halls waiting for lightning to strike. Most of them will wait a long time.

We don't mean to suggest that merely making the decision to approach music as a business solves all your problems. It's only the first step toward building a career, but it is a step many talented people never get around to taking. Of course, if you have half a dozen major labels bidding to sign you to a guaranteed-release, multi-album deal, you will have the luxury of choosing from any number of heavyweight managers on the lookout for the next Seal or Mariah Carey. But we all know that scenario is a fairy tale. Reality counsels that it's the artist's responsibility to seek out and sell his or her act to the music industry who will in turn sell it to the public. The most effective way to do this is to find a manager who has the contacts and know-how to put artist's careers in gear.

For the unknown act, this is not easy—it's an uphill struggle that can take years. But then it's not impossible either. If an artist has the talent, desire, and belief to make it, then there is simply no choice but to go out and do it. The alternative is either to quit or wait on a fairy tale. Not much of a choice, is it?

FINDING A MANAGER: THE ARTIST'S VIEW

Before we get into the specifics of how to *find* a manager, it is important to spend a little more time on what to do if a manager does indeed discover you. The odds of a top manager, agent, or A&R person finding you are slim indeed, although if you have been able to book yourself onto the stage of a showcase club in L.A., New York, Nashville, or another music center, your chances have increased. But more on that later. For now, let's say you are playing a medium-sized club in Miami, Kansas City, Sacramento, or any of a hundred other places boasting an active entertainment scene. Assuming you have talent and energy, your chances of being discovered have gone up dramatically. In fact, it happens every night of the week in clubs and lounges all over the country.

Unfortunately, being discovered under these circumstances could be the worst thing that could happen. The following is a true example. The names aren't important, but the lesson is. It's the story of a promising rock group that has been together for about a year and has finally started to create some excitement locally. All the group members are either freshmen in college or seniors in high school. As musicians, they're better than average, having played in smaller bands in high school. Over the past few months, they've become a hot attraction. For the first time since any of them started playing professionally, they're making some money. The scene: One of the top local clubs, where the group is playing to a packed house. The band is having a good set. The music is tight, their stage show has finally come together, the audience is enthusiastic—the group has never been better.

On their first break, they're surrounded by admiring fans. Suddenly, they're approached by a man who looks older and a little more hip than the rest of the audience. He introduces himself, telling them that he's a personal manager who just happened to be in the club. He thinks the group is one of the best he's ever heard. The manager is positive that a friend of his at a major record company would be interested in them if he heard their original material. In fact, if they'd sign a management contract with him, he could guarantee a recording contract and a concert tour as an opening act for a "major" artist. Throughout the conversation, he makes reference to all the different record companies and booking agencies he's worked for and all his contacts with entertainment industry executives in California and New York. One thing leads to another, and before the night is over the group has signed a seven-year management contract that they can barely understand.

For the next couple of weeks, things are fine with the group. They're sure that in a few more months they'll be the hottest new act in the country. But their optimism begins to fade when the group finds out that their manager's friend who was to sign them to a recording contract is no longer with the record company. Their prospects continue to dim when the manager tells them they're not quite ready for concerts yet and need more work in clubs.

Little by little, they find out that the manager who was to make them stars actually knows less about managing their career than they do themselves. Loss of enthusiasm is replaced by total disillusionment. The manager has lost interest in the group, but refuses to give them a release from their contract. All the while he eagerly collects his management commission on dates that were already booked, even though he has done nothing on behalf of his clients. Within a year, the group that had so much potential and high hopes breaks up because of dissension and mistrust brought on by this unfortunate situation. The group members go their own ways, cynical and hurt. They're turned off to the music business and to anyone who even mentions the word "contract." Does any of this sound familiar? It should, because it has happened too many times, and will surely happen again.

While there are many honest, capable young managers who approach artists in clubs or recording studios and go on to establish long and successful relationships, there are many more would-be managers who fit the mold of the fast-talking, over-promising con artist in our example. This is indeed unfortunate for the *legitimate* managers, because it makes their job more difficult.

The moral of the story is simple: Be careful. Never make impulsive decisions on a matter as serious as the management of a career. If you are an artist who is approached by someone claiming to be a manager who expresses interest in you and your career, look for the telltale signs of a con artist. Does this person want to sign you on the spot, despite being a total stranger? Does he or she promise you instant fame and money, or make success sound easy? If this is the approach, beware.

Legitimate professionals never offer to sign a total stranger; instead, they want to know as much about you as you would want to know about them. Prospective managers who are "for real" will want to set up a meeting away from the club or studio to get to know you better and to discuss your goals, motivation, and needs. They don't hesitate to give you background information about themselves which you can verify. Legitimate managers don't offer to bring artists instant success. They won't ask you to sign a contract until you have had a chance to discuss the terms with a lawyer. These are things any artist should consider and look for in a potential manager. If the would-be manager can't pass these basic requirements, chances are that he or she is a fraud at worst or a well-meaning incompetent at best.

One effective technique available to any artist who has been approached by a big-promising fast-talker is simply to ask: "How? How are you going to secure a recording contract for me? How are you going to get me a major concert tour? How are you going to make me a star?" A professional's response would be, "I can't guarantee you any of that, but from what I've seen and heard, I think you have potential, and I'd like to explore the possibility of working together toward realizing that potential."

Remember, all a legitimate manager should be trying to do when he or she approaches a new artist is open the door to establishing a relationship. The con artist, on the other hand, is pressuring you to sign a contract before you've done any research and is advancing no realistic plan for achieving your career goals. Most of the time, this type of manager won't even know or care what your goals are. All you represent to such a person is a quick commission or the chance to get rich if you get lucky enough to make it through your own efforts. The best advice in this situation is to take a long look before jumping on someone else's bandwagon.

TAKING THE INITIAL STEPS

The alternative to being discovered is to establish, through a well-planned program of action, a sound and successful management relationship. We assume that, at this point, you have recognized that your career needs some form of management, but you aren't sure what the next move should be. Before doing anything else, you must first determine what your specific needs are. Do you need total management or perhaps help with business management? Depending on the particular stage of your career, you may not need a full-time manager at all, but rather an attorney, accountant, banker, or business adviser.

A big part of this process is to define your career goals and objectives with questions such as:

Where do I want to go with my career?

Do I want to place more emphasis on recording?

Do I want to concentrate on personal appearances?

Do I want to spend my time writing songs?

Do I want to do all the above?

The answers to these questions will further define the type of help you need. This self-analysis may indicate that you need a record producer, booking agent, or music publisher instead of a manager. Likewise, your goals may indicate that you need a personal manager in addition to these other professionals. Yet another conclusion might be that building a complete artist's development team is premature. Perhaps your short-term emphasis should be on building a tighter stage show or writing more and better original songs. Most professionals give artists only one shot at an audition, so if you and your act aren't ready, a premature move to impress the right management team can close more doors than it can open. The key to success is not only being ready, but also knowing when you're not ready.

Once you determine your artistic and business objectives and conclude that your career requires full-time help, it is time to target potential managers. This brings us to a brief discussion of geography. There is an old maxim which applies to just about everything, but especially to the music business: "People in business do business where business is being done." If you are serious about making it big, that means Los Angeles, New York, or Nashville—these music centers are where the people are and where the deals are done. This is not to say that there aren't exceptions; there are other music centers outside the Big Three. It is also not to suggest that there are not competent, experienced managers outside these cities. But as far as making a serious run at the world of high-stakes record deals and songwriting, it's going to be a lot tougher in Oklahoma City, Indianapolis, or just about any place where deals are rarely if ever made. Making the decision to go where things can happen and to compete head-to-head with the best will really test your talent, desire, and belief.

Of course, telling you to uproot your life and move to a strange and sometimes hostile environment is easy for us to say and difficult for you to do, but it's a must. Circumstances may dictate a delay in making the move, but eventually you will have to do it if you are serious about a shot at the big time.

When you arrive in L.A., New York, or Nashville, make it a point to meet as many people and learn as much about the music scene as you can. It won't be long before you'll know who the players are, from managers and record people to lawyers and agents. Meeting people and building your knowledge base is also your best chance for visibility and exposure. Contrary to conventional wisdom, music people still go to clubs and showcases. If you are you trying to break in, people and information are the best and quickest routes to find a manager with contacts, savvy, and clout.

If you have more modest career goals or aren't ready to make the big step, that's fine. Putting the house up for sale and striking out for Hollywood, Broadway, or Music Row is not the only way to find quality management or earn your living in music. There are plenty of other avenues which can be taken, no matter where you live. One of the best sources of information regarding potential managers are entertainment industry professionals such as record company executives, booking agents, music publishers, entertainment attorneys, and accountants. These people possess knowledge of, and contacts with, successful managers and are in a position to recommend a few to you. Depending on the circumstances, they may even offer to make personal introductions or set up appointments between you and managers. For this reason, you should make an effort to get acquainted with those people involved in the business aspect of entertainment. They are easier to get to know if you live in the same town, but if you can't do that, you can still spend time in one of the major music centers and make friends without having a permanent address. A lot of very productive relationships began through a friend of a friend of a friend.

Other sources that may help are organizations such as the Conference of Personal Managers, which will provide information on member managers as well as instructions as to how and where they can be contacted. There are also a number of directories and listings of personal managers, such as the *Billboard International Talent and Touring Directory*. Such directories are usually published annually and contain valuable information regarding managers and management companies. They may also contain other types of useful information. For instance, the Billboard publication includes a section devoted to artists. Under each artist listing, there will usually be a notation of that artist's personal manager or management firm. Anyone in search of management can tell a great deal from analyzing a manager's clientele—how many and what type of artists, and the field of entertainment he or she is associated with, and how effective that manager is, based on clients' track records.

These directories, while helpful, don't tell the full story. Many successful managers aren't listed because of personal preference, especially those who are not seeking new artists because of commitments to their current roster. Attorneys or accountants who also serve as managers may, for professional reasons, not be listed. Artists should also note that a listing in a directory isn't necessarily an endorsement or assurance of a manager's competence. Most of these publications merely publish the names and addresses that are sent to them. A directory is just a compilation of information and should only be used as a point of departure. You should investigate the people you're interested in and never assume they're competent professionals just because they have a listing. And never assume they're the only managers available.

GETTING AN APPOINTMENT

With this preliminary information in hand, it's now possible to narrow the list of prospective managers you will want to pursue. Unfortunately, getting a name and phone number from a directory and getting an appointment are two very different tasks. As with any successful business person, a manager with a track record and a stable of established, income-producing artists will most likely be surrounded by secretaries and assistants whose job it is to screen out everybody who wants fifteen minutes of his or her time. That's why "cold calls" seldom work. The challenge facing the new artist, then, is to find ways to make the initial contact something other than just a cold call.

Because the music business is built on personal relationships, the best way to break the ice is through a mutual friend, preferably another entertainment professional whose opinion the prospective manager respects. This sets the stage for you by putting the manager in a receptive mood before the first meeting. However, unless you already have a a contract with a major record company, booking agency, or publisher who has a direct interest in helping you obtain a quality management situation, this method of getting in the door is generally not going to be available to you.

Another method that has gained in popularity over the past decade is the "hired-gun" approach. Many influential entertainment attorneys may be hired by new artists to make introductions and set up appointments and auditions with people in the business. Most charge an hourly fee for their services, though there are other forms of compensation, including percentage arrangements if their efforts lead to a deal. Be sure to ask around about fees and integrity. While lawyers are bound by a code of professional ethics, there is still the potential for abuse.

Before you start flipping through the Yellow Pages, a word of caution is in order regarding the hired-gun approach. Attorneys are no different from the influential people they introduce their clients to. Their reputations and credibility are their stock in trade. No reputable, connected attorney will risk that by taking on a client who does not appear likely to succeed. Top managers rely on the judgment of their attorneys, so you need to be prepared to sell yourself as if the attorney were a manager or a record company. If you aren't absolutely convinced you can do that, you're not ready yet.

If the friend-of-a-friend and hired-gun approaches aren't workable options, the next best (and about the only other) approach is for you to go directly to the manager through letters or phone calls. But be prepared for disappointment. Rarely will the switchboard put you through to the top on the first try. You will often have to convince a subordinate that the boss should talk to you personally. This can become an art form in itself. It can also pay big dividends. In the music business, as in most fast-paced industries, never underestimate the power of secretaries or personal assistants. Oftentimes, they can get you in the door if they want to. The key here is a combination of professionalism and persistence without becoming a pest. If every unknown artist gave up trying just because someone told him or her "no" or put him off, there would be very few stars around today.

On the subject of getting in the door, a high percentage of decision makers we talked to confided that they consider the barriers they throw up to be a test of persistence and self-confidence. "The people with the drive to make it will find a way to get my attention," was the way the president of a large and successful booking agency put it.

One last word on getting that all-important appointment: The more activity you can create, the better the chance you have of coming to the attention of people who can open the right doors. Country singer Dwight Yoakam is a good case in point. Back in the mid-1980s, the native Kentuckian moved to Los Angeles and developed a loyal following of fans, radio, and press people there by releasing his own record and playing top showcase clubs like the Palomino in North Hollywood. This was long before he was signed by Warner Brothers. He had created such a buzz on his own that the music establishment could no longer ignore him. That formula continues to write success stories each and every year.

Assuming you have secured the initial appointment, remember that the purpose is merely to introduce yourself to the manager and lay the groundwork that will lead to a more detailed exploratory conference. Be brief and to the point, and don't waste the manager's time. You want to make a good first impression and create curiosity about yourself. That means being organized, concise, and businesslike. Above all, be prepared.

THE FIRST IMPRESSION: YOUR SALES KIT

Before initial contact with any prospective manager, you should prepare a kit that includes a cover letter stating who you are and why you want to talk to the manager. It's important that you convey how you came to select him or her. If you have been referred by a friend of the manager or another industry professional, you should mention that fact in the letter. At the very least, you should cite recommendations or references from within the industry. You should mention the names of the individuals making the recommendations, especially if they are well known and respected. Do not mention a name if it would be meaningless. The cover letter should list your name, address, and telephone number, and should make reference to the enclosed kit.

The kit should contain pictures and information about you, including:

1. At least one 8 x 10" (20 x 25 cm) photograph of you
2. A brief one- or two-page biography. This sets forth the nature of your act, your past experience, and other relevant information (for example, whether you write your own material, have been associated with other name acts, and so forth)
3. A brief statement of your goals and management needs
4. Other supporting items, such as trade press or newspaper clippings, a list of important past appearances, and information on future bookings, especially those the manager could attend.
5. A tape of two or three of your best songs or routines. The tape should be as professional as possible

Remember, the manager will be forming a crucially important first impression of you based on what he or she finds in the sales kit. You rarely get a second chance to make a favorable impression.

This type of presentation, combined with your ability to conduct the first phone conversation or personal interview in an organized, articulate, and businesslike manner will improve your chances of the manager becoming interested in you. He or she will appreciate the fact that you are professional in your approach to the entertainment business, that you have at least a basic understanding of the importance of management and organization, and, above all, that you are realistic in your expectations of what a manager can and cannot do for you.

All this may seem like common sense, and it is, but you would be surprised how few artists take the trouble to make a good first impression in this way. Believe us, it makes a difference with managers. Just being professional is a prime indicator that you have the potential to be a long-term artist and that you are not just another thrill-seeker or somebody with a good voice and little else. Of course, all the slick presentations in the world won't compensate for lack of talent, but if the talent is there, this type of presentation will probably rate you a closer look by a pro. Face it, everybody is looking for talented, intelligent, persistent people. This kind of presentation is your best bet for setting yourself apart from the thousands of other would-be artists all vying for a few minutes of a top manager's time.

A word of caution about the all-important first impression: It cuts two ways. You can cause yourself immense harm in the initial interview by making fundamental mistakes. For instance, never be rude or arrogant, make demands for large advances, or voice unrealistic goals. Know when to talk and when to listen. Remember what has been emphasized before—talent alone is never enough. Attitude, cooperation, self-confidence, persistence, drive, and personality are just as important, if not more so. Talent is everywhere; these other qualities aren't. An experienced manager can usually tell a great deal about these intangibles from the first meeting. If your report card is bad, there won't be a second meeting.

TRY AGAIN AND AGAIN AND AGAIN

If you've managed to get a foot in the door and sell yourself effectively, things should begin to happen for you. If not, don't quit. Resourcefulness, ingenuity, and persistence is the only formula that will finally pay dividends for you. Nothing is going to happen unless you make it happen.

If you succeeded in making initial contact but failed to make the sale, seek the manager's advice as to how you can strengthen your weak points. You can obtain priceless information by listening to what an experienced manager has to say. If the manager feels the talent is there but personally hasn't adequate time to devote to your career, ask him or her to refer you to other managers or music business figures.

Regardless of the outcome of the meeting, strive to establish and maintain a good rapport with this initial contact. Often, it can be the first in a series of "breaks" that will lead to the realization of your goals. It's also possible that a manager who may not be interested today may very well be interested at some point down the road. Things change; never close the door.

FINDING AN ARTIST: THE MANAGER'S VIEW

Managers, especially younger and less experienced ones, have as many hurdles to clear as new artists do. Finding a promising artist who possesses talent, a realistic view of the industry, and a willingness to take advice and work hard is not easy. It's even more difficult when a manager doesn't have the same level of reputation and track record as more seasoned managers.

The question is often posed: "I want to get into management, where do I start?" Just as in any other profession, there are dues to be paid and contacts to be made. In this respect, an aspiring manager bears a close resemblance to a new artist. One should gain as much practical experience in the entertainment business as possible before trying to pay the bills by managing careers. Because good managers oversee the big picture of their client's careers, any experience in the business is valuable, whether it be in management, booking, recording, engineering, producing, music publishing, public relations, or a number of other capacities. All these training grounds provide a feel for the environment in which you'll be operating. They also allow you to make contacts that are essential to being effective.

One form of dues-paying is education. The good manager understands or is at least aware of many complex financial and law-related areas and must be able to make important business decisions and deal knowledgeably with attorneys, accountants, and bankers. The manager must be able to communicate with others, to express him- or herself orally and in writing on numerous levels. For these reasons, a college degree as well as some form of advanced professional training in law or business can provide a tremendous edge. As mentioned previously, professional education programs, such as the one offered by Belmont University's School of Business, in Nashville, is a proven path to a career as an artist and manager. Recording artist Trisha Yearwood is a Belmont graduate, as are a number top young Nashville industry figures.

Over the past decade, personal management in the music industry has come into its own in terms of professionalism and sophistication. There are more management agencies than ever before who employ entry-level managers to develop "baby acts" (artists with their first record deal). Starting as a junior or develop-mental manager is an excellent way to develop skills and make contacts while drawing on the resources and knowledge of more experienced personal managers in the firm. Today's baby acts and their developmental managers are tomorrow's superstars and power players.

Another pathway to an artist-management career is to serve as a road manager for a national act. Being out on the road with all the many responsibilities of a national tour is a tremendous training ground that has brought forward many of today's top-notch personal managers.

ATTRACTING CLIENTS

Aside from the matter of developing qualifications and gaining experience, the more direct question is: "How can I attract clients?" Probably the best way is through referrals from others in the business, such as record-label executives, publishers, booking agents, producers, entertainment lawyers, or accountants. These people have the inside line on promising new artists. Through personal contact with these people, a young manager can gain valuable information on these emerging artists.

Another method of attracting clients is through existing clients or other artists with whom the manager is acquainted. Artists frequently count other artists as their friends. The unknown manager's best calling-card is any existing client relationship. An artist who believes in and is satisfied with his or her manager will spread the word. The artist grapevine is an effective business magnet.

A third method of finding new clients is the direct, or discovery approach. This means personally scouting clubs or recording studios to find artists with the talent and personality that would merit an investment of time and effort to develop their careers. The problems inherent in this approach have already been discussed from the artist's point of view; many artists will mistrust managers taking this approach for the reasons mentioned previously. The young manager should not make overly bold statements that he or she may not later be able to back up. The initial approach should be businesslike and reserved, inviting the artist to meet at a later time, preferably at the manager's office.

The manager should be extremely cautious as to the type of artist he or she approaches. Many artists don't have the will power, maturity, or ability to make it. This type of artist can become a drain on the manager. Although problems are possible with any new artist, the likelihood is probably greater with artists discovered through the scouting method. In order to guard against this happening, the manager should conduct a thorough preliminary exploratory conference in order to increase the prospects for success of the artist–manager relationship. There are so many aspects of career development and management and only a limited amount of time to address them. The next chapter explores the all-important first meeting between artist and manager.

4

Asking the Right Questions

More than any other person, the full-service personal manager is the most influential force behind an artist's career. His or her input and efforts are often critical to the artist's ultimate level of success or failure. Given the critical role the manager plays in planning, execution, and day-to-day career control, it is essential that artist and manager be on the same wavelength both personally and professionally. The artist must have total confidence in the manager's motives and methods while, conversely, the manager must be totally committed to the artist and his or her music. Unless an overriding sense of reciprocity and trust is established at the outset, the relationship is, in all likelihood, headed for trouble. This is why it is so important for the artist and manager to enter into their partnership fully informed and with their eyes wide open. The only way to do this is to be sure that the artist and manager are both asking the right questions.

As previously suggested, a strong artist–manager relationship is analogous to a good marriage. Research indicates that the longer couples date prior to marrying, the greater the probability for a lasting marriage. We believe this principle applies to successful artist–manager partnerships. An extended "courtship" offers both artist and manager the opportunity to evaluate the other so as to develop the level of mutual commitment, trust, and respect necessary to make the collaboration work. Without these qualities, problems will undoubtedly surface at some point. Although time is almost always a luxury given the fast pace of the entertainment industry, both parties to a prospective artist–manager relationship should nonetheless be very sure about each other before taking on an obligation of this magnitude. A key element to ensuring a strong working relationship between the parties is the *preliminary exploratory conference.*

The purpose of the preliminary exploratory conference is to afford both artist and manager the opportunity to accumulate the necessary information to create a basis for commitment and trust. The information exchanged at this conference will also help to determine the type of management relationship that is actually needed. Furthermore, the information elicited at this early stage will aid the attorneys in the preparation of the final management agreement.

The purpose of this preliminary meeting should never be to negotiate the management contract, but rather to assemble data helpful to both artist and manager in evaluating the *advisability* of a formal relationship. If the initial conference ultimately results in an artist–manager relationship, a strong foundation for ongoing success will have been laid. If, on the other hand, the decision is not to proceed, for whatever reason, both artist and manager will have been spared the fate of writing yet another music-business horror story. There are already enough of those to go around.

THE ARTIST'S PERSPECTIVE

Assuming there is sufficient interest on the part of the prospective manager, the parties should set up a conference to explore the advisability of representation. Prior to this meeting, you, the artist, should take the time to formulate the answers to four key questions:

1. How did I get involved with this manager?
2. What is this manager's background and track record?
3. What exactly do I want from my career?
4 Is this the right manager for me and my career?

HOW DID I GET INVOLVED WITH THIS MANAGER?

Too often a manager is retained because it "just happens," or because the person has been a long-time friend who is a yes-man who'll tell the artist what he or she wants to hear. Being a close friend or relative should not necessarily exclude a person from being considered as a potential manager, but that person should be subject to the same objective scrutiny as any other potential manager. Because of the profound effect that a manager has on an artist's career, it's absolutely essential that you the artist investigate the potential manager as thoroughly as possible. To guard against just falling into a management relationship, you should always give consideration to how you got involved with the prospective manager. Was it through a recommendation or referral from someone else in the business? Good answers to these questions are essential.

WHAT IS THIS MANAGER'S BACKGROUND AND TRACK RECORD?

Another key topic for the preliminary exploratory conference relates to the manager's qualifications. What is this manager's track record in the industry? Who are his or her other clients? Even if a seasoned pro, does he or she have sufficient time to devote to my career? Will this person be a hands-on manager, or will an associate have some or all of the responsibility? Unless a manager's reputation is well-known, you should inquire directly, but tactfully, into the manager's capabilities and past experience.

Another often overlooked qualification is a manager's level of formal education. Although it isn't essential that a manager have a college degree to be qualified for artist management, it would certainly be a valuable credential. This is true not only in the entertainment industry, but in any business. Moreover, if the manager's degree is in business or psychology, the credential is potentially worth even more to the artist. And if the manager holds graduate or professional degrees, the value is higher still.

Probably the most critical factor in determining a prospective manager's credentials is his or her reputation. This can be easily determined, first, by asking others in the industry. Is this a person whose abilities are respected? What about his or her honesty, integrity, and fairness? Because the manager is an extension of the artist, these are critical questions. Reputation can also be determined by finding out who the manager's clients are. Having highly successful clients speaks for itself, although it doesn't always provide an accurate measure of integrity and honesty. That question should always be asked separately and verified to your satisfaction without regard to track record.

Another gauge is to observe manager's involvement in various organizations. Is he or she a member of the Conference of Personal Managers or other important trade organizations or associations? Does he or she serve or participate as a panelist at music industry forums and seminars? Answers to such questions will provide some indication of how plugged-in within the industry the manager is.

WHAT EXACTLY DO I WANT FROM MY CAREER?

If you as the artist don't have some conception of your career's future, you can hardly expect a manager do much better. Even more dangerous is turning your career over to a manager who might have divergent ideas or a conflicting philosophy of career development. Sooner or later, there will be trouble and a lot of wasted time.

You can be specific in requesting managerial help only if you have formulated clear goals. Although you may generally know *where* you want to go with your career, the *how* may be a puzzle. This is where a good manager earns his or her percentage. Once the goal has been established by the artist, and the manager has acknowledged that it's both realistic and within the manager's range of expertise, the discussion should turn to how the goal can be reached. This can include a preliminary timetable for action and the formulation of subordinate goals and proposed strategies for meeting them.

The parties should not try to map out the artist's career for the next five years at this preliminary stage, but the approach does provide a framework for substantive talks aimed at fleshing out goals, philosophies, and capabilities. It's a great way to find out if the prospective artist and manager are on the same wavelength.

Beware of a manager who has no answer to the "how" question. A lack of ideas regarding the preliminary construction of an artist's career plan could indicate a lack of interest or a deficiency in the expertise necessary to help the artist go in the desired direction.

IS THIS THE RIGHT MANAGER FOR ME AND MY CAREER?

This question will enable you to consider the services offered by the manager in the light of your preconceived needs. While deviation or disagreement over the artist's perceived management needs will not necessarily determine the advisability of a relationship, it will provide a starting point for preliminary discussions. Objectives and needs might change, or you might discover what's really needed is a lawyer, banker, producer, or publicist. Therefore, it is much more productive to discuss specifics rather than to have a conversation that goes something like this:

MANAGER: How can I help you?
ARTIST: I need a manager.
MANAGER: Fine. Where would you like to see your career go?
ARTIST: I want to be a star.
MANAGER: Good. I'm just the person you need.

Tells you a lot, doesn't it?

During the actual conference phase, discuss your goals and needs *in detail* and invite the manager to scrutinize them objectively and aggressively. In fact, you should be suspicious of anyone who does not ask you about your professional and personal goals early on. It is, after all, your career we're talking about. If there is going to be a personality conflict or just a failure to connect, the preliminary conference is the time to find out. Likewise, if the manager's ideas are off the wall or just not meshing with yours, it's better to know that before a deal is struck.

Compatibilty is also an issue here. Even if the manager has great ideas and an address book full of contacts, that is no guarantee that the two of you will connect personally. Because of the closeness of the relationship and the overriding importance of the trust factor mentioned earlier, we feel that personal rapport is essential. At the very least, there should be a basic comfort level accompanied by mutual respect and a sense of professionalism. If these are missing, you need to think twice about signing on with this particular manager.

MONEY

What compensation does the manager want for his or her services? This is an issue of obvious importance that should be confronted at the preliminary exploratory phase. Depending on the relative bargaining position of the parties, several alternatives are available. The commission arrangement, whereby the manager is paid a percentage of the gross earnings of the artist, is the most common. The percentage will vary from 10 to 25 percent of gross earnings. Some managers take an even higher percentage. The customary rate is 15 percent of gross earnings. A refinement of this approach is to base the percentage on net income; the problem here is defining the term "net."

Another approach is to set the manager's percentage at an escalating rate, depending on the amount of total gross income. As gross income goes up, so does the percentage. Or, depending on the status and negotiating position of the parties, a management percentage could decrease as gross earnings increase. Each particular arrangement is as unique as the parties themselves.

Sometimes a young artist may be in a very weak financial position, incapable of paying any management percentage, but be in desperate need of a manager. A possible solution here is the retainer method of compensation. Instead of a percentage of all monies received, a flat or fixed sum is paid to the manager on a weekly or monthly basis. Although the retainer may be much less than a set percentage of gross earnings, it may bridge the gap between artist and manager during the artist's early years of struggling. Perhaps, with the help of an effective manager, the artist's earnings will increase to a sufficient level to allow conversion to a percentage-of-gross-earnings arrangement.

In some cases, a manager might offer services for no compensation at all until the artist's earnings reach a certain level, and thereafter take a higher percentage than normal to make up for the earlier deficit. The attraction of this is obvious, but the artist should consider the "down side" as well. While it may appear the artist is getting a great deal, the actual net cost could turn out to be substantially higher than with other arrangements.

Another pitfall in the nonpayment situation is a lack of commitment of both artist and manager. An unsatisfied artist is in a weak position to voice complaints if he or she is not paying for the privilege.

POTENTIAL CONFLICTS OF INTEREST

Another question that should be raised during the preliminary exploratory conference pertains to a manager's potential conflicts of interest. Simply stated, he or she should be asked, "Do you have any conflict of interest that might have a detrimental effect on your ability to manage my career?"

For example, a manager may also be a producer or publisher. Although various state statutes as well as musicians' union and management association guidelines prohibit overlap of a manager's involvement in other areas, such as booking, such overlap does on occasion take place. While you should be cautious in defining such areas, they shouldn't necessarily be construed as negative in themselves. Many times, the manager owns or has an interest in a recording studio or production company, and such assets can be beneficial to the artist-client. You should be aware of any overlap and take appropriate steps to guard against potential problems arising out of any such conflicts of interest.

Another question to ask is, "How inquisitive is the potential manager during the preliminary exploratory conference?" In addition to your professional and personal goals, an experienced manager will want to know all he or she can about you. There should be a multitude of questions aimed at accumulating personal and business data in order to construct the preliminary career plan. Beware of the manager who doesn't seek information, for without it a plan cannot be formulated. And without a plan, there's no management foundation.

Specifically, an astute manager will want to know about the artist's career history and financial condition, both professionally and personally. Does the artist have a lawyer or accountant? Does he or she have life insurance, equipment-vehicle insurance, and so forth? Are there any outstanding contractual commitments with record companies, publishers, agents, or other managers? What about debts or other financial obligations?

Once you have been through the preliminary exploratory conference, you should have a great deal of information, coupled with a strong first impression with which to evaluate a prospective management relationship. You should take at least a week, if possible, to reflect on the preliminary exploratory conference, reviewing objectively the manager's ideas, proposals, and suggestions—especially if they are at odds with your own. Careful consideration should be given to the personal chemistry between the two of you, as well as the manager's credentials and reputation in the business. It's also important that you reconsider your own goals and preconceived ideas about the role a manager should play in your career development and direction. If there are any major areas of doubt or conflict, clear them up before going forward. If this can't be done, you would be well advised to continue your search for the right management situation.

THE MANAGER'S PERSPECTIVE

A good artist–manager relationship is a two-way street. This is why the preliminary exploratory conference is just as important for the manager as it is for the artist. Basically, the manager's questions during the meetings should center around certain key areas that correspond to goals and concerns of the artist. As in the case of the artist, the manager should ask, "Why did the artist come to me? Was he or she recommended or referred by one of my clients, an associate, or a friend within the industry?" Quite possibly, the artist and manager may have been working together in another capacity (for example, publisher–songwriter). Whatever avenue the artist has traveled to reach the manager, the specifics are important.

First of all, the prospective manager will want to know where the artist currently stands in his or her career. For instance, if the referral came from the head of a major label who had just committed to a multi-record guarantee, the manager would be in a much stronger posture to assess the advisability of getting involved. If, on the other hand, the artist was brand-new or had just been dropped by a record company, the manager would want to know that as well. In any event, one of the first calls a manager would make would be to people who could provide reliable information on the artist who is seeking career help.

The manager should next evaluate his or her managerial style, philosophy, and current client obligations to see if the potential for a compatible match exists. For example, a manager whose strengths are in the country music market would be extremely cautious of signing a hard-rock attraction unless the performers were seeking a change in artistic direction. Even then, a manager would be well advised to pass if he or she concluded that such a reversal was too much of a stretch. Unless the manager has the requisite knowledge of the particular music-industry segment required by the artist, he or she cannot adequately represent that client. A manager capable of wearing several hats is certainly not impossible to find; however, such versatility is not common. In short, the manager must be aware of his or her own capabilities and limitations when considering signing a new client.

In addition to other considerations, the manager's perception of the artist and art form must be analyzed. The manager must be on the same artistic frequency as the artist. Each must be in clear agreement on the career direction of the artist and be committed to taking that path. If, for example, a manager views his client as Coolio with subtle country overtones, while the artist envisions himself as hard country in the vein of an Alan Jackson—doing material with some social commentary—there is a serious gap in terms of image and direction, to say the least. Such a fundamental difference in image perception can only lead to problems. This is why it's crucially important to devote time to a detailed discussion of artistic goals and direction.

As noted above in considering the artist's view of the preliminary exploratory conference, the manager's compensation can take many forms. The primary point here is for the manager to know and understand his or her bargaining position. The same general considerations on compensation discussed earlier are equally applicable.

Additionally, if a manager is inclined to sign the artist, the goals and time requirements for accomplishing these objectives must be analyzed, especially if the manager has several other clients. Also, the financial arrangement must be equitable in terms of time expenditure versus compensation. Ideally, from a business standpoint, a manager should view clients as an investment portfolio—some being current revenue producers, others on the brink of financial maturity, and still others advancing through a building and growth stage with little expectation for immediate return. A mixed portfolio of clients can be a strong determining factor concerning a manager's flexibility in setting the amount and method of compensation.

A MANAGER'S CHECKLIST

In order for the manager to suggest a preliminary career plan for the artist, a wide range of business-oriented questions must be answered. This checklist of fundamental questions can serve as a basis for discussion. Every manager will want to customize and supplement it as individual circumstances dictate. This list is equally applicable to artists who want a full service manager.

1. What legal entity is the artist doing business as: sole proprietor, partnership, limited liability company, corporation, or joint venture? An ownership entity must be established, especially where the artist is a duo or group.

2. Are there any existing management, booking, recording, publishing, or corporate endorsement or sponsorship agree-

ments in effect? If so, what are the terms of these agreements, and what is the status of the artist with regard to the parties to those contracts? If there were previous agreements that are allegedly inoperative, are there proper releases evidencing this?

3. What are the artist's professional assets?
4. Is the artist a member of the applicable union, such as the AFM or AFTRA?
5. What is the artist's personal and business debt structure?
6. Does the artist own a registered servicemark on his or her name? And what about other legal safeguards relative to the Right of Publicity, Unfair Competition, and other applicable doctrines designed to protect one's name, likeness, and identity?
7. What is the artist's earning history over the previous five years, broken down into amount and source?
8. Does the artist keep proper financial records?
9. Does the artist have good banking relations?
10. Has the artist filed proper federal and state income tax returns for the last five years?
11. Does the artist have proper insurance coverage?
12. What is the artist's reputation and current image?
13. Does the artist write his or her own material? If so, is he or she a member of a performing rights society? Who controls and administers the artist's copyrighted musical compositions?
14. Does the artist have any affiliate companies (such as publishing or production concerns)?
15. What is the artist's past recording experience and track record?
16. What has been the artist's exposure and experience as a live performer?
17. What current industry trends might influence the artist's career?

As stated earlier, these questions are fundamental. While they don't indicate the entire spectrum of inquiry relating to business planning that a manager could delve into, they do provide the basics. As each question is raised, additional questions will undoubtedly be suggested. Prior to drafting a final management agreement, the expertise of an attorney and accountant will probably be required, depending on the training and background of the manager.

Finally, as suggested earlier, the most important aspect of the potential management relationship is the personal one. The manager must determine what kind of personal relationship will be established with the artist. He or she must ask, "Are we compatible? Is the artist willing to work toward the stated goals or does he or she expect me to do everything? Is the artist realistic? Does he or she have the ability and discipline to face the hard times as well as the good? Is this artist dependable? What is his or her reputation in the industry?" Answers to all the questions related to talent, potential, and business considerations may be positive, but unless the same can be said of the personal dimension, the manager should seriously question any decision to proceed. The real-life stories of personal problems wrecking a promising career have been amply documented. Be mindful that the opportunities aren't outweighed by the potential problems, and act accordingly.

DECISION TIME

The formal vehicle of the preliminary exploratory conference provides both artist and manager with a comprehensive tool to evaluate each other's talent, personality, and capabilities. At this stage, should a management relationship result, the manager ought to have enough data to begin to design a career plan for the artist, while the artist should have a much better understanding of his or her management needs. No matter how long the preliminary exploratory phase takes, be it several days or several weeks, it should be thorough.

Once the questions have been asked and answered, approaches and ideas shared, both manager and artist have a decision to make. Procrastination doesn't enhance a good artist–manager relationship. If both agree on goals, direction, and methods, and most importantly, on each other, they should be eager to begin. If the answer is yes, put it in writing, then go to work. If it's no on either side for whatever reason, then keep looking.

5

The Management Contract

Assuming artist and manager are right for each other, the next step is to resolve the details of the relationship. The end result of this process is the management contract.

It's often difficult for an artist and new manager to sit down and address delicate areas relating to the financial and legal rights and responsibilities that flow out of their newly created relationship. Both parties are eager to get started on more creative matters, and neither wants to jeopardize the fledgling association by bringing in lawyers and reducing a personal relationship of trust to pages of legal fine print. This is certainly understandable, but putting off a formalized contract or, worse yet, proceeding without one is the wrong move. It is absolutely essential that a formal management contract be negotiated and finalized before anything else is done. Handshake management deals, despite their good intentions, are nothing more than open invitations to disaster.

The first step in negotiation of the management agreement lies with the parties themselves. The preliminary exploratory phase should have provided the forum in which to exchange viewpoints on how each sees the relationship, including the respective roles each will play. Specific subject areas relating to financial, business, and legal aspects of the management relationship should have also been addressed. Depending on the depth of those discussions, the parties should now move to finalize the basic areas of their agreement. Undoubtedly, many unanswered questions and new subjects for discussion will surface. Listed below are the broad subject areas on which the parties should focus during their initial discussions:

- Manager's duties
- The artist's role
- Length of the agreement
- Manager's compensation
- Manager's expenses
- Accounting procedures
- Prior contracts still in force

Once the parties have reached a general understanding of what they want their relationship to be, the next step is for each to retain separate legal counsel. This suggestion in no way implies a lack of trust in each other, but rather a mutual willingness to articulate the relationship in clear, unambiguous terms. Most disputes between parties to any contract come not from lack of trust, but from a failure to anticipate likely issues and resolve them apart from the pressures and circumstances that are sure to crop up in any business relationship. Spending money for contract specialists at the outset is the best way to ensure that litigation counsel is never needed. Once the deal is signed, sealed, and delivered, the parties are best advised to file the contract away and proceed as if it were a handshake deal, referring to the contract only to clarify what the parties have already agreed to.

When choosing an attorney, each party should make sure his or her lawyer has experience in the entertainment industry. Law has its specialties like everything else. A good music lawyer will save you time and grief later on by anticipating issues and potential problems that might be overlooked or not fully appreciated by a lawyer who does not specialize in the entertainment industry.

The standard method of billing for negotiation and contract drafting is to compute charges on an hourly basis. Be sure to ask your lawyer to provide his or her hourly rate along with an estimate of the number of hours anticipated for completion of the project.

Part of what you are paying for is advice and help in nego-tiating the specific aspects of the management agreement. Therefore the artist or manager shouldn't be concerned if every point is not worked out before counsel is retained. Your lawyer will have some very good ideas along these lines, especially regarding some of the trickier or more sensitive provisions. After artist and manager have reached a basic agreement on the major points, they should turn negotiations over to the attorneys. Attempting to negotiate and draft a management agreement without assistance of counsel is one of the biggest mistakes one can make. There are several reasons for this.

The most important is that an experienced entertainment lawyer will make sure all necessary points of the contract have been addressed and included in the final document. He or she will be able to counsel and advise the client on the merits of all relevant subject areas, whether previously discussed or yet to be considered.

Secondly, the lawyer is able to act as a negotiator, sparing artist and manager any direct confrontation over delicate matters, thus allowing the parties to preserve their close personal and artistic relationship while ensuring that essential points are covered.

Finally, the entertainment attorney has the ability to draft the final agreement in clear, concise language that will help avoid ambiguities that could lead to disagreements while also ensuring that the parties have a legally enforceable document.

We can't stress enough that one should never adopt a "do it yourself" approach when it comes to legal matters. It is tempting, especially when an artist or manager is trying to save money and one of them has access to a form management agreement. However, every artist–manager relationship has its unique aspects or special twists that a form agreement may not be capable of fully anticipating or expressing. It's worth the extra money on the front end of the relationship to ensure that the management contract accurately reflects the true intent and complete agreement of the parties.

AN OUTLINE OF BASIC TERMS

The unique nature of each relationship makes it difficult to draw generalizations regarding specific legal provisions. However, there are certain subject areas common to all management agreements. We outline and discuss these topics as a point of reference concerning subjects that should be dealt with in the preliminary negotiations. Moreover, a better understanding of the terms, provisions, and intent of the management agreement by the parties will assist the attorneys in drafting an instrument capable of accomplishing the objectives of the parties.

Most management agreements can be divided into nine major subject areas:

1. Appointment of authority
2. Manager's compensation
3. Exclusivity
4. Term, options, extensions, and blackout periods
5. Disputes
6. Artist warranties
7. Accounting and trusts
8. General legal clauses
9. Definitions

APPOINTMENT OF AUTHORITY

Generally speaking, there are four basic areas to look for in the management agreement regarding this topic: appointment, manager's duties, power of attorney, and employment agency disclaimer.

APPOINTMENT DESIGNATION

This provision usually does just what it states: It designates the manager to perform certain specified acts. It is important that the appointment language be clear and specific. This provision can be used to specify the type of management relationship the parties desire—for example, personal management, business management, consultant, and so forth. Also, the issue of exclusivity or nonexclusivity of management services can be dealt with under this section.

MANAGER'S DUTIES

The manager's duties should be spelled out under the appointment of authority. The general phraseology used in many management agreements sets forth a number of specific duties. Here are phrases that are traditionally used:

- To represent the artist as an adviser in all business negotiations and other matters relating to his entertainment career
- To supervise professional engagements
- To consult with employers in the entertainment and literary fields
- To cooperate with and supervise relations with any booking and literary agents whom the manager may from time to time employ with the artist's consent

- To be available at reasonable times at the manager's office to confer with the artist on all matters concerning his or her artistic career, including but not limited to publicity and promotion
- To use best efforts to arrange interviews, auditions, and tryouts designed to further the artist's career
- To perform, wherever and whenever possible and whenever called upon, and such other functions as may be consistent with any of these duties

It must be emphasized that these subject areas are generalizations. The duties of a manager can be made more or less specific depending on the desire of the parties. The needs of the artist or the manager's capability may totally alter the sample language listed above; nevertheless, they are listed to help stress the importance of specifying duties and responsibilities of the manager.

POWER OF ATTORNEY

A power of attorney is an instrument authorizing another person to act as one's agent or attorney. The power of attorney clause can be styled to fit the needs of the parties. It can be general or specific in its form. For example, in most cases, the artist rarely signs personal performance contracts, endorses checks received in the course of business, deals directly with union organizations, or corresponds with royalty collection societies. These are normally the duties of a manager. However, in order to make binding the documents the manager signs on behalf of the artist, it's necessary to have a power of attorney authorization in the management agreement.

As stated previously, such a clause can be general, pertaining to all business matters of the artist, or specific, relating to a narrow segment of the artist's business affairs. The artist can limit the power of the manager by restricting or omitting the power of attorney clause.

EMPLOYMENT AGENCY DISCLAIMER

Most management agreements clearly disclaim any duty to obtain employment for the artist. While the American Federation of Musicians has lifted its regulation against agents acting as managers, other professional management organizations still oppose the dual function.

The duties of a manager and agent are separate. However, during the span of an artist's career, the manager may find him-

or herself devoting a substantial amount of time to developing agency outlets for the client or, if necessary, to seeking engagements directly with promoters or purchasers of entertainment where permitted by law. So, while the functions of manager and agent are distinct, there can be overlap. This is an important point that must be carefully studied by the manager prior to entering an agreement with an artist who needs help in obtaining engagements. The artist should clearly understand that the manager has no obligation to seek employment directly if efforts toward motivating agents to book the client fail. Of course, if the manager is also acting as an agent pursuant to another agreement, then an obligation would exist.

It should be re-emphasized at this point that certain states, the most notable being California, restrict and regulate this dual function. The manager should therefore consult an attorney to determine the legal consequences of acting as a manager and agent. He or she should also inquire into any licensing requirements of the particular state in which he or she is a resident or is doing business.

MANAGEMENT COMPENSATION

Once the artist and manager have agreed on the compensation to be paid for the manager's services, there are still certain issues to be resolved. These include establishing the percentage base, time of payment, reimbursement of expenses, and other matters connected with the term of the agreement.

ESTABLISHING THE PERCENTAGE BASE

Once the management percentage has been established, assuming this is the form of compensation utilized, the parties will need to determine the base to which the percentage will apply. Will the manager receive a fee on gross or net earnings? Will the fee be calculated only on personal performance income and record royalties, or will endorsements and songwriter income also be included? In short, on what sources of income will the manager's percentage be based? Although managers normally charge a fee ranging from 10 to 25 percent, with the customary figure being 15 percent, the areas of income to which this fee applies will vary. To some artists, the compensation clauses won't be as important as the manager's authority and designated duties or some other provisions of the agreement.

Special attention should be given to the artist–manager relationship when the artist wishes to use an affiliated firm in which the manager has an interest, such as a booking agency, record label, or music publishing company. The manager may voluntarily waive management fees pertaining to incomes the artist derives from the affiliated company, since he will already be receiving indirect compensation from those firms. Alternatively, the manager may argue that the incomes earned by these companies should be treated as any other income and therefore be commissionable to the manager.

In discussing the compensation provisions of a management agreement, the artist must not only consider the percentage to be charged, but also the areas of his or her income to be affected. Many artists are overly concerned with the percentage while ignoring those provisions that could substantially reduce the significance of a higher percentage. An artist should always consider the percentage and the base to which it applies simultaneously.

Although common in the industry, management compensation certainly need not be limited to a percentage of income. In some instances, the artist may want to retain the manager on a fee arrangement, a guaranteed amount payable at predetermined times. Such an arrangement may be more economically feasible or advantageous to the artist (or manager) than a percentage of the artist's income. Again, different circumstances will influence the final arrangement.

TIME OF PAYMENT

Another important consideration is determining when the management percentage will be paid: monthly, quarterly, or semiannually. When attempting to resolve this question, attention should be given to the artist's type of work. For example, an artist performing primarily on the nightclub circuit would have regular cash-flow capable of paying management fees on a monthly or even weekly basis. However, an artist playing one-nighters may elect to perform only during certain months, making it hard to maintain a monthly payment schedule. In addition, the accounting problems associated with a popular one-nighter attraction may necessitate payment of all management fees at the end of the quarter or at the conclusion of a tour. For a recording artist/writer, the bulk of income is paid in record and songwriter royalties, usually twice a year. All these considerations, along with the tax consequences attached to each, should be examined before a final decision is made on when commissions are paid. It may be advisable to consult an accountant on this particular issue.

REIMBURSEMENT OF EXPENSES

Normally a manager is reimbursed for all direct expenses incurred on behalf of a particular artist. This amount is apart from and in addition to the management commission. However, this area can be structured in many ways.

Where it is the artist's money at stake, he or she might want to incorporate controls over the manager's discretion to incur reimbursable expenses. Amount, type, time, and geographic limitations on these expenses are just a few of the many controls that may be imposed on the manager. For instance, the manager may have the authority to spend up to a certain amount without the artist's approval—for example, any expenditure less than $500. Or the manager may be granted the right to spend any amount necessary for certain purposes. Yet another approach allows the manager to spend up to a certain amount each month in artist-related expenses without artist approval. This approach is normally used after a budget has been established and usually becomes a matter of simply paying the regular monthly bills.

Still another approach provides that the manager be reimbursed for expenses incurred only beyond a certain radius of operation. By way of illustration, let's assume artist and manager are based in New York City, but that it's necessary for the manager to spend time in Los Angeles. All expenses associated with Los Angeles trips could be recoverable, but trips within a 250-mile radius of New York, representing the majority of the manager's travel activities, are not recoverable from artist earnings. These are just a few of the many alternatives that could be incorporated into the reimbursement clause under the compensation provisions.

Certainly, trust is at issue here. The manager's hands shouldn't be unduly tied, nor should the artist be subjected to unduly expensive surprises.

EXCLUSIVITY

In most management agreements, the artist grants the manager an exclusive right of representation. However, the manager is normally not obligated to the same exclusivity provisions as the artist. Although this type of practice is standard within the industry, it can still be the subject of negotiation, in some instances.

The basic premise supporting this one-way exclusivity is the unique talent of the artist. It's virtually impossible to duplicate the style and personality of an artist, especially one who is established with a loyal following. On the other hand, the manager's talents are normally business-oriented, which can be more easily duplicated or substituted. Of course, this is a generalization, and there are certainly managers who are stars in their own right because of their unique image and talents. But generally speaking, it's the artist who has the one-of-a-kind characteristics. Therefore, the manager will normally insist that the artist be the one who is exclusively bound by the agreement.

Of course, there have been some notable exceptions to this, with a manager committing to one artist. Colonel Tom Parker always maintained that managing Elvis Presley was a full-time job and thus devoted all his time to his famous client. But such one-to-one relationships are rare.

A frequent argument supporting the manager's right to represent other clients is that his or her compensation represents only a fraction of what is earned by the clients. For a manager to lower overhead and stay in business, it is necessary to have several clients, all of whom are paying commissions on their income. This is especially true with regard to new artists who might not be top income producers when they first seek artist management. So unless the manager derives income from other sources, it might be impossible for him or her financially to represent a young, inexperienced artist. Of course, some of the most successful managers don't represent newcomers at all, because they don't have to.

From a practical standpoint, the manager must have the ability to make important career decisions with the assurance that others who have a stake in the artist's career won't have the power to countermand or interfere in the process. While agents, publishers, producers, and publicists are empowered to make decisions affecting the artist's career, they are usually made within certain boundaries established by the manager, or with his or her direct approval. Any other approach to final decision-making would result in confusion, if not catastrophe. Everyone with a stake in the artist knows this to be the case and depends on a strong manager to act as the glue to an artist's career—thus the exclusive representation clause.

While it would be difficult for artists to compel managers to work full-time on their behalf, there should certainly be a demand that adequate time be spent. Special care should be taken by the artist to ensure that a manager is both willing and able to do the kind of job that is required. A manager who is extremely successful might not have the time to spend on a new addition to the artist roster. This is precisely why it might be a good idea to consider a manager who might not have a top-tier track record or client list but does have the time and dedication to do the job for a new client.

Another approach is to insert a "best efforts" clause and reduce the term of the agreement if there are doubts about a busy manager's time constraints or level of commitment. Better yet, if doubts are strong, the artist should reexamine the advisability of the entire relationship.

TERM

The term, or length, of the management agreement is one of its most important points. Because there are numerous advantages and disadvantages attached to this provision, special attention should be devoted to coming up with the right formula for both parties. From the manager's viewpoint, a long-term agreement is beneficial in protecting his or her investment, especially when dealing with a new artist requiring a long development phase. A manager usually won't be inclined to invest substantial amounts of time to develop a newcomer, only to lose that artist once results are achieved. Conversely, a manager may be wary of a protracted development phase and may seek a short-term agreement with option provisions exercisable only on one side.

On the other hand, the artist may prefer not to be bound for an extended period with a new manager, or may want to enter into a long-term agreement with a well-known manager who is capable of developing the artist to his or her maximum potential.

The term of most management agreements ranges from one to five years with options. The *option* term usually consists of one to six consecutive one-year periods: This means that at the conclusion of the original term, the agreement will continue if one party, normally the manager, exercises the option(s). Options are often tied to certain levels of performance by the artist and/or manager.

Options exercisable by the artist are recommended as a way to ensure performance by the manager, especially where he or she may represent a full roster of other artists. Likewise, options are advisable for the manager as an effective control device.

The artist should be wary of committing to a manager for a term longer than three years. Time changes people and circumstances. Regardless of the strong belief an artist may have in a particular manager, it is always advisable to maximize flexibility by limiting the agreement to a three-year span. If the artist is successful, a contract of short duration will allow a renegotiation with the manager on more favorable terms. If the management relationship is not successful, the shorter term will allow the artist to terminate the agreement and seek alternative management representation.

In reality, the original term and option provisions are based on bargaining power, of which new artists have little and powerful managers have plenty. But there are always compromise positions. Use of a short-term agreement with mutually exercisable options or option terms based on performance of the parties is an approach that potentially provides artist and manager with a workable middle ground that affords sufficient protection for each.

RENEWALS AND EXTENSIONS

One provision somewhat misunderstood by many artists deals with renewals and extensions. Simply put, the typical provision states that if a manager negotiates a contract for the artist and revenue from that contract is received beyond the term of the artist-management agreement, the manager is still entitled to a commission on that portion of the artist's income. For example, let's assume that an artist wants to secure employment in a major hotel in Las Vegas. He contacts a manager specializing in that market and requests an audition. After the audition, the manager informs the artist that his or her act is not suitable for the Las Vegas market. However, the manager is interested in working with the artist and believes Las Vegas dates could be secured by using their joint business and creative talents. They enter into a three-year management agreement calling for the artist to pay a 15-percent management commission. One year later, the artist and manager have developed a show suitable for the Las Vegas market. The manager utilizes certain contacts and secures a one-month engagement for the artist in a major hotel. The artist does well and the Las Vegas employer books a return engagement the next year. The second engagement is so successful the employer now wants to book the artist for periods of sixteen weeks a year for three years. The manager would obviously be entitled to a commission for the engagement played during the final year of the management agreement. But what about the two additional sixteen-week engagements following the termination of the agreement? The manager could argue that he or she is entitled to the fee on the monies received by the artist for the dates played after termination of the management agreement.

There are various ways to control, compromise, or limit the extension and renewal clauses. An attorney familiar with the repercussions of these types of provisions will seek to obtain the most favorable wording possible for his or her client. Both manager and artist can advance strong arguments for removing or retaining these types of provisions. However, unless this potential problem is dealt with in the agreement, a costly lawsuit could ensue, especially if manager and artist were to part under strained circumstances. This is just another example of why a clear, complete management agreement should be welcomed by the parties rather than avoided.

TERMINATION AND BLACKOUT PERIOD

Related problems arise in the event that the management contract is terminated by one or both of the parties prior to the end of the term, consistent with the language of the agreement. While every new artist–manager agreement is entered into with hope and anticipation, the reality is that most of these relationships end at some point. The reasons for parting company are as diverse and different as the relationships themselves. People, circumstances, goals, needs, and abilities are constantly evolving—such change is just part of the game.

When change dictates that artist and manager go in different directions, it is wise to have already prepared for it. Specifically, we are referring to the sensitive problem of how long and under what circumstances the manager will be entitled to continue to receive commissions from residual sources of income after the termination of the artist–manager relationship.

In the case of a new artist, a manager is likely to be instrumental in getting a record deal as well as setting up booking agency and music publishing relationships and helping obtain endorsements and corporate sponsorships. It is also likely that these sources of income will not begin to produce substantial management commissions until later in the term of the management contract. Clearly, the manager deserves to earn commissions from those income sources he or she was instrumental in creating. But what is the result if an artist finally begins to earn substantial sums only toward the end of the term of the management contract? After years of effort and patience, the manager finally begins to be compensated by substantial management commissions only to have the original or option term of the agreement expire, freeing the artist to seek a new management arrangement. Because of the long lead time involved in launching an artist's career, a manager will want to protect him- or herself from falling victim to this all-too-common situation. This is done by inserting language in the contract often called a *blackout* clause. This precludes an artist from finding new management for a predetermined interim period during which the manager is entitled to continue receiving commissions from income sources he or she was instrumental in helping to set up.

There are numerous variations to the blackout clause. One is to allow for new management while setting an upper-level dollar amount of commissions the original manager may collect after termination of the agreement. Another is to automatically extend the original or option term of the management agreement for a specified period that is measured from the date the artist gives the manager notice of termination. As with other management clauses, this is subject to negotiation between the parties. But in light of the substantial investment of time a manager makes in an artist, coupled with the likelihood that the investment may never be recouped, the manager is well advised to have the protection of a blackout clause.

REDUCTION OF FEE IN THE EVENT OF
THE MANAGER'S DEATH OR DISABILITY

Another provision often included in the management agreement involves the amount of commission paid in the event of the manager's death or disability. If the management agreement is with a partnership or corporate entity, this clause probably will not be included unless other circumstances dictate. Assuming, however, that the agreement is with an individual, language is often included to protect the manager or the manager's estate from a total loss of all income on contracts made on behalf of the artist–client prior to death or disability. For example, a clause is often inserted whereby the estate of the deceased manager would receive a reduced percentage of management compensation derived from contracts negotiated for the artist by the deceased manager. Similar clauses can also be added to cover disability. These types of clauses can be used in conjunction with the provisions previously discussed regarding contractual extensions and renewals.

DISPUTES

It's good practice to include a clause in the management agreement whereby, if either party has a grievance against the other, written notification must be given and then a certain time period allowed for rectifying the dispute before the offending party can be held in default. This is often referred to as a *cure* provision. In the event that an artist–manager controversy does arise that can't be settled, then it may be wise to insert an arbitration clause.

Arbitration is a procedure for resolving disputes without having to resort to litigation in a court of law. The person conducting the arbitration hearing is not a judge, but rather someone knowledgeable of the subject matter in controversy. The arbitrator is usually chosen by mutual agreement of the parties from a list submitted by organizations such as the American Arbitration Association. Once the arbitrator takes jurisdiction, he or she has wide discretion to conduct a hearing and make any ruling deemed appropriate under the circumstances. The arbitration clause will normally grant the prevailing party the right to recover any and all reasonable costs including attorney fees. Depending on the wording of the arbitration clause and governing state law, the arbitration award may or may not be subject to appeal. Given the unique character of the entertainment industry and the crowded court dockets across the country, the arbitration clause may be beneficial to both artist and manager as a speedy, inexpensive manner of resolving disputes.

ARTIST WARRANTIES AND INDEMNIFICATION CLAUSES

A warranty and blanket indemnification clause is usually included in the management agreement whereby the artist guarantees certain facts. For instance, let's assume that an artist, believing that he has been fully released from a previous management agreement, when in fact he is really not, enters into an agreement with a new manager. Assume further that this new management contract happens to contain a clause that warrants that the artist is free to enter into this new agreement. A short time later, a major recording contract is secured. The artist's previous manager believes that her efforts on behalf of the artist were the reason the contract was obtained, while the new manager strongly contends that his efforts alone resulted in the contract. The result is a lawsuit between the two managers. Regardless of the outcome, under the indemnification clause contained in the second agreement the new manager would still be entitled to be reimbursed by the artist for any losses incurred by him as a result of the artist's breach of warranty. This is because the artist guaranteed that he was free to contract with the new manager and agreed to protect him from any loss if the manager relied on the contractual warranty.

This type of clause makes it important for an artist to understand the full implications of any prior contractual commitments. More than one potentially rewarding artist–manager relationship has failed because of previous legal entanglements.

ACCOUNTING AND TRUSTS

The artist should always include an audit provision in the management agreement, giving him or her the right to examine the books of account kept by the manager. Conversely, if the artist (or a representative of the artist) keeps the accounting records, then obviously the manager would want the same privilege. The management contract should contain a specific provision stating exactly whose obligation it shall be to keep the books of account. As a regulatory provision to the right of examination, the audit clause should provide for a written notification and a time period for the examination (for example, within ten days from notification during normal office hours). To avoid unnecessary or vexatious examinations, the party to be audited will often seek to limit such examinations to no more than one per year.

A trust provision places a duty on the artist or manager to hold and preserve monies that might be collected by one but that belong to the other. The party in possession of these funds is obligated to protect said monies until the other party is paid. Legally, this establishes a trust or fiduciary relationship which carries a greater degree of accountability between the parties to a contract than is normally the case. Over the last decade, the trend in state law has been to regard the entire management agreement as creating a fiduciary relationship much like an attorney–client relationship. This imposes upon the parties the duty of utmost good faith, fair dealing, and full disclosure of all matters materially affecting the relationship. Here, as with any legal matter, an attorney can provide in-depth advice appropriate to the situation at hand.

GENERAL LEGAL CLAUSES

All formal management agreements contain various general legal clauses. For instance, a *jurisdiction* provision characteristic of all such agreements states that the contract will be construed under the laws of a particular state or country. A *modification* clause states that once the agreement is reduced to writing and signed, then all subsequent changes must be reduced to writing and signed by both parties in order to be enforceable. An *assignment and delegation* clause may be found in the agreement regulating transfer of rights and duties under the contract.

Many other general legal clauses may be included, depending on the desires of the parties and their attorneys. While these clauses may not appear to be important to a layperson, they can be of great importance with regard to legal interpretation and the construction of the agreement, should the need arise. This is one more compelling reason to retain an attorney rather than take a do-it-yourself approach to legal matters.

DEFINITIONS

Some management agreements contain definitions of specific words and terms used in the body of the agreement. This is done to guard against an ambiguous meaning being attached to a frequently employed word or phrase. If the parties to the agreement are unclear as to the meaning of any word or phrase, then it should be defined. As with the other provisions of the contract, care in drafting of the document can alleviate greater problems later on.

THE IMPORTANCE OF A WIN–WIN CONTRACT

Different things are important to different people. Consequently, each artist and manager will be motivated by different needs when negotiating the management agreement. Much of the final product will be determined by the parties' mutual desire for a positive, workable relationship, though some of it will be the result of hard bargaining and the respective levels of negotiating leverage. The delicate balance of maintaining a good personal relationship in the midst of hard-nosed bargaining is where the services of a good music business attorney can be invaluable. While the artist and manager should both feel comfortable about the management contract, neither party should be timid about having it tailored to meet needs specific to him or her. In a successful negotiation, everybody wins, but sometimes one party wins a little more than the other. Consequently, both parties must be prepared to give, take, and compromise to make the final agreement acceptable to both artist and manager. If it's not, then what you might think is a legal blueprint for success is really a time bomb bound to explode. When that happens, nobody wins.

PART TWO

Planning the Artist's Career

6

Taking Care of Business

O nce the terms of the management contract have been negoti- ated and the document drafted and signed, the manager can finally get down to business. The manager's first matter of concern is to determine where the artist's career currently stands. This means the manager, in effect, must take inventory of the client's business and creative assets. For sophisticated acts that earn sub- stantial amounts, the business side of things will most likely be handled by a separate business manager who is a specialist in business and financial matters; we'll cover this more in the next chapter. On the other end of the income spectrum, for those newer artists who are employing principles of self-management, the need to inventory is the same.

In order to simplify the material in this chapter, we refer to whoever has the responsibility for the business side of things as being the manager. But regardless of what this individual is called, a basic truth stands out: Simply stated, it is impossible to plot a course to the future if you don't have a clear grasp of where you currently are. This chapter is devoted to the business portion of this evaluation.

Generally, the manager's analysis should cover the following: the form of business, employment agreements, service mark, banking, insurance, bookkeeping and tax planning, budgeting, and legal overview.

THE FORM OF BUSINESS

The starting point of any business evaluation are the questions, "What form of business is my client currently working under?"

and "What form of business should my client be working under?" Basically, there are three traditional forms of business entities available. They are proprietorship, partnership, and the corporation. In recent years, a fourth has come into being. Most states now recognize the limited liability company, or LLC, which has the limited liability advantages of a corporation combined with the ease and informality of management of the partnership.

Each of these four forms of business has distinct characteristics, advantages, and drawbacks. The manager should analyze the various entities in view of the artist's circumstances and needs before making the appropriate selection. Often the advice of an attorney or accountant will be necessary to make a proper determination of which form to select. As we've advocated before, if the manager has any questions regarding the selection of a particular business entity, he or she shouldn't hesitate to seek appropriate counsel or even recommend the use of a business manager, provided that the artist's income and business warrant such a move.

Let's briefly review the advantages and disadvantages of the four basic entities, or forms of business.

SOLE PROPRIETORSHIP

A sole proprietorship is an unincorporated business operation owned by an individual. The advantages of the proprietorship form of doing business are numerous. The primary advantage is that the owner is the boss. He or she makes all decisions regarding the operation of the business without having to consult others, such as a board of directors (a body associated with formulating policy matters and the business direction of a corporation). There's little formality or cost associated with the formation of a proprietorship. The business is free to trade and operate anywhere without having to comply with various qualification statutes in each state where it does business. The proprietor is not subject to liability for the actions of others, which is inherent in partnerships and with officers of a corporation. Moreover, the individual proprietor is not subject to as many regulatory and reporting requirements as other forms of business enterprise. Finally, a proprietorship may be granted borrowing power beyond the value of the business, to the extent of the owner's assets outside the proprietorship will allow.

A primary disadvantage of the one-person business is that no one other than the owner can act on behalf of the enterprise, except as an agent. Consequently, the business has limited decision-making capability and expertise. More disturbing is that the owner is subject to unlimited personal liability for all the obligations of the business. Furthermore, the amount of the investment in the business is limited to the resources of the owner. Another distinct disadvantage is that the proprietorship is subject to termination upon the death or incapacity of the owner. In addition, the other entities or forms of business provide certain tax advantages not found in the one-person business structure.

PARTNERSHIP

A partnership is created when two or more people agree to combine their property, talent, or other resources to establish a business in which each is to be an owner sharing the profits or losses of the enterprise. While the characteristics of a partnership are similar to the proprietorship, there are major distinctions, the foremost being the general agency feature of the partnership. Each partner can act on behalf of the business, thereby rendering the enterprise liable for any partner's action within the scope of the firm's operation. Therefore, it's extremely important that each partner have the utmost confidence in the integrity and ability of his or her associates. Generally, the partners are liable not only collectively but individually for all the obligations of the business, including liabilities that result from wrongful acts of the other partners.

The growth of a partnership can be restricted because all its members must consent before any additional members are included. However, termination of the partnership takes place upon the withdrawal of any one party. If the withdrawal is in violation of the partnership agreement, it may give rise to an action against the withdrawing party, but the partnership is nevertheless terminated. Dissolution of the partnership also occurs upon the death or incapacity of one of the partners. The effect of the death or incapacity of a partner can be minimized by various provisions embodied in the partnership agreement or by a collateral agreement between the parties. Nonetheless, if some provision has not been made, then the death or incapacity of a partner terminates the business.

CORPORATION

The corporate form of doing business is more complex than the proprietorship or partnership. The formation of an incorporated business creates a new entity capable of doing business in its own name. This new entity is viewed as an artificial person in the eyes of the law. The major positive characteristic of the corporation is freedom of the shareholder (owner of the corporation) from personal liability for the obligations of the business. Other desirable aspects of the corporate entity are the ability to easily transfer ownership through exchange of stock shares; to exist for a set period of time without being impaired by the death or incompetency of individual shareholders; and to raise large amounts of capital through investments of many shareholders.

On the negative side, the corporation is more costly to form compared to proprietorships and partnerships. In addition, corporations are subject to more governmental regulation, such as requirements of periodic filing of reports and various statements. Because ownership and control of the business corresponds to ownership of corporate stock, minority shareholders are subject to the control of the majority shareholders. This is a potentially frustrating fact of corporate ownership.

An additional drawback to the corporate form is that the credit available to a corporation is limited to its own assets, and not those of the individual shareholders, without some form of personal guarantee.

LIMITED LIABILITY COMPANY

In recent years, legal experts have invented a fourth basic form for conducting business called the limited liability company, or LLC. This hybrid of a partnership and corporation utilizes the best attributes of each while disposing of many of the more cumbersome and expensive characteristics of those alternatives. Specifically, an LLC combines the advantages of limited liability found in corporations with the flexibility, ease of management, and lack of formalities found in a partnership. This form of business, which is increasingly controlled by state statute, requires two or more principals. This makes the LLC an ideal vehicle for duos and groups in the music business.

OTHER BUSINESS ENTITIES

As stated at the outset, the proprietorship, partnership, corporation, and limited liability company are the four *basic* forms of business available to an artist. However, there are other entities that derive from the four basic ones, including the limited partnership and joint venture. Since their use is limited and extremely complex, these business arrangements are beyond the scope of this discussion.

To assist in the proper selection and formation of any of these entities, the advice of an attorney and an accountant is recommended. It should also be noted that the corporation will normally require the services of an attorney to ensure that proper records are being maintained and reports required by law are being filed. The adoption of one of the derivatives of the basic entities also requires counsel in its formation.

SELECTING THE FORM OF BUSINESS

The manager can recommend selection of any one of the various business entities available. The choice will depend on the circumstances of the client and the advice of professional counsel. For example, a young artist recently signed to a major recording contract would probably select the sole proprietorship form of business. However, as an artist's career develops, the need may arise to transform the proprietorship into a corporate entity depending on increased exposure to liability, tax consequences, and other considerations. For another example, let's assume we're dealing with a four-man rock group. On first glance, this would seem to suggest the creation of a partnership arrangement. However, because of the desire to limit exposure to legal liability, which could stem from something like a traffic accident on the road, or to breach of contract, a potential result of missed club performances, or to any number of other unfortunate yet real possibilities, the band might well be advised to form a limited liability company.

Depending on the circumstances, there may well be a third option. Let us suppose that one member of the band is the financial strength of the entire group, while another possesses all the creative, writing, and vocal talents. Given this situation, the best arrangement might not be a partnership between all four members; instead, those members with the financial and artistic strengths may want to consider the formation of a partnership between themselves and then employ the other two members. The possible variations are limited only by the circumstances of the applicable situation.

In short, the manager must assess the artist, or the group as a whole, and its circumstances to determine what the appropriate form of business should be.

SUPPORT PERSONNEL

Once the manager has assessed the artist's business-entity status, consulted counsel, made the appropriate recommendations, and taken measures to set up the appropriate business vehicle, the first step is completed. Next comes a review of the personnel requirements of the artist. For instance, if the artist is a single act, will he or she require a full-time backup group? If the artist tours regularly, will a road crew be required? Does the artist need a road manager? Regardless of specific career objectives, he or she will require the services of other people on either a regularly or irregularly recurring basis. These people might be regular employees or contract personnel.

Certainly, the creative and economic circumstances of the artist, along with the career plan the manager will help formulate, will greatly affect the number of people the artist will have to employ. The manager must analyze the existing situation in view of how many people are currently employed and how many are contemplated for future projects. Are all employees necessary? Does the artist have employment contracts with them?

Making personnel recommendations to the client and subsequently negotiating employment contracts can be a big job. It can spell the difference between annual profit and loss, given the spiraling costs of hiring backup and studio musicians and vocalists, musical directors, arrangers, a road manager and crew, sound engineers, stage directors, wardrobe designers, lighting technicians, drivers, pilots, bodyguards, promotion people, publicists, and the other supporting cast that help get an artist to the top. Only through this type of coordinated approach to personnel management can an artist track overhead, which is one of the keys to controlling profit and loss.

SERVICE MARK

An often overlooked aspect of the business inventory is the value of an artist's or group's trade name. There are many nightmarish stories about the hit group who found out they didn't have full right to use their own name. Even more common is a situation in which no partnership agreement has been executed between members of a group and subsequently the group breaks up. When the former members create new groups and utilize the original trade name, the result is often protracted, expensive litigation. The best way to avoid problems related to one's trade name is to seek federal *service mark* protection.

Whereas the *trademark*—such as Ivory for soap or Coca-Cola for soft drinks—indicates origin of goods, a service mark denotes origin of services. In this context, the mark relates to entertainment services provided by the artist, such as the live performance and recording of music. Federal service mark protection is obtained by the use of a specific name in connection with the rendition of services provided that the usage is made in interstate commerce. In 1988, the Lanham Trademark Act added an "intent to use" provision whereby applicants could reserve a name without actually going to the expense of using it in commerce. In both instances, federal nationwide protection is obtained by registration of the proper application with the Commissioner of Patents in Washington, D.C. The artist and manager are advised to simultaneously file for state service mark protection or its equivalent, if available.

The advantages of registration under the Lanham Act are numerous. A service mark indicates the origin of the artist's services. It's a vehicle for building and valuing goodwill in the artist's business. It helps protect the artist from mistake, confusion, or deceit fostered by other artists who may subsequently adopt the same or a similar name. It ensures that the artist may exclusively perform under his or her professional name. In addition, it can be included on the artist's financial statement as an asset. It's a potentially marketable commodity.

The only disadvantage is the out-of-pocket cost associated with a service mark search and the filing of the application. When consulting an attorney as to the various forms of doing business, the manager should ask about securing service mark protection. At the same time, the artist should specify both the ownership of the name and what is to happen in the event of a breakup. This is especially important in the case of groups. The partnership agreement or a corporate resolution is the appropriate vehicle for clarifying this potential problem.

BANKING

When examining the condition of the artist's business, the manager needs to ascertain the borrowing power of the artist, whose relationship with lending institutions will either be good, bad, or nonexistent. Given the last two situations, the manager must convert his or her client into a good risk in order to establish a solid banking connection.

If the artist has never dealt with a bank before, the manager can arrange for him or her to meet the proper banking officer not only to establish a business relationship, but also to ensure that the artist's personal banking needs are fulfilled. On the other hand, if the artist has a poor record with a particular bank, the manager should attempt to clear up the problem, if possible, or embark on a new relationship with another institution. As a last resort, the manager may choose to utilize his or her own borrowing capacity to assist the artist in starting a bank relationship.

If the artist has maintained a good banking relationship in the past, then as the manager you should seek to build on the existing financial base. A sure way to solidify the relationship is to meet with the artist's banker and explain the artist's career direction, goals and objectives, strategies for success, and contracts, budgets, and forecasts.

Some progressive banks in music centers have special departments to deal with the needs of entertainment clients. But even when it is unnecessary to explain the high profile and often unstable environment in which your client operates, it's still essential that you do your homework and present the artist to the bank *as a business.*

The banker will be the first person to recognize professional business management, so an immediate benefit will be derived from presenting an artist to a banker in a businesslike fashion. Beyond performing the normal function of moving money for routine transactions, the bank can provide a host of additional services once the artist's career advances past the breaking-in stage. These include preapproved lines of credit, open-note signature loans, credit cards, foreign exchange, long-term equipment or vehicle financing, mortgages, and so on.

Banking is a fact of life; it's important not to overlook it or take it for granted. Being organized and talking the bank's language is at least half the battle.

INSURANCE

Like it or not, insurance is another fact of life in the business world. Any well-managed business maintains a variety of insurance policies as a hedge against economic or personal disaster.

The artist's business is no different. The manager should examine the areas of vehicle, liability, equipment, and life insurance.

VEHICLE INSURANCE

The bank will normally require insurance protection if it has provided funds for a vehicle; from a financial standpoint, it's simply good business. But the need doesn't stop with the bank. If an artist or group has invested substantial amounts in vehicles, a total loss could have catastrophic financial consequences. Replacement problems are magnified considerably if the artist is in the middle of a tour and suddenly finds him- or herself without vehicles or the cash to purchase new ones.

LIABILITY INSURANCE

Liability insurance protection is a necessity. Just as vehicle insurance protects a property value, liability coverage insures against negligent acts of the driver of the vehicle.

The possible consequences of operating an uninsured vehicle are obvious. They are magnified if the artist is doing business as a proprietorship or partnership, with personal exposure for his or her own negligent acts, those of employees, and, in some cases, those of independent contractors. And while the shareholders of a corporation or limited liability company would be protected from personal liability, the assets of the corporation or LLC are vulnerable to a lawsuit stemming from negligent operation of a vehicle owned by the business. To put the problem in perspective, if it is a stretch to make payments on a used Greyhound Bus, how much tougher would it be to come up with a million dollars to satisfy a wrongful death judgment when that bus has been involved in a fatal accident caused by a driver who fell asleep at the wheel? Sadly, it's happened all too often.

EQUIPMENT INSURANCE

Artists must invest considerable sums of money in their musical equipment, sound, lighting, and staging to maintain artistic quality and stay competitive in today's market—primarily, giving audiences what they demand for their entertainment dollars. Substantial equipment investments require insurance protection from fire, theft, and other potential damage or loss. The artist must have the assurance that in the event of damage or destruction activities can resume as soon as possible without financial disaster. The cost of equipment, along with high annual premiums, can be a good reason to rent or lease equipment on an as-needed basis, but the artist can still expect to pay the insurance premium—either directly (albeit for a shorter period) or indirectly, as part of the agreed-upon rental charge.

LIFE INSURANCE

Life insurance coverage is another protective device that should be used by the artist. As one's career develops, so does one's income. The manager and other group members (if the artist is in a partnership) become vulnerable to substantial loss of income in the event of the death of the artist or another group member. In order to protect against this contingency, life insurance can be maintained on the artist or other key members of the group. Such a policy would normally name the manager or the other members of the group as beneficiaries. The amount of life insurance carried can be adjusted from year to year to provide sufficient protection.

It should be noted that this coverage would be in addition to life insurance acquired to provide for the artist's family in the event of his or her death.

Insurance companies offer an assortment of business-coverage policies. The manager should seek the advice of an insurance expert in formulating a plan to protect all the various areas of the artist's business exposed to potentially crippling loss. Insurance premiums are no fun, but they are certainly preferable to losing everything.

BOOKKEEPING AND TAX PLANNING

Is the artist maintaining a set of financial records? Have books been kept in the past? It's very important that the manager ascertain the adequacy of the artist's record-keeping system. Not only does the manager have to be concerned with the current bookkeeping system, but he or she should also review the artist's records for at least two previous years. This will help prevent any unannounced surprises from the IRS or the state tax commission.

Knowledge of a client's haphazard bookkeeping practices or of any failure to file required tax reports doesn't mean that the manager can wave a magic wand over these problems if tax officials raise questions. But the manager can help avoid problems in the future while taking steps to rectify past problems.

Unless the manager has special expertise in this area, an accountant should be retained to help the manager install a new bookkeeping system or to review the adequacy of an old one. The accountant is usually responsible for filing all state and federal income tax forms and corporate franchise and income tax returns. An accountant will also be helpful in reviewing the artist's business as it grows, to determine whether a switch to a different business entity is desirable. One of the primary motivations for changing the legal structure of a business is to take advantage of the most favorable tax treatment. The accountant will be the first to recognize the tax ramifications of a particular business entity. As the artist's career and income moves upward, the tax consequences will become more of a factor in the overall career plan.

BUDGETING

A budget is a financial road map. Just as the road manager plots the route for an upcoming tour, the manager must map out the artist-client's financial route.

The first step in budgeting is to prepare an income forecast: The manager must attempt to project the artist's earnings for a given year by studying the previous year's income. Once it is clear how much was earned the previous year, when it was received, and what contracts are in effect for the upcoming year, the manager can make a forecast for the coming year.

Given the objectives of the artist, in view of the earnings forecast, the manager then determines the amount of money that will have to be generated during the year and starts balancing the various factors (banks, agents, record companies, budget) in an attempt to reach that goal.

For example, let's say that an artist grossed $500,000 from personal appearances and wants to increase his earnings by $100,000 for the upcoming year. The manager would have to analyze several factors. Can the client command an increased performance fee? Can the agent deliver higher priced dates? As an alternative, should the artist's overhead be reduced? Should he or she shift markets? On the basis of these findings, the manager will attempt to formulate an economic plan capable of fulfilling the artist's wishes.

Let's take another example. Assume that an artist earned $200,000 the previous year by performing her act in the nightclub market. For the upcoming year, she would like to reduce the number of night-club performances to devote more time to song-writing and recording. However, she wants to maintain her previous year's income. The manager has to answer several questions in designing a budget. Can the artist maintain her previous year's income by working less? Should they cut overhead? Can the artist afford to pay the increased studio bills? Just exactly how is the manager going to help her accomplish this objective? Is it possible?

Again, the first step is to formulate a financial plan based on a forecast and budget. The manager must be able to look into the artist's economic future. From this point, he or she can juggle the figures and, usually, structure a plan to achieve the artist's objective. But if it is evident that it can't be achieved, the process that yielded this conclusion will be helpful in explaining to the artist why it is not achievable at present.

In this scenario, some options immediately come to mind: Cut fixed overhead by reducing the size of the backup band or nonstage personnel; raise the asking price to clubs, knowing that it will probably result in approximately the same amount of income on fewer dates; help offset the income deficit by seeking an advance from a record company, music publisher, or performing rights society; sell equipment or vehicles to raise money and then rent or lease on an as-needed basis.

All these solutions rest on the premise that the artist's talents and abilities can command these options. If not, the answer might be that a reduction in dates isn't currently possible. The focus then shifts to finding ways to create those options in the months ahead.

Artists are like everyone else in that they have both personal and business financial needs. It's the manager's responsibility to help fulfill those needs, or at least explain convincingly why the artist's desires cannot be fulfilled. It's also the manager's job to help the artist spend his money wisely in order to ensure that there's something to show for the years of effort once his or her popularity wanes.

LEGAL OVERVIEW

We've previously discussed the importance of attorneys during the negotiation and preparation of the management contract.

During the business inventory stage, any legal question regarding the artist's business status should be reviewed by legal counsel. The artist's manager and attorney need to be aware of all business planning, pending litigation, existing contractual obligations, and all other pertinent legal data. The manager should consult the attorney on any matter of which he or she is unsure. Once a financial and legal inventory of the artist's business has been taken, the manager should be ready to take a creative inventory, which is followed by formulating the career plan—the specifics of which will be discussed in subsequent chapters.

The final result of the business inventory phase should be a well-organized, efficient business vehicle, complete with all the protection that contracts, service marks, and insurance can offer. By creating a stable and predictable business environment, artist and manager will gain a clear understanding of where they are financially and, more importantly, exactly where they're going in the future.

7

Attorneys, Accountants, and Business Managers

While the personal manager is instrumental in structuring and administering the artist's creative and business affairs, many aspects of the artist's business will require the expertise of the professional support team. This is especially true when the artist is making substantial sums from record royalties, personal appearances, songwriting, and corporate endorsements and sponsorships. The professional support team normally consists of attorneys, accountants, and business advisers, or, in some instances, a business manager. We have already alluded to the important role these people play in the initial stages of defining the management relationship and in business planning. Their involvement becomes even more pronounced as the artist's career begins to take off with hit records and sold-out concert tours.

The entertainment industry is a highly sophisticated and complex system. As the level of investment and corporate participation continues to increase, so does the complexity. A manager and artist can expect to be confronted with a wide range of legal and financial decisions over the span of a career. Just from a legal standpoint, a successful artist will probably be involved in contractual relationships with his or her manager, booking agents, record company and producer, music publishers, book publishers, corporate sponsors, advertisers seeking product endorsements, and, possibly, motion picture, television, and video producers. Multifaceted successful artists will often own all or part of some entities—music publishing, booking and concert promotion companies, and so on. The artist will certainly be involved with the protection and licensing of his or her name and likeness, as well as the exploitation and administration of copyrighted musical compositions and other literary and intellectual properties. And as if that weren't enough, there is the seemingly endless entourage of musicians, road managers, drivers, roadies, wardrobe personnel, and publicists who comprise a sizable overhead expense.

There is also the matter of the ownership or leasing of sound and lighting equipment, musical instruments, vehicles, props, and wardrobe. Besides business responsibilities, the artist will also be concerned with the administration of his or her personal finances and personal property. Sound complicated? It certainly is—and that's only a quick overview of routine matters requiring a good lawyer, accountant, and business adviser or manager.

ATTORNEYS

The preceding two chapters outlined the role that an attorney plays during the initial stages of the artist–manager relationship. General legal counsel, contract expertise, and negotiation skills are all staples of a successful career, but that only begins to explain the role of a top-flight attorney.

When selecting an attorney the artist and manager should seek a person with experience in the entertainment field—indeed, with an active involvement specifically in the music business. Don't assume that all attorneys possess the special knowledge and training to adequately handle the peculiar requirements of the music business. The trend today is toward greater legal specialization, and the entertainment world is no exception. In fact, music law is a subspecialty as distinguished from motion pictures and television or sports law. Unless a lawyer regularly deals with management, recording, and music publishing contracts; copyright protection and administration; and licensing of intellectual and artistic property, chances are he or she won't sufficiently understand or appreciate the industry and its peculiar legal problems.

When seeking a qualified music lawyer, other managers and industry professionals are good sources for recommendations. Professional directories such as the *Martindale–Hubbel Law Directory* (Martindale–Hubbel, New Providence, N.J.), which is found in most law libraries, may also be consulted as a starting point if the artist or manager is totally unfamiliar with members of the legal profession and their qualifications. Ask the librarian to show you how to use it.

Because of the high degree of specialization in music law, the majority of practitioners are located in industry centers such as New York, Los Angeles, or Nashville. However, they may be found in other cities throughout the country, too.

Artists and managers should be cautioned against the natural inclination to use a friend, relative, or family lawyer to fill their entertainment law needs. This is fine if the person is qualified, but the manager could be doing the artist-client a great disservice by retaining an attorney without a music industry background.

When contacting an attorney for the first time, the manager or artist should discuss the fee at the outset to avoid any misunderstanding. Often, the attorney will schedule an initial conference to discuss the artist's particular legal needs or problems on either a flat-fee or an hourly-rate basis. During this initial meeting, the artist or manager and the attorney should discuss their financial arrangement, which will usually be based on an hourly rate that can range from as little as $100 an hour to hundreds of dollars for each sixty minutes of billable time. In some cases, attorney's charges are based on a percentage of the artist's income, depending on the circumstances of the artist and the preference of the parties involved. In certain instances, attorneys will charge a flat fee for specified assignments such as drafting contracts or other legal instruments.

While it's understandable that a new artist must necessarily be cost-conscious, he or she shouldn't let price be a reason to neglect seeking competent and experienced legal counsel. Our advice is to shop around for legal representation just as you would for any other service. Attorney's fees vary with the experience and client load of individual lawyers. Often, a younger, less experienced though competent entertainment attorney may be just the right choice for the new artist or manager. And finally, cost aside, it's important to find an attorney with whom you feel comfortable.

Whatever the final decision, the artist or manager should never try to be his or her own lawyer just to save money. This is a guaranteed path to trouble which can result in having to hire an attorney for substantially more money later to deal with what should have been a routine matter. That's where suing and getting sued comes in. Either way, you lose. It is always better to avoid litigation, if at all possible, and concentrate on more productive pursuits. For this reason alone, it is worth digging into your pocket at the outset to pay for quality legal talent that can help you avoid an expensive mess later on.

ACCOUNTANTS

We've already discussed the importance of the accountant in helping to select the artist's business entity and in reviewing and developing a workable bookkeeping system. One of the worst things that can happen to an artist is to experience financial success without being properly prepared for it from an accounting standpoint. There are many sad stories of artists who made fortunes only to lose everything as a result of ineffective income management, negligent recordkeeping, nonexistent tax planning, and failure to save and make proper investments. A good accountant can help avoid all this and more.

Sadder yet is the fate of those artists who've operated under the mistaken impression that filing tax returns was an optional exercise. Obviously, it is essential that timely and accurate tax returns be filed with the Internal Revenue Service as well as state and local governments.

As the artist's income increases, the need for professional accounting and tax planning becomes more important. Of special importance to a recording artist and songwriter is the ability of the accountant to interpret and verify royalty statements and, when necessary, to conduct audits. A good accountant will see to it that none of this falls through the cracks.

As with the attorney, the value of the accountant increases dramatically as he or she becomes familiar with the ongoing developments in the artist's business. Therefore, the manager should keep the accountant regularly informed of the artist's financial activities.

The same general rules regarding selection and compensation of an attorney also apply to accountants, with some exceptions. While it's helpful for the accountant to have a background in the entertainment industry, especially with regard to audits and royalty accounting, it's not generally as crucial as with attorneys.

Compensation will vary with the expertise and experience of the accountant. Certified public accountants (CPAs) usually command a larger fee due to their special training and wider range of knowledge and expertise. Compensation is usually set on either a flat-fee, hourly-rate, or retainer basis. As with attorneys, you shouldn't be shy about the subject of fees. And don't hesitate to shop around for the right person as well as the right price.

BUSINESS ADVISERS

We'll refer to bankers, estate planners, and insurance professionals under the heading of business advisers. Their services are essential in maintaining an efficient business.

Again, the banker can play a central role in the development of a young artist's career. Finding the right personal banking connection should not be overlooked when time comes to put together the professional support team.

The estate planner is a highly specialized professional whose function is to plan the most efficient distribution of the artist's assets in the event of his or her death. While most artists are not concerned with this aspect of business planning at the outset of their career, it does become important later. An artist must exercise caution when choosing an estate planner. There are many firms and individuals who profess to have such skills. Attorneys, certified public accountants, and chartered life underwriters are generally qualified to render this important service. Whoever is chosen, the artist and manager must be certain they select a well-qualified professional.

BUSINESS MANAGERS

Everything we have said regarding accountants and business advisers can be rolled into one individual called a business manager. The more complex the career and the higher the earnings of the artist, the more appropriate it is to delegate all of the artist's business and accounting needs to a full-time business manager. In addition to the functions of an accountant, a business manager will be responsible for receiving all monies, paying all bills, and investing what is left. The standard fee for a business manager with solid music business experience is 5 percent. Alternative compensation schemes include a flat-fee, hourly-rate, or retainer basis—or some combination of those.

A WORD OF CAUTION

Attorneys, accountants, business advisers, and business managers are no different from personal managers when it comes to making choices about whom you will assign leading roles in your career. In fact, when it comes to legal commitments and money, you should be doubly careful. All the creative and commercial success you have ever dreamed of can be destroyed by an incompetent or dishonest lawyer, accountant, business adviser, or business manager.

Whereas all lawyers must be licensed by the state in which they practice, the same cannot always be said of business managers or financial advisers. In addition to knowing whom you are bringing on board, lean toward CPAs, chartered life underwriters, and other individuals who have credentials beyond a big office, a flashy car, and a toothy smile. The unfortunate fact is that there are unscrupulous people in the world who gain people's trust only to steal their money later. Because you are, in effect, handing over your checkbook, you need to be very, very careful about whom you hand it to. That is why you should maintain a sense of healthy skepticism when it comes to the subject of money. That means asking hard questions and always insisting upon references. You and your bank account will be glad you did.

8

Taking Creative Inventory

Having taken stock of the artist's business organization and assets, the manager should next focus on taking creative inventory. Before getting into the details of the creative inventory, a brief word about how to get the most out of the process: A meaningful artistic evaluation requires total honesty between the manager and artist. This is no time for the artist to get his or her feelings hurt or to let ego stand in the way of a process that will ultimately prove beneficial. Of course, this is easier said than done, but nonetheless it's vitally important.

Because this is a touchy subject, the manager should take steps to sufficiently prepare the artist. The artist should be reminded that any criticism is meant to be constructive in nature. The manager should point out that he or she wouldn't be involved with the artist if there weren't a strong dedication to the artist's talent and ability to succeed. Finally, the manager should stress the need for complete honesty and mutual trust. The manager's tone and interpersonal skills are all-important when it comes to making this process work. Both parties should be aware that this will probably be the first juncture in the relationship where there's the possibility of confrontation and friction. Both parties should know that and be ready. If the necessary rapport and trust are in place, things should go okay. If not . . . well, maybe it's time already to re-evaluate the relationship.

ARTIST EVALUATION

The first level of inquiry by the manager should be a personal assessment of the artist. The same general types of questions will apply to both individuals and groups.

The process should begin with basic questions involving the particular talent or talents of the artist. Because this is primarily a book for aspiring artists in the music industry, we know that singing and performing will be a common element, but beyond that, what are the basic questions that should be asked?

DOES THE ARTIST HAVE A UNIQUE SOUND?

In the case of an aspiring recording artist without a record deal, the first item of concern relates to the artist's sound. Does he or she have a unique vocal style, or is the sound reminiscent of other well-known recording artists? One of the primary complaints of record producers and record company A&R people is that otherwise talented, would-be recording artists often sound too much like someone already on the radio. If an artist is merely a clone of someone else, there is little chance a record company will be interested. No label wants or needs another Tom Petty, Whitney Houston, or Reba McEntire when they have the original. Record buyers are no different. That is not to minimize the importance of an established star influencing an aspiring new talent. It's up to the manager to help the artist see the difference between an influence and a clone.

WHERE WILL THE HIT SONGS COME FROM?

Another critically important factor for singers has to do with material. Does the artist write his or her own songs? If so, chances for a long-term record deal are greatly enhanced. First of all, an artist-writer is more likely to have a distinct sound or style by virtue of songs that are custom-tailored to his or her own performing abilities. Secondly, an artist-writer is assured of a stable source of material. This enhances longevity and in the eyes of the record company reduces the risk of signing the artist.

Of course, there are many notable exceptions: Elvis Presley depended on other writers for material; over the span of her career, Dionne Warwick has always been a pure singer who has relied on songwriters Burt Bacharach and Hal David for a steady stream of classic hits. Many country acts have sustained careers for a decade or more while depending almost exclusively on Nashville songwriters for material. But even this is changing. The conclusion is clear. If an artist doesn't write, it's time to start.

THE ROLE OF PHYSICAL APPEARANCE

In today's market, recording artists are in reality multimedia artists. Like it or not, with some exceptions in the rap, heavy metal, and alternative-music fields, physical appearance is a critical factor to career success. Starting in the 1980s, MTV first changed the face of the music industry so that viewers could not only hear, but see an act as well. Since then, VH-1, CMT, BET, as well as the video production units of the major labels, have solidified what was a trend into an industry standard. The commercial music industry is a sight and sound business, and it's not going back to just audio anytime soon. Like it or not, how you look and project yourself in video and live TV is, in many instances, every bit as important as the song and how you sing it.

Traditionally, the visual mediums of television and motion pictures demanded that a leading man or woman be either blessed with natural good looks or, alternatively, very, very interesting physically. Fortunately or unfortunately, the music business with its increased video emphasis has moved in that direction. A survey of managers, publicists, and record people we interviewed evoked the following response to our question, "What kind of physical appearance must an artist have to enjoy success in today's music industry?" *Pleasing, different,* and *interesting* were the top answers. However, almost all agreed that the odds were against someone who was physically unattractive.

A related factor is age. Because the baby-boom generation is aging, this is less of a factor than it once was, but it is still a factor for artists in their mid-thirties who are not yet established. Fortunately, the miracles of diet, wardrobe, and cosmetic enhancement can work wonders with almost anybody. But the fact remains that much of commercial music appeals to a youth market, even after you factor in the forever-young baby boomers, who still buy records in large numbers. While there are always exceptions, a brand-new forty-year-old artist might be able to get by on a CD, but he and especially she start showing their age on video. Of course, none of this applies to Mick Jagger or Rod Stewart, but then they already have record deals and loyal followings. Call it unfair, but that's the way it is in today's video-driven, multimedia world.

POISE AND PRESENCE

Certainly, physical appearance is important, but it's really only one element in the artist's total image. Today, more than ever, poise and presence are dominant elements in building and sustaining a successful career. Because it is often a 24-hour-a-day job, it's important for an artist to adopt an image that is both comfortable and consistent with his or her personality and values. Playing the part of someone else, especially someone who doesn't ring true, will backfire sooner or later, given the intense media scrutiny that comes with being a high-profile artist/celebrity. Coming across as genuine and credible while generating charisma unique to the artist is a must in a long-term career. Audiences want more than just good records. They want personalities. The substance of that personality (good, bad, weird, strange, and so on) is far less important than the unique qualities that define the celebrity to the public.

Image and how effectively that image is projected are virtually identical. Like the tree that falls in the forest, all the charisma in the world amounts to nothing if it is not properly and effectively projected to the public eye. Publicity photographs, video clips, interviews, wardrobe, and even the artist's choice of charities and political causes all combine to tell the public who the artist is and what he or she is all about. That image, whatever it might be, and how it's projected should never be left to chance. This is why it's essential to retain a first-rate publicist to formulate and control the image that goes out to the record-buying and concertgoing public. For inexperienced artists in the early stages of their careers, the cost of hiring a seasoned media consultant to help sharpen their celebrity skills is often money well spent. Because of the record label's investment in the artist, there is a very good chance that the manager can squeeze out some extra dollars to offset the consultant's fee.

THE TOTAL IMAGE PACKAGE

At the risk of offending the aesthetic soul of managers and their clients, the artist should be viewed as a total image package. Career survival requires both artist and manager to constantly and objectively measure the overall impression the artist makes on its target audience on and off the stage.

It goes without saying that one's strengths should be accentuated whenever possible. But what about deficiences or perceived weaknesses? An astute artist and manager will first acknowledge them, but only to each other, and then either mask or minimize them or find a way to turn them into an advantage that will make the artist different or unique. A wonderful example is Tony Bennett, who has blended style and material in such a way as to retain his core audience while winning over whole new generations of younger fans at an age when many of his contemporaries have long since been pushed off the charts and out of the lime-light. The Grammy Award winner has only recently enjoyed some of his greatest successes by turning a potential liability into an asset.

The mark of a resourceful manager is the ability to recognize weaknesses and, if possible, convert them into points of distinctiveness or, at the least, minimize them. More than one sex symbol has dazzled audiences with capped smiles that would never betray the secrets of stage corsets, lift shoes, and tinted hair. Remember, show business is just like magic in that it is the audience's perception of reality rather than the reality itself that counts. Good managers live by that fact.

WHERE THE ARTIST IS GOING

Part of the artistic inventory should involve sketching a detailed historical profile of the artist. The artist and manager will want to take maximum advantage of the artist's past successes and experience while avoiding repetition of past mistakes and failures. Knowing in detail where the artist has been both professionally and personally makes it possible to formulate the right career plan and image for the future. The historical profile should include the artist's past triumphs as well as the failures, and the motivations behind both. Insight into the personal and psychological makeup of the artist along with the past circumstances or life experience can be very helpful in selecting goals and structuring a plan for career development.

For instance, singer-songwriter Merle Haggard's now well-chronicled experience with prison, as well as a love for the traditional country music of Bob Wills and Jimmie Rodgers, played a big part in shaping his image when his career was in the breakthrough period. Emphasis on these factors, combined with good timing, helped give Haggard a unique identity that the public embraced, thus launching a legendary career. Once again, a shrewd twist turned what would usually be considered a negative into a positive.

PERFORMING EXPOSURE

Once the overall picture is in place, the manager should begin to break it down into its component parts and analyze them. For example, the artist's present status and past history with regard to personal appearances should be subjected to scrutiny. This includes the type and amount of performing experience; the type of stage show the artist puts on; a list of the artist's contacts with agents, promoters, and club owners; and the present status of bookings. All this information is useful in helping the manager structure an immediate network of contacts and possible return engagements that could be turned into immediate income for the artist.

RECORDING EXPOSURE

Similiar questions should be asked in the area of recording, beginning with a review of the artist's present status—his or her current producer, recorded material in the can, and affiliations with record companies and executives. Previously released material, sales and airplay history, and contacts with radio program directors and disc jockeys should also be thoroughly discussed and noted. The parties should touch on anything relevant to furthering the artist's career via recordings, especially producers, A&R people, and other record executives who have previously expressed interest in the artist. In addition, the parties should review and critique all the artist's recordings, both released and unreleased, in order to determine a future strategy.

OTHER SIGNIFICANT CAREER AREAS

As with personal appearances and recordings, the process of evaluating the artist's present and past should be repeated for every substantive area of his or her career—songwriting, music publishing, television and motion pictures, commercials, merchandising, endorsements, and so on.

Once the detailed information concerning artist and career has been compiled in the creative inventory, the manager can begin the formulation of the artist's image.

IMAGE FORMULATION

We've already touched on the issue of image. The concept isn't hard to understand, but the reality of shaping, projecting, and maintaining the artist's image in a way that will strike a chord with the public while allowing the artist to retain some semblance of a private life is among the most difficult tasks confronting the artist–manager team. Here are some suggestions for going about it.

The image will be determined in light of the artist's goals, abilities, values, resources, and the existing commercial setting. Using the information gleaned from the foregoing inventories, the starting point is to set career objectives.

IMAGE

Every artist must decide what image he or she wants to project. That sounds rather obvious, but an alarming number of very talented people only know that they want to be "stars," or that they have a driving desire to "make it" in the business. That is all well and good, but it tells us nothing about who they are and what they stand for. As previously stated, image must be consistent with these very things.

What is the artist's identity, then, and what do his or her fans value? With some notable exceptions, a too-dissonant image runs the risk of losing credibility with fans. For instance, heavy-metal fans expect a certain degree of rudeness and aloofness from their favored type of artist. The warm-and-fuzzy approach would surely shatter the image of a rebel who has a harsh message for society and couldn't care less about how it is received.

On the other hand, if a contemporary "family values" type of country artist were to preach toleration for drug use and sexual promiscuity, he or she would find it difficult if not impossible to maintain a wholesome image—much less get or keep a record deal in today's country market. This is in many respects curious, given country music's history of drinkin' and cheatin' songs, sung by Hank Williams, George Jones, and a score of others. Times and tastes change, and the most likely victims are artists whose images aren't consistent with the shifts in public expectations.

IMAGE VERSUS TRENDS

There is no doubt that much, if not all, of the music business runs on trends. Classical music is probably the least buffeted by trends, but even there fashionable ideas and sales strategies take hold of the industry. To ignore a trend could mean saying goodbye to a tremendous career opportunity. However, if an artist is too trend-conscious, there is a risk that the public will forsake him or her when the trend passes.

There are numerous examples of long-extinct careers that once flourished and then failed to survive the demise of the disco, urban cowboy, or new wave movements. The correct answer to this potentially tricky problem seems to lie in perfecting a balancing act between being original and commercial while maintaining sufficient flexibility to change with the times. Trends shouldn't control image, but neither should they be completely ignored.

Again, one of the textbook examples is Elvis Presley. There was the young rock-and-roll Elvis, the movie star Elvis, and the Vegas-jumpsuit Elvis. Each distinct phase of the entertainer's career was wildly successful. Why? Elvis and his manager, Colonel Tom Parker, were willing to let go of the previous career phase in favor of change. Some would say it was genius, while others would argue it was a matter of survival, but the one consistent theme in the story is that at the center of each shift was the unmistakable personality, unique voice, and undeniable appeal of Presley himself. This is a prime example of originality and commercial viability tempered by flexibility.

It is not always as easy as trading in swiveling hips for a rhinestone-festooned suit, but you get the idea.

EXISTING IMAGE

Aside from the artist's professional and personal goals, a major consideration is his or her existing image. The manager should ask: "How is my artist presently perceived by the public as well as by others in the entertainment industry?" If an artist is new or relatively unknown, current perceptions won't present a problem—nothing much has been established. However, existing image can be a problem for an artist who wants to renew an established but slipping career with an image change. The veteran artist runs the risk of alienating those fans that he or she already has. And a radical change carries the danger that it simply won't be accepted by the public at all. This can be especially true of an artist long known for a particular style of recording or performing.

The trade press and industry decision-makers, as well as the fans, are obsessed with labels. In the increasingly short attention span world in which we live, labels are a necessity. They are an effective short reference that allow us to categorize and deal with a complicated world. But once accepted, labels are difficult to change. Consider how difficult it was for people to accept the fact that a former Monkee, Mike Nesmith, could produce serious music videos. This should illustrate why an artist and manager should pay careful attention to formulation and development of image.

Flexibility should be built in to allow for shifts in direction or development of an artist's music that will be accepted by the public without turning off hard-won fans. Walking this fine line requires a great deal of managerial dexterity.

ISSUES OF IMAGE-CRAFTING

Manager and artist must craft an image that will not only complement the talent, appearance, and personality of the artist, but also have commercial potential. For instance, let's assume that an artist's songs and style are compatible with the image of an early 1960s Greenwich Village folksinger. Projecting such an image would be a blunder if there's no substantial market for that particular style of music in the contemporary market. Yet by taking some basic elements of folk music—such as "message" songs with contemporary social themes and basic acoustic guitar accompaniments—and blending them with a unique voice and a striking personal appearance, you have innovation. We have just described Tracy Chapman, who used these basic ingredients to become a Grammy Award winner in 1989. Today, Chapman sells big numbers and at the same time is considered to be a critical success as well. This demonstrates the important role played by image and illustrates the fine line between recycling a trend or genre that is passe versus truly innovating with time-tested elements that can succeed again and again.

The lesson here is that nothing ever actually repeats itself to the letter, yet almost everything hailed as an *innovation* is a hybrid of styles and influences that have gone before. Jerry Lee Lewis, Chuck Berry, Little Richard, and the rest of the 1950s pioneers didn't just sit down and invent rock and roll; they had influences and role models to draw from—just as the Beatles, the Rolling Stones, and the rest of the "British invasion" drew from those pioneers. One of the most striking examples in the late '80s was the obvious influence that the early James Brown shows, a staple on the Deep South black nightclub circuit, had on the current performance styles of Michael Jackson and Prince. Very few fans of these two mega-entertainers ever sat in a Mississippi Delta juke joint in the early '60s, yet today they are witnessing many of the same approaches and styles developed by the "hardest working man in show business," as Brown was known in his early days. Despite Brown's strong influence, Jackson and Prince (or the artist formerly known as Prince, speaking of image) are rightfully hailed as innovators.

All this just underscores the fact that the artist who leads the field by carving a truly unique niche is usually a perceptive student of recent music history. The gift of innovation is to add a personalized touch that connects with a target audience. These lessons should not be lost when it comes time to assess artistic strength and create an image that projects musical innovation, star quality, and all those other intangibles that translate into gold and platinum records and SRO concert appearances.

Because image is so important to the success of an artist, the manager must constantly be aware of the various factors that comprise it. They include the artist's recording style and sound; selection of material; songwriting; the content and style of his personal appearances; mode and style of dress, speech, and physical appearance; the types of interviews granted; the television and radio-show appearances; and even the way the artist behaves offstage. These are all components of image that must constantly be monitored, reviewed, refined, and kept current and consistent by the manager.

CHARISMA

A prime ingredient in an effective, commercial image is the element of *charisma*. Charisma is best described as an exceptional quality or magnetic power generated by an individual that causes him or her to stand out in a crowd or draw followers or fans. Charismatic qualities are often intangible in nature, yet they can spell the difference between being just another artist and a superstar.

Although charisma is difficult to manufacture, managers should try to distinguish their artists from others by developing or maximizing any unique characteristics they might possess. For instance, if an artist is from a distinctive region of the country, such as some part of the Deep South or Texas, emphasizing this may create curiosity about the regional characteristics of the artist; this might, in turn, result in increasing his or her appeal. The same principle can be used by artists from foreign countries or who tour countries other than their own. Another example of a possible charismatic trait is a slight imperfection. Here a manager can use an apparent handicap, such as blindness or a scar, to advantage.

A personality trait may also furnish a form of charismatic appeal, as with a reclusive artist who refuses to be interviewed or photographed. These are characteristics a manager can use in image formulation and projection.

WHAT'S IN A NAME?

Even names that roll easily off the tongue are touched up to reinforce the image an artist seeks to project. Stage names are an obsession in Hollywood, though there is not quite as much of it in the music business,

Music groups, however, really don't have a choice. They have the often difficult responsibility of finding a name that will project and promote the collective identity of its members and their music. Individuals enjoy the same option, of course, but they often choose not to adopt a stage name. When it comes to names, the key is to make sure that a good fit exists between name and image. If it doesn't, a change is in order. Considering the images of the following artists, which name sounds better to you? Conway Twitty, or Harold Lloyd Jenkins; Elvis Costello, or Declan McManus? As with everything else, use good judgment. Recognize what works and what doesn't.

OTHER SKILLS OR TALENTS

What about other talents that can be blended into the act to set an artist apart? Many artists who are ostensibly vocalists often possess other talents or skills that can be developed and incorporated into the overall image. For instance, a great guitar player like Vince Gill makes it a point to showcase this skill on his live shows. Michael Jackson has sold tens of millions of records, but a large part of his appeal derives from an electrifying stage show built around his dancing ability. These special talents translate directly into revenues from music videos and touring in addition to record sales. The creative inventory will uncover those talents and skills that will allow the artist to incorporate them into his or her overall image.

Another important factor for multitalented artists and their managers to consider is career flexibility. During the decade of the '80s, the career crossover artist became prominent as never before. Cher is an excellent example of a multidimensional artist who achieved success on movie and TV screens and even in product-retailing in addition to her traditional sources of income in record sales and concert tickets. Eddie Murphy is another example: Starting as a stand-up comedian, he parlayed his talents into a phenomenal television, movie, and music career. With the increased pace of technological development and the continuing trend toward the integration of show business genres, more opportunities than ever exist for a diversified entertainment career.

With increased opportunities for multimedia exposure— television, cable, and print—there is and will continue to be a demand for celebrity personalities who can cross the traditional entertainment-career boundaries. Expect to see more music artists who act in feature motion pictures and TV movies, act as corporate spokespersons, appear in commercials, write books, and so on. The smart artist and manager will consider these opportunities for diversification when taking creative inventory.

A manager should carefully evaluate all the elements we've discussed affecting the artist's image and coordinate them for a consistent and credible pattern. Neglect in this area can lead to public confusion about who the artist is and what he or she is trying to do. Another possibility is that the artist may develop a bad public image as a result of unfavorable press or a distorted perception. The manager and artist should always be on guard to protect against this type of situation.

PROJECTING AND MARKETING THE IMAGE

Once the image is formulated, the next step is to project and market it. This process never stops. Given the heightened sophistication of marketing techniques and greater competition for coveted chart positions, coupled with an increased number of avenues through which to promote an artist's career, the task of image projection has become a very complex, full-time job. Record labels, full-service booking agencies, corporate sponsors, and even music publishers are all involved in the process. However, the artist still has primary responsibility for promoting the image that has been so carefully crafted.

Clearly, the first step is to hire a publicist whose sole job is to promote the artist in the media. The down side of doing this is cost: Depending on reputation and range of services, a publicist can cost $500 to $5,000 a month. Over the past decade, the publicist has become a fixture in any established artist's career. Because this comprises so much of what artist management has become, we will deal with the role of the publicist at length in our discussion of the artist's development team (see Chapter 11).

For now, let's focus on a new artist who doesn't have an extra $500 to $5,000 lying around. There is still plenty he or she can do and, indeed, *must* do before the day when the giant publicity and promotion machines of the record labels and booking agencies become part of the equation. It is crucial that the artist make enough noise to get noticed and signed. The following are some basic image-projection techniques any artist can put to work immediately.

THE PRESS KIT

This kit should contain at least two 8 x 10" (20 x 25 cm) black-and-white glossy photographs of the artist, a professionally written biography, some reviews, a copy of the artist's latest recording or demo cassette, and other pertinent information or quotes regarding the artist. You should not enclose color photographs, although it is a good idea to have some color slides available on request for certain kinds of duplication. While it can be expensive, a short video biography can be a great help when it comes to pitching television shows, major magazines, and top-rated showcases. Optimum time for a video bio is seven minutes.

Even if financial limitations preclude the video component, a well-written, professionally produced press kit is a relatively inexpensive image-projection tool that is both essential and highly effective in presenting the artist in the most positive light possible.

PERSONAL APPEARANCES

One of the most effective methods of image projection is through live personal appearances at concerts, clubs, or showcases. This means arranging for the artist to appear in the right market at the right venue before the right audience, and that his or her appearance, speech, actions, material, and onstage performance all come together to reinforce the image that has been formulated. The same considerations naturally apply to radio or television appearances. At the break-in stage, exposure should take precedence over all else, and certainly over money.

If you are an artist in the break-in phase, or if you've ever been there, you are probably laughing. How many times have you heard, "It doesn't pay much, but it's great exposure." In fact, it may pay nothing, but the trick is to know the difference between valuable exposure and charity. It doesn't take half a brain to calculate what an appearance on "The Tonight Show" or "Late

Night with David Letterman" could do for a career, even if the AFTRA-scale payment to the performer would barely make a dent in expenses. It is much tougher to decide how much to invest in showcases or how much of a financial hole to go into for the right club appearance.

The other word of caution here is to be ready once the financial sacrifices of an exposure appearance have been resolved. New artists seldom get a second chance to impress the "right" people, whether it be a live performance or demo tape. Make sure the image is right and that all the pieces for putting the artist across are coordinated. If there is any doubt, *don't* take the risk.

DO-IT-YOURSELF PROMOTION CAMPAIGNS

Another valuable and effective means of image projection for new artists is the do-it-yourself promotion campaign. Popular and effective examples include artist-released recordings, fan clubs, newsletters, even organized word of mouth ensuring a club owner a guaranteed audience for a personal appearance. These techniques have proved successful in focusing attention on artists who were then able to parlay that attention into a record deal, an agency contract, and even representation by a name manager.

Any contact an artist has with the public, either personally or through record sales, print, or electronic media via the Internet, constitutes image projection. Maximizing public exposure while avoiding the dangers of overexposure should be a key item on the artist's agenda at all career levels, but especially during the breaking-in stage.

DOING IT RIGHT

It bears repeating that when it comes to formulating and projecting an artist's image, nothing should be left to chance. Do it thoroughly and with deliberation. It is difficult enough to convince a record company to accept the gamble in taking on a new artist. Assuming you are successful, you will likely have one shot to make an impression on a fickle public whose attention span and precious entertainment dollar is limited. The key to making that impression is by projecting a high-impact, unforgettable artistic image. The process starts with taking a complete and thorough artistic inventory, then taking the time and finding the money to do it right.

9

Mapping out the Career Plan

All successful people share a common attribute, and it's not necessarily talent. It is, rather, the ability to see the future and find the way to make that vision a reality. In short, successful people know where they are going and how they intend to get there.

Of course, talent is important, but there are a lot of talented people in the world who never seem to fully realize their potential. Luck also plays a role in success. Most top artists can point to a lucky break that transformed them from aspiring artists into stars. At the same time, many of these artists will also tell you that their breaks were created at least in part by their own efforts. Even when a lucky opportunity materialized out of the blue, the really successful people have been able to take advantage of it because of planning and preparation. In the world of show business, just like any other pursuit, success seldom, if ever, just happens. It is rather the result of conscious, calculated, ongoing effort.

If you doubt the validity of planning to a successful career, consider the alternative. If you have little or no idea of where you want to go beyond some hazy notion of wanting to make it—"I want to be a star"—how will you know if and when you have arrived? How will you know how to adjust to changing circumstances to achieve goals that were never set? Attaining the specifics of success is the function of the career plan.

We've referred to the career plan at numerous points in previous chapters. Now it's time to discuss fundamental concepts of business and creative planning and some of the considerations that go into formulating a realistic and workable career plan that is both artistically and commercially sound.

The career plan is the artist's and manager's blueprint for attaining the success they both seek. In an earlier chapter, reference was made to a young group who was approached by a would-be manager full of promises about the pot of gold that awaited them at the end of the rainbow. The group made a key mistake when they failed to ask that all-important question: "Just how do you propose that we get to the end of the rainbow?" The career plan is the "how" to mastering the art of artist management.

THE PLANNER'S VISION

The most important dimension of any plan is the human one—the planner. The personality, values, talents, and vision of the planner are always reflected in the finished product. For instance, if the planner is an enthusiastic, free-wheeling optimist, the resulting career plan is likely to reflect those traits by setting goals that boldly shoot for the moon. While this may be great on paper, is it realistic and will the follow-through be there to make the plan a reality? On the other hand, if the planner is a cautious, steady type, the plan is apt to be realistic and a bit conservative, but will it be sufficiently ambitious? One must always be willing to question one's own assumptions if the career plan is to be of any value.

In addition to the qualities of vision, degree of realism, and the level of risk-taking reflected in the plan, one must be prepared for setbacks. Any business driven by the promise of big-time fame, glamour, and money will draw many more would-be players than there are places on the record charts. Let's face it, the world will surely survive into next week without another rock star, movie idol, or television personality. The higher the reward and the greater the competition, the easier it is for the industry gatekeepers (record company execs, publishers, agents, and managers) to say "no." And don't doubt it, the music business is a "no" business. Nobody, absolutely nobody, is immune. The Four Tops, for example, labored thirteen years becoming "overnight" successes. Every record label in Nashville passed on Alabama at least twice. More recently, hit artists like Alanis Morrisette and Vince Gill endured indifference and rejection before finally breaking through. We repeat: Nobody is immune.

The hated and feared "no" is not just reserved for new artists. In the mid-1980s, Bonnie Raitt and Van Morrison, viewed as being washed up, were dropped by their record company despite their unbroken strings of hit albums and millions of record sales. Of course the record execs were eventually proved wrong after both Raitt and Morrison went on to record some of their best work for other labels. Still, that didn't make their potentially career-ending rejections any less painful. To their credit, they picked up the pieces and kept moving forward with their careers.

The lesson here is that no matter how sound an artist's career plan may be, it will surely encounter problems, obstacles, and delays. It is here that the qualities of persistence, discipline, and follow-through will pay off. The planner with those qualities will surely have incorporated them into the career plan as contingencies and backup devices. The naive optimist who believes talent and hard work are always enough is setting him- or herself up for disillusionment at the first appearance of trouble. Of course, there's a fine line between thinking positively and blindly ignoring obstacles. This is where belief in self, commitment, and dogged persistence combined with contingency planning will pay big dividends. Why not deal with the prospect of resistance at the outset of the planning process rather than in a month or a year into your efforts to convert your plans into reality? If "no" never comes, so much the better. If it does, and we bet it will, you won't be surprised. Better yet, you will be able to do something about it.

A COLLABORATIVE PROCESS

In the realm of artist management, the career plan is by necessity a product of the manager's and artist's collaboration. Each must not only contribute to the overall plan, but also must be able to deliver on their promises and realistically attain the goals they set. Consequently, the melding of personalities and aspirations of artist and manager are of critical importance. The preliminary exploratory conference, contract negotiation, business and artistic evaluation, and other meetings and discussions should have provided manager and artist with insight into each other's vision and strengths and weaknesses, as well as preliminary answers to some very basic questions. Nonetheless, both should take another look at their own chemistry before undertaking the career planning or revising process. Each should again ask:

- Am I a positive-minded person who is willing to do what it takes to reach my goals?
- Do I still totally believe in this artist–manager relationship?
- Do I still want the same things from this relationship?
- What are my personal strengths and weaknesses?
- How can I best exploit my strengths and improve my weaknesses?

This self-appraisal will greatly assist in the formulation of the career plan, or it may add new insight and perspective into an existing plan.

A word of caution: Because formulation of the career plan is a collaborative effort, there is always a danger that one strong personality may dominate the other. The dominant planner may resist compromising his or her position even though some level of accomodation might be advisable. This is often the case with impatient, overly-ambitious people who might equate a more cautious, less ambitious approach with weakness or lack of commitment. Sticking to your guns is important, but at the same time, remember that all the grandiose visions in the world will come to nothing if the goals are unattainable or the plan unworkable.

By the same measure, striving for a dime makes absolutely no sense when a dollar is easily within reach. Honesty, openness, and realism will ensure the right balance.

FOR SELF-MANAGING ARTISTS

The artist without a full-time manager will be forced to plan alone. Nevertheless, the same principles and concepts apply. To guard against the dangers of unrealistic optimism or overly cautious aspirations, the artist going it alone would be well advised to find someone with business savvy and industry exposure to act as a sounding board. The worst possible consequence is to take the time to plan, only to base the future on flawed or unworkable premises or conclusions. Having an objective and knowledgable person to bat around ideas with you is always a big help.

ESTABLISHING GOALS

A first element of planning revolves around goal setting. Goals may range from getting a record deal; succeeding on the nightclub circuit; making the charts with a top-10 record; or earning a million dollars in income. Goals vary, depending not only on the particular circumstances, needs, and desires of the artist, but also on the mutual talents, abilities, and resources of artist and manager. An appropriate goal should stimulate and motivate the artist toward a particular, focused achievement.

As we said earlier, you should avoid setting your sights too high, thus making the goal extremely difficult or impossible to achieve. Unattainable goals can bring on frustration and disillusionment. Neither should the goal be so low that it's quickly accomplished, consequently losing its motivational value. A happy medium must be reached.

Similarly, setting too many goals may create a lack of focus or direction as you try to do too much, with the result being that nothing gets accomplished. Of course, not setting enough clearly articulated goals is just another way of shooting too low. Artist and manager are advised to study the feasibility of each goal and rank it according to priority. Open discussion and honest self-evaluation will result in the right balance.

GOAL TIMELINES

Goals are worthless unless they are accompanied by a realistic timeline for realizing them. The emphasis here is on *realistic*. You would do well to start with the old but true adage that everything takes longer than you think it will. This means planning for unexpected events, obstacles, and setbacks that all combine to delay the scheduled accomplishment of certain objectives.

Because it is difficult, yet necessary, to keep a number of balls in the air at one time in a music business career, goals should be staggered over long, short, and intermediate periods. One objective can be set for achievement in six months, thereby giving the artist something to work for with immediate results. Another goal can be set for achievement in one year, and still another for three to five years. All the goals, of course, should be designed to lead to some ultimate objective. The short-term and intermediate objectives give the entire plan a logical stair-step effect. Although the timetable is different for each level of achievement, the overall design is geared to the ultimate goal.

SELF-IMAGE AND GOALS

Psychology plays a role in the goal-setting process. While we have previously discussed the role of the planner and how personality and management style can affect the planning process, we are concerned here with how the less obvious dimension of self-image can manifest itself in goal setting.

Some individuals have a subconscious fear of failure. This fear may reveal itself in terms of easily attainable goals over a very short period. There are others who have a hidden fear of success. This fear is camouflaged by choosing goals that are almost impossible to attain. These individuals do not have to worry about success, since their goal will never be accomplished, but then they have a built-in excuse: "I knew I couldn't reach that goal—it was just too high," or, "I would have succeeded, but. . . ."

Another important point is the psychological assistance that goals give in the pursuit of success. The fact that a goal exists provides a good reason to start. Writing down goals is also valuable. Periodic reading or repetition of the goal will imprint that objective in the subconscious. Thus, conscious actions which are mandated by the career plan are supported by these subconscious thoughts. This can be very helpful when things don't seem to be going well and self-doubt sets in. At this point, a positive frame of mind can help put an artist back on the route toward the goal.

GOAL STRATEGIES

If the goal is the target, the strategy is the *how* part of hitting that target. Assuming that realistic goals have been selected, the next step is to develop approaches for reaching them. We'll refer to these approaches as goal strategies.

The goal strategy is what the planner conceives as the shortest, most effective route to a particular point, the goal. The manager should realize that the goal strategies will almost always differ from artist to artist, depending on the artist's particular talent, needs, and circumstances. Past experience, personal motivation, expertise, knowledge of the overall structure of the music industry, and timing all play an important part in strategy.

For instance, many artists wish to break into the national concert market. Several strategies could be employed to accomplish this goal. The artist could work on recording with the aim of having a hit record that would lead to concert bookings as an opening act and later as a headliner. As an alternative, the artist could record and release records through a small regional label in the hope of developing a market as a concert attraction in that region, consequently gaining attention from a major label or national agents. Yet another approach would be to invest more time in developing a high-energy stage show that would win the attention of agents or established concert artists who might book the artist as an opening act.

All these strategies could ultimately achieve the desired result. The pivotal question for management is, "Which strategy will be the most desirable for this particular artist?"

Strategies, then, may be designed to follow just one route, or change directions on numerous occasions throughout the artist's career. Nonetheless, they should all clearly lead in the same direction—toward the artist's goal.

DEVELOPING TACTICS

Career tactics, the means of implementing the predetermined career strategies, are the actual moves you make, the day-to-day activities of an artist's life. These seemingly unimportant details may account for a month's or even a year's work toward the accomplishment of certain goals. The control of these activities is a critical aspect of goal achievement. Many people enjoy the talking, planning, and dreaming phase of planning. But the tactical phase isn't concerned with tomorrow; its focus is today. The manager and artist should ask what's being done right now toward accomplishing the predetermined career goals. It's at this point in the career plan where many lose control of their future. If a successful future is the goal, then start with being a success today.

To have high aspirations and realize them takes hard work. To work efficiently and consistently takes discipline. Daily tactics inject discipline into the career plan. That can mean rehearsal, writing, recording, interviews, visits to radio promotion people, and so on. Any tangible movement toward the objective is a career tactic.

An important factor here is the planner's ability to use time efficiently. Because of the rapid fluctuations in popular trends and styles in the entertainment business, time is of critical importance. The artist who has achieved success must maximize it before a new style emerges that may divert his following to a new rising star. Too many artists think that once they have a hit record, the work is over and the fun begins. Nothing could be further from the truth. Established artists and managers will tell you that getting there is tough, but staying there is a lot tougher. This is especially true for a young artist. Every major label executive, record producer, and personal manager we interviewed said the same thing: No new artist is ever aware of the work and overwhelming demands on an artist's time that go with stardom. The hour a day on stage during a concert tour is the easiest part of an artist's schedule. Every day is filled with people who want a part of the artist: fans, reporters, radio people, promoters, retailers, road managers, corporate sponsors, record company promotion people, and the list goes on. This doesn't take into account the pressures inherent in making sure that the next record has hit potential and that the next concert show is the best it can be.

Another surprise that comes with stardom relates to the overhead associated with being a success in the business. Studio rental fees, publicists, attorney's fees, accountant's bills, union stage hands, sidemen for recording, concert halls, and so on and so forth, are part of the back-handed reward for hard-won success. Working efficiently means knowing how most effectively to handle people and control costs. This, to a great extent, is accomplished by controlling time, which in turn is a function of effective planning and scheduling.

UPDATING THE PLAN

Once career goals, strategies, and tactics have been determined, the plan should be reviewed periodically. A review enables the planner to gauge results and to determine if a strategic or tactical change is necessary. Periodic review is a necessary function of success. Once goals are accomplished, new ones must be formulated. Career momentum has only two directions, up or down. Failure to keep a career on an upward path means it's actually going in the opposite direction.

Often you hear someone comment, "How did that record make the charts?" or "How could that artist be successful?" If you look behind the record or artist to the people planning the career, the success in question may become more understandable. Determined, positive-minded people with a well-developed, realistic career plan can greatly affect the prospects for success. In a nutshell, they know where they're going and how they're going to get there. This is the essence of career-planning.

PART THREE

Making the Plan Work

10

Making Your Own Breaks

Talent, organization, and planning are all essential elements of a successful career in show business. However, unless an artist has access to industry decision-makers and receives the proper exposure, the artist is no better off than when the management program was conceived. One way to do this is to wait for a break. A better way is to make your own breaks.

Making things happen is the most demanding part of a manager's job. It requires daily attention to detail and constant follow-up. It means creating opportunities that will turn dreams into reality. This is where a manager really earns his or her money.

The break-in phase of an artist's career is probably the most difficult and frustrating. This is when the commitment of artist and manager is tested severely. Tremendous amounts of persistence, drive, and skill are needed to cope with the inevitable obstacles that stand between an unknown artist and the ultimate goal of recognition and success. Many talented performers and their managers are not equipped financially or emotionally for the heavy duty dues-paying associated with this career phase. As a result, many promising artists who receive initial rejections from agents, producers, and record companies become discouraged and quit.

If there is anything that is an absolute certainty in the music business, it is rejection. Artists and their managers are best advised to be prepared for rejection not *if* but rather *when* it comes. Success comes to those capable of rising above certain adversity. Those who cannot will never make it. That is a guarantee.

Even artists who do enjoy a measure of recognition and financial reward soon learn that success is always relative. Beyond that, there's always the possibility that hard-earned success will disappear as quickly as it materializes. Every artist is only as successful as the most recent accomplishment. The competition for the limited number of slots on record-company artist rosters and the Billboard charts is fierce and getting fiercer. For every newcomer, somebody must lose a place. It is a perilously short distance between being a star this year and a has-been the next.

The material in this section is designed to acquaint the manager and artist with the problems they'll undoubtedly face in implementing their plan. These chapters also suggest approaches and techniques for overcoming problems with a proactive style calculated to make things happen.

ACCESS TO THE GATEKEEPERS

Talent is always the starting point. Unfortunately, too many talented people who never quite seem to make it to the big time mistakenly think that talent assures success. Unfortunately, nothing could be further from the truth. Certainly, without talent, the most experienced manager, working with the best plan conceivable, won't succeed in making an artist successful. But talent alone is never enough by itself.

The first dynamic for success, after talent, is access to the industry. Ultimately, it is the general public who will decide an artist's fate, but it is record companies, booking agents, video channels, and all the other gatekeepers who make the crucial decisions concerning whether the public will ever get that chance. Since talent and commercial potential are so subjective, record companies as well as the other distribution channels often rely on top-flight managers to prescreen talent. If a manager is sold on an artist's potential, chances are greatly improved that the artist will at least rate a listen at a record company. It is for precisely this reason that a prime means of access for you as a new artist lies in getting a top-rate manager interested in you.

While even a top manager can't ensure success, he or she can certainly improve the odds that the industry will pay closer attention. If a record company or an established producer agrees with the manager's assessment, the prospects for a record deal dramatically increase. In fact, of the record executives we talked to, every one of them agreed that a manager with a track record was a significant factor in their decision to sign an artist. By contrast, a strong artist with weak or ineffectual management can sometimes lose a potential deal for that reason alone. On the other hand, lack of any management is never fatal to an artist's chances of getting signed. However, the commitment of an artist to finding acceptable management can in fact be a condition to a deal. In this situation, helping the artist to find strong management becomes a top priority for the record company.

THE MANAGER'S BASIC ASSETS

All this leads to an obvious question: What separates the great managers from all the others? Certainly, this question is the theme of the entire book. We have alluded to some of the distinquishing elements from the perspective of the artist looking for a manager. While is impossible to answer this question completely and fully in the next few pages, here are the basics from the manager's viewpoint.

KNOWING THE INDUSTRY

The first prerequisite is a thorough understanding of the various aspects of the entertainment industry. Intelligence and judgment are no substitute for a working knowledge of the particular field of entertainment in which the artist is involved. This knowledge takes many forms. Every manager should know the mechanics of the particular area in which he or she is involved, be it recording, publishing, performing, or merchandising. This means knowing the inner workings of each, knowing what the prevailing industry practices are, and having the ability to speak the language of that particular aspect of the business.

If you are an aspiring manager, doubtless you bought this book to gain hands-on knowledge of the many complex areas that make up the music business. In addition to this book, there are publications like *Billboard* and the other trade magazines that are devoted to keeping managers and artists informed of current happenings and trends in the business. We recommend that you become familiar with these resources. A more complete listing of such materials is provided in the Appendix.

FORMAL EDUCATION

In an earlier chapter we spoke about the value of an education. Having a college degree, a law degree, or an MBA, or being a certified public accountant (CPA)—all these are paths that can lead to a successful career as a manager. Increasingly, there are college-level commercial-music programs that can help aspiring managers prepare for a career in music business management. You can never know too much.

While books and trade publications and a good education are highly recommended, they can't establish personal contacts or provide the intangible qualities of insight, judgment, and timing. The key to making it in artist management is experience, experience, and more experience. This is the only way to gain the requisite knowledge and contacts that will make you a player. Because the music business is relatively small in terms of numbers, decision-making tends to be concentrated primarily in a few entertainment centers, such as New York, Los Angeles, and Nashville. Consequently, it's possible to meet a wide cross-section of music industry figures by working and living in one of these centers. People advance themselves by accumulating practical experience and establishing personal relationships, so chances are good that an acquaintance who's struggling today might be one of tomorrow's top decision-makers. This all adds up to one inescapable conclusion: There is simply no substitute for being in the middle of what is happening where it is happening.

KNOWING THE PLAYERS

In a business where access means everything, it is essential that the manager know and have access to the decision-makers within each branch of the industry. The music business is a "people business." Personal contacts can mean everything when it comes to getting a deal for an unknown artist. Again, the key to success, after talent, is access to the gatekeepers—the recording executives, agents, producers, and publishers. They depend on word-of-mouth reports or personal recommendations to reduce their risk and help them screen the new and unproven because of the sheer numbers who are drawn to show business by the promise of fame and wealth. The truth is that as more artists try to break down the barriers to a show business career, industry pros tend to build those barriers higher and stronger as a defense mechanism. Naturally, this reality of industry access is often criticized by new artists and many managers. However, in practical terms it means that for a manager to present an artist to a decision-maker who can "green light" a deal, it becomes even more crucial for the manager to know someone. Without that resource, the most knowledgable manager representing the most innovative artist means nothing.

HAVING A FEEL FOR THE BUSINESS

While it's clear that knowledge of the industry and personal contacts are necessary tools of any effective manager, they don't guarantee success. The winning manager possesses the intangible quality of "having a feel for the business," which allows him or her to craft a strong career plan and make the right decisions at the right time. Having a feel for the business is a combination of perception, understanding, judgment, and timing which can't be acquired from books or at cocktail parties. It means knowing how to calm a temperamental artist; how to sense the artist's under- or overexposure by reviewing his or her itinerary three months ahead of time and adjusting it accordingly; and how to read the subtle professional and personal interrelationships that make up the business. An illustration of this intangible ability is an accurate prediction by a manager of how a certain television appearance or video production will affect an artist's concert drawing power and record sales. All top-flight managers share this talent for making the right move at the right time.

BUILDING A CAREER

Unfortunately, great managers are like great artists, they are few and far between. Given that only a handful of newcomers will be able to attract a name manager prior to getting a record deal, what can the unrepresented artist or aspiring manager do to build a career? The answer is, plenty. Let's look at the career building blocks that artists and managers at any point of development must have in place if they are to "make their own breaks":

- Preparation
- Follow-through
- Persistence and determination
- Realism
- Flexibility
- Luck

PREPARATION

Preparation by the artist and manager is a fundamental ingredient for success. Planning, which has already been discussed, is one form of preparation. Always being ready to carry out that plan is another. The music business is unpredictable. Opportunity often knocks when least expected. Both artist and manager must always be in a position to capitalize on a break when it appears, because it might not present itself again. Many of today's stars attribute their success to being able to take advantage of an opportunity. These brief and often chance events are the best reasons for constant preparation, planning, and rehearsal. If the artist and manager are ready, it will just be a matter of doing what both have prepared themselves for when the right opportunity presents itself.

FOLLOW-THROUGH

Follow-through may be the single most significant factor standing between adequate managers and great managers. So much of the day-in, day-out job of management involves sitting in meetings, returning phone calls, making decisions, responding to proposals, answering correspondence, reading reports—in a word, keeping the artist's professional life on track. Follow-through isn't always glamorous, fun, or easy. That is precisely why it is so important.

PERSISTENCE AND DETERMINATION

Persistence and determination are needed to stay with it, of course, so these are in many ways the most important qualities of all. The ability to keep going and accept disappointment and setbacks without giving up, marks the difference between stars and ordinary people with talent. This type of single-purpose drive is necessary not only to unknowns, but to established artists as well.

One of the best examples of persistence in action is in recording-artist Kenny Rogers's experience. Rogers enjoyed early success with a solo hit record in the late 1950s. After a fast start, he faded from the charts. He later came back with a group, the First Edition, which enjoyed a string of hit records in the late '60s and early '70s. After what seemed to be a period in which success was guaranteed, another dry spell hit. The group broke up, and Rogers moved to Nashville, where he began recording country-oriented material. After a few years of absence from the charts, he enjoyed a second comeback, recording the biggest hits of his career.

During the decade of the 1980s, Rogers and his manager, Ken Kragen, consolidated this hard-won success through a variety of outlets—records, concerts, and videos, charitable activities, corporate sponsorships, and commercials, and even a national chain of restaurants. The underlying reason for Rogers's success is that he never gave up. He was determined to find a new approach that would put him back on the charts. The roller-coaster effect of his career is typical in show business. The artist and manager should accept this from the outset. If the talent is there and the commitment is strong enough, something will usually happen sooner or later. The time in between is for paying dues.

REALISM

Maintaining a realistic attitude is a must. The music business seems to run on big promises that have a way of never material-izing; "firm commitments" too often dissolve into "maybes." Part of the manager's job is to sort through these promises, offers, and alternatives and make a realistic assessment of the value of each. He or she must help the artist keep a clear-eyed perspective while also sustaining a personal enthusiasm and commitment. This means being able to recognize a true commercial opportunity and taking steps to turn it to the artist's advantage. It also means rejecting offers that may look good on the surface, but probably have little real merit. It's often difficult to perform this function, especially in light of the many glamourous offers that "can't miss." Unless the manager can retain perspective and make accurate judgements, the chances of the artist making it to the top and staying there are slim.

FLEXIBILITY

Our Kenny Rogers example also illustrates the virtue of *flexibility*. The artist and manager should always be willing to change the game plan to fit the circumstances. Trends in entertainment can change overnight. Being able to anticipate and change with them is essential to achieving and maintaining success. Rogers's willing-ness to move from rock to country underscores this principle.

Flexibility is not only important for the established artist but applies equally to the artist in the breaking-in stage. What might have been in vogue a year ago means nothing if the public won't accept it today. The unknown artist must constantly adapt to existing commercial opportunities.

LUCK

Of all the "career-builders" described in this chapter, luck can least be controlled by the artist and manager. Luck is as much a part of entertainment as talent. It's being in the right place at the right time. There are many artists who have been in that fortunate position but were not properly prepared to make the most of the opportunity. And so we have come full circle to being prepared.

This is the essence of making your own breaks. Although a good manager can't make a lucky break materialize, he or she can help create the circumstances of commercial opportunity through contacts and an understanding of the industry. The manager can, through preparation, follow-through, persistence, determination, realism, and flexibility, help open a door and then ensure that the artist will be ready to step through it. This is what this business of artist management is all about—helping the artist to make his or her own breaks, rather than leaving success to chance. It's the difference between an artist sitting back waiting for a break that may never come and an artist with a well-planned and executed management program constantly working to find a place on the record charts and in the hearts of fans who haven't heard of him or her . . . yet.

The Artist's Development Team

P revious chapters have dealt with the importance of organization, planning, and action by the artist and manager to help create commercial opportunity. In the increasingly complex and interrelated world of entertainment, it is impossible for any artist or manager to adequately exploit a show business career without a lot of help. This is where the artist's development team comes into play.

The term "artist's development team" refers to the various entities or people within the entertainment industry who have a direct monetary stake in the artist's career and with whom the manager and artist must deal on an ongoing basis. For instance, let's assume the artist's income is derived primarily from the sale of records, songwriting royalties, personal appearances, and commercial endorsements. Those entities or people who stand to directly benefit from the artist's success would include the record company, music publisher, booking agent, publicist, and corporate sponsor with whom he or she does business. They comprise the artist's development team. All are vitally concerned that the artist succeed because their fortunes are tied, at least in part, to that artist; they have certain resources and assets they are willing to expend in order to further various aspects of the artist's career.

Any experienced manager knows that without the help and resources of these various entities, achieving the artist's career goals would be almost impossible. However, maximizing the contributions of each member of the team in a coordinated, efficient manner consistent with the artist's career plan can ensure that those goals are attained. When it's done right, everyone benefits.

THE TEAM CONCEPT

The concept of the *artist's development team* relies on a fundamental principle of the entertainment industry: No one can ever hope to achieve success alone. Even the most resourceful manager, working with the best plan conceivable and the most talented artist imaginable, must also have the support and help of others in order to make it.

The concept of an artist's development team, by its very nature, suggests a positive, proactive approach. The manager's role is that of a coordinator and motivator. He or she is the glue that holds the team together while getting the most out of each team member. To do this, the manager must first establish harmonious, one-on-one working relationships with those individuals and companies who make up the team. This requires an open-minded, cooperative person who is willing to listen to recommendations and suggestions. This is not to suggest that the manager be just a follower. It also does not ignore the manager's responsibility to assert and protect the artist's rights. However, a successful application of the team approach should allow the manager to maximize the benefits for the artist-client without having to make compromises that are unnecessary or that would be detrimental either to artistic integrity or the long-term interests of the artist.

DIFFERENCES AND DISAGREEMENTS

We are realistic enough to acknowledge that disputes between team members and management are sure to arise, and that compromise will be called for, as it is in any collaborative effort. In a creatively driven industry like the music business, where personal taste and preference play such an important role, differences of opinion and disagreements are inevitable. When disputes do crop up, a good manager will shield and insulate the artist as much as possible, while seeking resolutions through the art of pragmatic compromise or alternative approaches. This is where imagination, savvy, and personal style are essential elements that separate the great managers from those who are merely adequate.

Most unnecessary disputes arise as a result of ego. Managers should remember that the profession exists not to enhance their own self-image but to build artists' careers. The manager's sense of self-discipline and restraint will play a key role in helping to avoid many petty, time-consuming disagreements. By the same measure, the manager's ability to communicate and counsel can help avoid artist-related ego hangups. One help in avoiding these types of problems is to anticipate and weigh the counter-productive effects of such disputes before a potential problem surfaces. By anticipating problems and consequences, both manager and artist will often realize that the dispute is simply not as important as they originally thought.

There's a motto worth remembering here: You can't die in a ditch over every issue. In other words, pick your fights carefully. To illustrate, assume that you are the manager of a successful recording artist who has just released a new CD four months earlier. The record company is about to release the second single from the album, and the artist would like the label to throw a single-release party to note the occasion. You know that a party will cost $5,000 to $10,000. You also know that if you push hard enough, the record company will probably do it, even though they gave an album-release party four months earlier and are reluctant to throw another party so soon. Their reluctance is further based on an expensive promotional program later in the year that will spotlight your artist. The question is, how hard do you push for a party your artist wants? The up side is that the party will surely massage the artist's ego while giving your publicist and the label's publicity department an event they can use to promote the artist and the new record. The down side relates to long-term considerations. A begrudging "yes" from the record company will certainly justify a future "no" or two when it comes time for the artist and manager to ask for financial help. It could even mean scaling back or cancelling the special promotional program. The manager must objectively ask whether the short-term benefit of stroking the artist's ego and using the party to promote the single outweighs the almost certain long-term negatives.

In other words, is the party worth dying in the ditch over? Only the manager knows the answer to that question. However, when making the call, it should be remembered that everybody has a "personal favor account" with other members of the artist's development team as do they with the artist and manager. This is very much like a bank account. The wise manager and artist will know how to manage those "funds" effectively.

Continuing our example, once the manager weighs the relative pros and cons of the party, that decision must be followed through to a conclusion. In this case, it will mean either pushing the record company or convincing the artist that it is best for the long term to skip the party and focus on making a success of the special promotion scheduled for later, knowing all the while that there is a favor or two left in the account. In either event, the manager is best advised to remain cool and logical while keeping the lines of communication open. By doing this, he or she will gain far more than is lost, not only with other team members, but with the artist as well. This process is repeated dozens of times every week.

FORMING THE TEAM

When it comes to putting together an effective organization to develop an artist's career, the first step is to identify the team members or potential team members. For example, if the artist is presently affiliated with a record company and a music publisher but not a booking agent, the former two companies would be team members, while any of a number of booking agents would be potential team members. Provided that the need exists and the artist is ready, the manager's next move would be to secure affiliation with an agent or agents to fill the vacancy on the team. Other members would be added based on the overall career plan and needs of the artist.

Other possible team members might be a record producer and a publicist. Members of the team will often be added or dropped, depending on their involvement with the artist at any given point in his career.

ESTABLISHING PERSONAL RELATIONSHIPS

Once the various entities that will constitute the team are identified, or essential members are subsequently added, the manager should move to form a personal relationship with each individual who will have a role in the development of the artist's career. We stress the importance of each person who has a contribution to make, not just the president of the record company or the responsible agent in charge of booking the artist. Every person within an organization is potentially important to the artist's career, from secretaries to department heads to the top executives. For example, at a booking agency, this means taking the time to meet and get to know not only the agent primarily responsible for booking the artist, but his or her assistant as well as other agents and supporting personnel in other departments, especially publicity.

Besides just getting acquainted, the manager should be selling these people on the artist and what he or she is trying to do creatively. This will help the team members to better understand the artist. A better understanding can be the beginning of genuine excitement and belief in the artist and his or her music.

Though it takes time, the successful manager makes the extra effort to establish personal relationships with as many people as possible. It makes a difference when it comes to getting things done or having quick access to information. It's human nature for people to give a little extra or be more responsive or cooperative when they are dealing with a manager they know and like on a personal level. People appreciate being appreciated; they like knowing that the manager thinks their input is worthwhile. The difference will become apparent in a hundred little ways, each one of them important to advancing an artist's career.

Besides the manager's efforts in building personal bridges, it's often a good idea to introduce the artist to these same people. This is what we call "working the office." When it comes to creating excitement, there is no substitute for connecting the artist with those responsible for pushing his or her career.

COORDINATING THE TEAM'S ACTIVITIES

A managerial prerequisite to dealing effectively with the artist's development team is a detailed understanding and appreciation of the structure and function of each part of it. In short, this means that the manager should not only understand what record companies do and how they do it, but also have insight into the inner workings of the particular company that records the artist's music. The same is true with every other component of the development team. Beyond this, the manager must also understand team politics—how each member relates to the other.

One of the most frequent criticisms of managers by record company executives, producers, agents, and publishers is that they don't understand enough about the various aspects of the business and, as a result, are unprepared to work effectively with the different members of the team. Even if a manager understands the business, but not a particular company or individual with whom he or she is dealing, the results are likely to be disappointing. People get fired, budgets are cut, companies are constantly being reorganized. More than one artist has been caught in a crossfire of company politics. It's the manager's job to spot trouble on the horizon and take the appropriate steps to either convert it to an advantage or steer the artist away from potential problems. When it comes to dealing with the artist's development team, the manager must keep a watchful eye for trouble while always having the artist poised to respond effectively when opportunity knocks.

Once the manager has done the necessary interpersonal groundwork, the actual process of artist development begins. The manager should strive to maximize the resources available to the artist from the various components of the team. To do this, he or she must help the team members achieve their specific objectives while ensuring that those goals fit into the artist's overall career plan. This requires a high degree of coordination and communication with each team member to make sure that everybody is pulling toward the same objective. For instance, the manager will want to see that an extensive personal appearance tour is timed to maximize the promotion of the artist's latest record release. This requires coordination between the marketing, advertising, publicity, and promotion departments of the record company along with the booking agency and publicist. Serving as the liaison between the team members, the manager can help each of these players to realize each of their specific goals. The personal appearance will reinforce the record company's promotional efforts, thereby resulting in increased CD sales. Because of the new release, there's increased interest in the artist, thus making him or her more appealing to promoters. This, in turn, makes the agent's job easier in booking the tour. The efforts of the artist's publicist complements the work of everyone.

To be an effective coordinator, the manager must maintain communication with the appropriate development team members, keeping them constantly informed of the artist's activities and plans while also monitoring the plans and objectives of the various team members. The manager should remember that as the focal point for all information concerning the artist and all communication between the team members and the artist, he or she should be readily accessible to everyone involved.

Additionally, the manager should try to anticipate the specific directions the various team members will seek to exploit. For example, by anticipating the record company's marketing strategy for the artist, the manager can plan accordingly. If that meshes with the artist's career plan, the manager can arrange the artist's schedule accordingly to gain maximum benefit. And if the company's plans don't fit into what the manager and artist have determined to be the proper direction, the manager is positioned to offer alternatives or compromises, before time pressures lead to a confrontation or serious disagreement.

The manager should make an effort as well to understand and appreciate the limitations and specific problems of the particular team members as they relate to any given project. By knowing what's possible and what's unrealistic, he or she can phrase requests in a way that will help get what the artist really needs and wants.

The resourceful and proactive manager will always take the initiative to help the team members achieve their goals by submitting proposals and ideas. It's the manager's job, whenever possible, to act as a catalyst without appearing overly pushy, inflexible, and critical. Working effectively with the artist's development team should be a cooperative process aimed at trying to give team members the benefit of a different perspective or alternative viewpoint from which to choose.

To be successful at this requires tons of good judgment. It's only natural that some team members might feel a manager's initiative is a criticism of their abilities or a threat to their egos. The manager should be sensitive to and respect the wishes of these individuals and treat them accordingly, while still protecting the interests of the artist. It bears repeating, however, that there will be inevitable conflicts. When that happens, the manager must ultimately do what he or she thinks necessary, taking into consideration the long- and short-term best interests of the client.

WORKING FOR A SHARED SUCCESS

Almost every manager we've talked to has cited the concept of the artist development team as one of the key factors in promoting an artist and keeping him or her on top. The business of creating and sustaining a career in today's entertainment business is just too complex and sophisticated for any one person or firm to adequately handle. Ask the managers of the major artists and they will tell you that success depends on the interrelationship of a lot of talented, hard-working people. The driving force that motivates, informs, and guides this process is that of the artist's manager. The bottom line is that the manager should strive to deal as effectively and efficiently as possible with each individual concerned with the artist's career. Every manager will have personal and particular techniques for getting the job done. These techniques will necessarily vary with each particular person with whom the manager deals. Common sense, flexibility, and follow-up are the key words here. Regardless of the approach used, the more the manager contributes to helping the various development team members achieve their own success, the more he or she contributes to the success of the artist.

The
Record Deal

A successful record company affiliation is the key to any career in the music industry. Besides being a potentially lucrative source of income, the record is the most effective career development tool the artist possesses. It can reach millions of potential fans via radio airplay—national and international exposure that translates into record sales, a demand for concert and television appearances, offers for endorsements and commercial work, and songwriting income. In short, the ability to make and sell hit records is the engine that drives every other aspect of an artist's career.

Getting signed to a major label has never been easy. Given today's spiraling production, marketing, and promotion costs, the always tight radio playlists, and the increased numbers of talented and sophisticated artists competing for the relatively few places on a label's roster, the task is more difficult than ever. Record company A&R departments are swamped with new artists and their managers or attorneys all trying to "get a deal." The division head of a major label's Nashville operation told us that his office alone receives over a thousand submissions a year. Out of this number, he'll sign four or five new acts.

The good news, if there is any, is that over the last decade the music business has experienced a broadening in musical tastes. This has translated into specialized markets and formats and greater opportunity for those with the talent and vision to respond to what consumers want to buy. The rap-music phenomenon is an example of one of the music industry's new self-contained subcultures which has created a growth market complete with its own video programming, fan magazines, and charts in *Billboard*. The obvious question raised by any fad is: Will it last? While it's impossible to know with any certainty, the odds are that it will survive in some form. A look at the current charts suggest a greater variety of commercial genres than ever before, all of which seem to be coexisting nicely. For instance, the disco explosion of the late '70s is still going strong under the alias of dance music. Newer R&B artists Boyz II Men and Whitney Houston share the *Billboard* R&B Album Chart with legends like Bobby Bland and Aretha Franklin, which is an indication that there is room on the charts for the old and the new. Country music playlists accommodate the lean, traditional styles of Randy Travis, George Jones, and Alan Jackson next to the innovations of Lyle Lovett, the Mavericks, and Lee Ann Rimes. The Rolling Stones are past 50 and are bigger than ever.

All of this seemingly spells opportunity. However, it's probably worth pointing out that while the number of specialty charts have increased, there are also more artists than ever before fighting for those chart positions and the radio airplay that can help them get there. As far as the *Billboard* Hot 100 goes, it is still the barometer for measuring an all-purpose hit single, and it has, obviously, still only a hundred slots available to accommodate a big world of innovation and ambition.

This chapter is designed to help familiarize the new artist and manager with the recording phase of the artist's career. This information, we hope, will help them to achieve a successful record company affiliation.

MAKING A QUALITY RECORDING

The first objective in this phase of the artist's career is to produce a recording of professional quality and commercial value. There are two approaches the artist can take. The first is to try to record a finished master recording that can be sold or leased to a record company. The other is to produce a high-quality multitrack demonstration recording, or *demo,* that will create interest in the artist by a record label. There are pros and cons to both approaches.

THE FINISHED MASTER RECORDING

A finished master recording is desirable from several standpoints. If the record company likes what it hears, the tape can be pressed and released in a short period of time. Some companies prefer to listen only to finished masters because they know what they're buying and won't be required to spend additional time and money on re-recording. This allows the company to concentrate on the marketing and promotional aspects of the business.

As a practical matter, almost every major label will regard your recording as a demo, no matter what it sounds like or how much you spent on it. The business today tends to be driven by name producers with a track record that companies hope can be parlayed into a hit, so the major companies will most likely want to match the artist with a hot producer and re-record the tracks. The recent exceptions have been in the alternative and rap areas where the labels have had to catch up to music that was coming "from the street." Of course, like everything else in the music business, this is a trend that is subject to change.

A negative aspect of the finished-master approach is the expense involved. Despite the astounding developments in recording technology, such as sampling, DAT, and so on, recording and mixing two finished sides can cost the artist several thousand dollars or more in studio time and musician payments. Depending on the format, an album of finished master quality can cost $10,000 and up—as much as the artist wants to spend. The average rock or pop album released by a major label can run $150,000 to $250,000. Budgets for established acts capable of selling double or triple platinum have been known to exceed a million dollars, and a few have flirted with the two million dollar mark.

Because of lower production values, country albums are significantly less, but on average they still cost between $75,000 to $125,000 and more. That's a lot of money for any artist to put up.

Another problem with this approach is that many new artists lack the recording experience necessary to turn out first-class commercial recordings in the early stages of their careers. A finished master makes it difficult to make changes a record company may want. As a result, the company may reject the recording entirely.

THE MULTITRACK DEMO

An alternate approach is for the artist to record a quality multitrack demo that will give the record company a chance to listen to the artist's material and singing style. The company may make suggestions to improve the recording or suggest other material the artist could record. This approach allows the label to get involved in every detail of the artist's recordings at the outset of the artist's career.

THE DEVELOPMENTAL DEAL

There are cases where a label recognizes the potential in an artist, but does not feel he or she is ready for a full-scale release. This interim step is called a developmental deal, where the label advances money for the artist to record sophisticated demos as a way of getting recording experience and finding the right material. Once the artist is deemed ready, the developmental deal ripens into a recording contract.

The problem with this approach is that some companies prefer not to commit the time needed to develop an artist from a recording standpoint. Rather, they prefer that the artist be capable of recording a finished product before they'll offer a contract. Unless a demo is of professional quality and has a high degree of commercial potential, the record company may choose not to get involved with the artist.

Signing an artist is a business decision. As a result, the companies are looking for the "sure thing" when they can get it. Since the demo isn't a finished product, the risk factor is increased for the company. This means that whatever you show the record company had better be good—not only the vocals and instrumental performances, but also the arrangements and, most of all, the song. As we've pointed out before, artists seldom get a second listening by a record company. The competition is too stiff. The advice here is to make sure you are taking your best possible shot with the record company. If you can improve any aspect of the presentation, take the time to do it. You may never get another chance.

FINDING A PRODUCER

Assuming the artist or group does not produce its own records, the first challenge is to find a producer. If a major label is interested in a new artist, they will certainly be involved in the choice of producer and at the very least will want veto power over the choice.

It's the job of the record producer to mold the elements of artist, song, arrangement, studio, engineer, and musicians into a finished product. Many experienced artists are producers themselves; others don't feel capable of performing this important function. In some cases, the manager may be qualified to serve in this capacity. The new artist is probably best advised to retain the services of an experienced, independent record producer. Whether the artist attempts to fill a dual role or retain the services of another as producer, it's essential that someone be in charge of the recording.

Of course, artist, manager, and producer must be able to work closely with each other to help develop the artist's recording career in a manner that is consistent with the artist's ability and career plan. Choosing a producer is much like choosing a manager. Producers all have their own way of doing the job, but their methods aren't nearly as important as their results. The qualities an artist and manager should look for in a producer are experience, track record, and an ability to understand the artist's musical direction and work with him or her on a creative level.

Contractually, there are two basic approaches to the artist–producer relationship: the exclusive personal services agreement and the producer-for-hire approach.

THE EXCLUSIVE PERSONAL SERVICES AGREEMENT

One approach is for the artist to sign an exclusive personal services agreement with an independent producer who becomes responsible for payment of a negotiated royalty to the artist. The producer, in turn, seeks a recording affiliation by offering him- or herself and the artist to the company as a package. Under such an arrangement, the producer signs an agreement with the record company, who pays all advances and royalties directly to the producer, who in turn accounts to the artist.

A major advantage to this approach is that a well-known independent producer, through professional contacts, may be able to make a deal that the artist or manager might not otherwise have been capable of obtaining. In addition, the name value and experience of a hot producer can make a big difference in breaking a new artist once a deal is made.

The major disadvantage is that the artist is exclusively tied to the musical tastes, production style, and fortunes of the producer. If the latter encounters a cold streak, the artist doesn't have the option of looking elsewhere for recording guidance. If a disagreement arises between the label and the producer, the artist's career could suffer as a result.

THE PRODUCER-FOR-HIRE APPROACH

The alternative is for the artist to be signed directly to the record company. In this situation, the artist would employ a producer on a project-by-project basis for a flat fee, or a percentage of the artist's royalties, or a combination of both.

This approach is certainly preferable from the standpoint of giving the artist and manager more control over the recording aspect of the artist's career. The fortunes of the artist are not tied to one producer. However, the producer-for-hire approach is not always available to the new artist because of the expense involved and the inability of the artist to get a deal without the help of an independent producer.

Should the artist enter into an exclusive production agreement, he or she and the manager should try to limit the contract terms to provide for termination of the agreement should the relationship become no longer beneficial to the artist. This is a negotiable point and will depend on the bargaining positions of the parties.

After becoming familiar with the artist's ability, style, and goals, the producer will help the artist select the material to be recorded. The right song can play a crucial part in the success or failure of the artist's recordings. The producer will first look at any songs the artist might have written. If the artist doesn't write, or if the material is not appropriate, the producer will consult music publishers and other writers for suitable material.

After songs with sufficient commercial appeal have been selected, the artist and producer will work on an arrangement of the song that complements the artist's style and enhances its commercial appeal. If needed, the producer will employ the services of a professional arranger, usually on a flat-fee basis.

FINDING A STUDIO AND PERSONNEL

The next decision to be made is the selection of a recording studio, engineer, and, if any, other musicians, including background vocalists. Today, fully-equipped, professional recording studios can be found not just in recording centers such as New York, Los Angeles, and Nashville, but throughout the country. Million-selling records have been recorded in such small towns as Macon, Georgia, and Muscle Shoals, Alabama, as well as in big cities like Chicago, Miami, and Detroit. Because of technological advances, it is now possible for artists to build state-of-the-art facilities in their homes at a fraction of what it would have cost just a few years before. Because of this diversity of facilities, geographic location of a recording studio is not really as important a consideration as it once was.

Most facilities furnish a recording engineer as part of the studio rental cost. This person's job is to attend to the technical end of recording, working under the supervision of the producer. Often, an established artist or producer may want to bring in his or her own engineer. In other instances, the producer may double as the engineer.

From both a quality and cost standpoint, experienced studio musicians can make a difference in the artist's recordings. A studio pro works faster and with better results than a musician not accustomed to studio work. The same can be said of background vocalists. Here, in contrast to the location of the studio, geography can play a significant role in obtaining quality. The quality of musicians and vocalists won't be crucial in the case of self-contained alternative and rap acts, but in the pop and country worlds, using top studio sidemen and vocalists can be critically important to the finished product. Experienced studio musicians and vocalists are found in recording centers because of the opportunity for steady work. Nashville and Los Angeles are both known for the quality of their support people. Other large centers such as New York, Detroit, Philadelphia, and Memphis are home to quality session artists. Many studios have their own staff musicians who can provide solid basic rhythm tracks. Another approach is to employ the artist's band members on the session. Because of the uniformity of equipment, it's not uncommon for an artist to record basic tracks in one city and later add horns, strings, and backup vocals in a studio located in a recording center.

Studio rental is usually handled on an hourly basis, depending on the number of tracks used and other specialized equipment available. Most master sessions employ 24- or 32-track professional recording equipment. The basic hourly rate will vary, depending on equipment, location, and volume of recording activity. The rate for a top-flight, multitrack studio can be as much as $200 per hour and up. The artist, manager, and producer should shop around for the best rate available. Studios often will "block book" time at cheaper rates or offer a reduction for non–prime time periods.

Musicians who play on master sessions are paid in accordance with applicable American Federation of Musicians (AF of M) scale rates. Vocalists' payments are governed by the American Federation of Television and Radio Artists (AFTRA). These respective organizations should be contacted by the manager as to applicable rates and procedures.

REHEARSALS

An artist recording for the first time shouldn't tackle a full-scale master session until he or she has gained recording experience. The demo session is an excellent means to gain experience while trying out different material and production techniques. Most studios offer less-expensive demo rates on 8- or 16-track equipment. Band members or other less experienced musicians can be employed for this purpose. Union rules provide for a reduction in scale payments on demo sessions.

Once an artist has sufficient recording experience, commercially viable material, and satisfactory arrangements, he or she should try to rehearse this material with the other musicians, if possible, or prepare written charts that they can study. Because of cost considerations, the studio is no place to rehearse.

Multitrack equipment employed in professional studios allows each separate instrument and voice part to be recorded separately, making it possible to refine and perfect a recording until it captures the exact sound desired by the artist and producer. After all the parts of a song are recorded, the producer will mix the volume levels, tones, and effects on the various tracks into the final master product. Like anything else, experience and familiarity with the recording process contribute to better, more commercial recordings. The new artist should gain as much experience as possible before undertaking a full master session.

SECURING A RECORDING CONTRACT

Assuming that producer, artist, and manager are satisfied that they have recorded a commercially viable master or a high-quality demo, the next step is to "shop" the tapes with record companies in order to secure a recording contract. This aspect of the manager's job is one of the most difficult, especially if the artist is new or relatively unknown.

It's important for the manager or other persons charged with the responsibility of shopping tapes to know how to approach a record company and appreciate what they're looking for in a new artist. This knowledge, used wisely, will improve the chances for success.

WHAT DOES THE RECORD COMPANY WANT?

Managers must try to put themselves in the shoes of the record company, which is in business to do one thing: sell records. As noted earlier, when a label signs a new artist, they're making a business decision that involves the commitment of substantial expenditures, not only in the form of royalty advances to cover recording costs, but also the costs of manufacturing, promotion, and tour support. One label executive estimates that every time he signs a new act, his company will spend a minimum of $500,000. He goes on to point out that this figure would be low in most cases and doesn't include any extra promotional efforts or take into consideration the countless labor-intensive hours put in by his staff. Because of this expense, the company wants to be sure that they're dealing with an artist capable of recouping this amount and earning a profit for the company. Thus, many factors go into deciding whether to sign an artist. The manager should be aware of all of them.

First and foremost, the record companies are looking for artists with talent and ability, capable of making records that will appeal to the mass record-buying public. But, as we have said repeatedly, being good or just having talent isn't enough. Record company A&R people hear hundreds of good tapes by talented artists every year. They're looking for more: a unique voice or a distinct sound—something that isn't already on the market. The worst thing a manager can say to a record company is, "I've got an artist who sounds just like. . . ." The companies just aren't interested.

When evaluating a recording, the company is listening primarily for the lead voice. In all but exceptional cases, musicianship can be recreated by experienced session men; the voice, however, cannot. The record company is also interested in the artist's material. Even if the voice is unique, the material must be commercial. "Commercial" is a fluid and subjective concept that depends on many variables. The producer, artist, and manager must be aware of the marketplace when making an assessment of what is acceptable and what is not. This will depend on the circumstances of each individual artist and the trends that exist at a given time in the entertainment industry.

The record company will also be asking: Does the artist write his or her own songs? If not, what is the source of the material? The ability of an artist to write songs is generally viewed as an asset, for it ensures a constant source of material for future recordings. While we're not suggesting that an artist *must* write his or her own material, in some cases this could be a factor in the company's decision to sign an artist–writer if a nonwriting artist of equal ability is available.

A critical aspect of the artist's career from the record company's point of view is the live personal appearance. Most labels won't sign an artist who's not a working act. Concert and club appearances remain one of the most effective means of promotion a record company possesses. If the artist isn't able to perform the recorded material in a live performance situation, this promotional tool is lost. This illustrates the importance of obtaining live personal appearance experience before approaching a record company.

Aside from the creative components of an artist's career, record companies want assurance that they'll be dealing with an artist who is articulate, poised, and presentable, capable of being before the public in a variety of contexts. This includes press interviews, television and radio appearances, and music videos. If these promotional elements aren't present, many companies will choose to pass on an artist who may have met all the other criteria.

Another critical area of inquiry from the record company's point of view is the artist's management. A good record company, just like a good manager, thinks in terms of careers, not just one-shot hit records. This is especially true because few first albums recoup the total investment the company has made. Often, it may take two, three, or even more album releases to break an act. If an artist has ineffective management, or no management at all, the company will often choose to pass on that artist. In some cases, the record company will prefer to help an unrepresented artist establish a management relationship. Whatever the artist's status, the major labels uniformly consider strong management to be a must; nothing of any substance will happen for any artist until an effective management situation is in place.

As with management, the record company will want to inquire about the status of the artist's booking-agency affiliation. This goes hand-in-hand with ensuring that the artist has a tight, well-rehearsed concert and club act. Other members of the artist's development team are also of interest to the label: the record producer, music publisher, publicist and others.

The artist's attitude and experience will weigh heavily on the company's ultimate decision of whether or not to offer a deal. The record company must be able to work with the artist on a very personal level. Unless he or she is realistic and willing to help build a career, neither record company, management, nor anyone else will be able to make that artist a success. A company would rather pass up a promising artist than take on the potential headaches he or she may cause later.

The foregoing considerations have dealt with factors within the artist's control. However, there are other elements in the decision-making process that have nothing to do with the merits of the artist and manager. A record company may be overcommitted to artists already on the label. In some cases, the company's budget may have been expended on signing new acts during the then-current fiscal year. There may be an overabundance of artists already signed who are similar, in style and appeal, to the new artist trying for a deal. In some instances, a company may have recently gone through an internal restructuring, resulting in a halt on acquisitions of new artists.

A manager can improve the artist's chances for a deal by studying the rosters of various labels to determine the needs of the various companies. For instance, a label may be overloaded with female rock singers, but may need a male country artist.

The manager should read the trade magazines for news about company shakeups, shifts in emphasis, and expansions. Often, knowing when to approach a label can mean the difference between a rejection and a record contract.

HOW SHOULD THE COMPANY BE APPROACHED?

As stated earlier, record companies aren't interested in dealing with amateurs or thrill seekers; they're in business to make money, not to educate people about the entertainment business. Record executives want to deal with professionals. To do this, they often rely on recommendations from others in the business they know and respect. The best way to get an appointment is by knowing someone personally at the label or someone else in the business who can recommend the artist or help set up an appointment.

Often an entertainment attorney or someone associated with the artist, such as the producer, will be more effective than the manager because of a personal contact.

It's generally a good idea for the artist to let the manager or some other party make contact with the record company, rather than try to do it him- or herself.

If a manager has no personal contacts, he or she should get the name of someone in the company's A&R department and try to make an appointment. It is the A&R person's job to listen to tapes submitted to the record company. When communicating with an A&R contact, the manager should be as professional as possible. This means being organized, brief, and to the point. Some A&R people will set up an appointment, while others will ask the manager to mail them a copy of the tape. Of course, an appointment is more desirable. However, if the A&R person wants to listen in a privacy to the tape—and most do—the manager should at least try to deliver the tape personally and establish some sort of rapport with him or her. The manager must be persistent, without becoming a pest.

According to all the record-company executives we surveyed, unsolicited mailing of tapes to record companies, almost without exception, is a waste of time.

Generally, when submitting an artist to a record company, the manager should make a tape copy of the three or four most commercial-sounding numbers the artist has done. It's also a good idea to submit a lyric sheet, especially if the songs on the tape comprise original material written by the artist. In some cases, the manager may want to submit an entire album, depending on the preference of the company. Just keep in mind that an A&R person doesn't have time to sift through a number of recordings. If interested, he or she will ask to hear more after listening to the submitted tape.

The manager should also submit a press kit that includes photographs of the artist, a professionally written biography, a list of past appearances, an itinerary of upcoming performances, and any other relevant information that will help the company better evaluate the artist.

If an interview is obtained, the manager should give the A&R person basic information about the artist in a straightforward manner. Record companies don't want hype. Neither do they want to hear qualifiers and excuses about the tape, such as, "You have to take into consideration that the mix isn't very good," or "The artist had a cold when this tape was recorded." If the tape is a demo, the manager should convey that information. If it's a master, the manager can say so, if it would be helpful. If there's immediate interest in the tape, the manager might offer to take the A&R contact to a live performance. The key to a successful interview is to be firm and remain in control, without becoming obnoxious.

Even if someone in A&R shows interest, he or she will almost always want to play the tape for others at the record company. The manager, leaving a business card, should promise to follow up the interview after the A&R person has had a chance to hear and consider the tapes.

At the worst, the manager will get an on-the-spot rejection. In this case, a cool demeanor is best; there's no sense in arguing. The A&R person's mind is made up. Instead, the manager should ask how to improve the artist's recordings and try to establish a rapport that might help get him or her in the door the next time. Then, regardless of the outcome of the interview, the manager should write a letter thanking the A&R contact for taking the time to consider the artist's work.

In the event the tape is rejected, it's important that neither manager nor artist become discouraged and give up. Rejection by record companies is just part of the game. There are many stories of record companies rejecting artists and material that later went on to become hits. Remember the Beatles. We're sure all the record executives who passed on them do. That should serve as a positive inspiration to any artist and manager who have been turned down. Just make the best of it, and move on.

NEGOTIATING THE RECORD CONTRACT

Believe it or not, record companies will sometimes say "yes." Better yet, more than one record company may be interested. At this point, the focus shifts to negotiation of a record contract.

The first step is to retain an experienced attorney specializing in music law who will be able to advise the artist and manager of the points to be covered and the complexities involved. Even if the manager has knowledge and experience in this area, it's still best in most cases to let the attorney do the negotiating. This course of action shields the artist and manager from the bargaining process, which can often be tedious and sometimes damaging to the artist/manager/record company relationship.

Whichever approach is selected, both artist and manager should keep in mind that a record company affiliation is a business relationship, regardless of how enthusiastic or friendly the A&R department has been. The record-company negotiator, who is usually someone from the label's business affairs department, will be trying to get the best terms possible for the company. From their point of view, signing a new artist is a dollars-and-cents proposition, so they will take advantage of their relative bargaining strength wherever possible. Naturally, the company will be in a better position when attempting to sign a new artist than it will be in negotiating with someone with a considerable track record or in renewing a contract with their own established artist.

With this basic premise in mind, we'll briefly discuss some of the points that should be considered by a manager in a record-contract negotiation. This is by no means intended to be a comprehensive or exhaustive discussion but only a general outline of relevant considerations—the subject is far too complex for an in-depth exploration in the context of this book. It is especially not meant as a do-it-yourself shortcut to avoiding legal fees. The manager should seek the advice and counsel of his attorney in any record negotiation. Remember that once the contract is signed, the artist and manager will likely have to live with its terms for a long time. This should give the artist and his or her representative more incentive to make sure that it's the best possible deal that can be negotiated under the circumstances.

CONTRACT TERMS

Generally, the recording contract is an exclusive personal services agreement whereby the artist furnishes master recordings embodying unique vocal and/or musical performances to the record company. In turn, the label becomes obligated to manufacture, promote, and market these records to the public and to pay the artist a royalty on the records sold. While this sounds simple enough in the abstract, the process is quite complicated and involved.

ROYALTIES

One of the most important provisions of the contract, from the artist's point of view, is the artist's royalty. Royalties are usually based on either a percentage of the suggested retail price or the manufacturer's wholesale price. Almost all the major labels calculate royalties on the suggested retail price. The royalty range for a new act generally runs around 11 to 14 percent. Established acts can command 14 to 16 percent; some superstars are able to get as much as 20 percent. It should be noted that in recent years, independent labels that specialize in niche formats and markets have increasingly become players. The royalty rates for the independents can range from 9 percent to 14 percent of retail for a new artist. Often, when a contract contains option periods, as most do, an escalating royalty rate is provided. It's also possible to negotiate rate increases or bonuses based upon sales performance. As this book went to press, the suggested retail price of records with their general corresponding percentage of retail sales by configuration was as follows:

Compact Disks $16.98   Tape Cassettes $9.98

Eleven to fourteen percent sounds pretty good, doesn't it? However, before you start totaling up the bankroll you'll get from your first platinum LP, let's talk about various deductions and rate reductions for specific types of sales.

Until recently, industry custom provided that royalties be computed on 85 percent to 90 percent of records sold. This 10- to 15-percent deduction was originally devised to cover breakage. Although breakage is no longer a problem because of improved manufacturing techniques, the custom has stubbornly persisted until only recently. Today, almost every label pays on 100 percent of records sold. While this is seemingly a victory for artists; it can be deceiving in light of other reductions record companies customarily make in the "royalty base," the figure upon which royalties are calculated. Standard deductions are as follows.

PACKAGING DEDUCTION
There is a customary deduction made before calculating royalties to cover jacketing or packaging costs. This figure usually runs from 10 to 15 percent for vinyl records, and from 15 to 25 percent for cassette tapes and CDs. The packaging costs should be limited as much as possible and specified in the contract.

EXCISE TAXES
It's standard to deduct all excise taxes and duties applicable to the records. In the same vein, for foreign sales record companies

pay the artist at separate royalty rates that range from 50 percent to 85 percent of the royalty rate payable on domestic sales.

FREE GOODS

In general, record companies give away 15 percent of every hundred records shipped to distributors. This is a form of discount to distributors, to give them some incentive and flexibility when it comes to coaxing retailers into stocking the artist's latest CD. Since royalties are only paid on records *sold*, not shipped, this in effect represents a sizable reduction in the artist's royalty base.

RESERVES FOR RETURNS

If that weren't enough, the artist and manager should be aware that it is standard in the record industry to pay royalties only on records sold at retail and not those returned by the wholesale distributors. In recent years there have been attempts by major labels to modify a longstanding "return privilege"—an industry custom that has allowed distributors to get back 100 percent of the wholesale price they paid for any product they return unsold. Whatever the rate of repayment, there are still such returns, which can further erode an artist's earnings. Consequently, companies will often put into escrow a percentage of the artist's royalties as a reserve to cover these return repayments. The artist's attorney should try to limit the impact of returns as much as possible and provide for prompt liquidation of the reserve after a stated number of accounting periods.

ROYALTY REDUCTIONS

Besides deductions from amounts payable, there are also various reductions in the applicable royalty percentage payable in certain specialized sales areas. For example, a lesser royalty rate—50 percent of the normal royalty assigned to retail sales—is applied to sales made to record clubs, sales of budget-priced records, special mid-price marketing programs, educational sales, sales made to military bases, and seemingly whatever else the record company can conjure up and get the artist to accept.

Generally, no royalty is paid on disc jockey or promotional copies or bonus goods given away to distributors or to record clubs to generate orders or new memberships. The artist's attorney will strive to minimize these reductions whenever possible, as well as limit the discretion of the company in areas of budget records and free goods.

RECORDING COSTS AND ROYALTY ADVANCES

When it comes to the subject of advances, too many inexperienced artists and their managers harbor unrealistic expectations. As with everything else in the record business, there is no such thing as easy, no-strings-attached money. Ultimately, it is the artist who will bear the cost of making the recording. There are two approaches to addressing the costs associated with making a record. One is the funds approach; the other is cost plus.

With the *funds approach,* the record label allocates a negotiated amount representing recording costs that it will advance to the artist. Any part of this amount the artist doesn't spend on delivering the finished album goes into the artist's pocket to be spent without restriction. These monies are recouped by the company out of artist royalties based on record sales.

With the *cost plus approach,* actual recording costs are paid for by the label. Additional advances, if any, are made to the artist for specified or unspecified purposes as determined by negotiation between the label and manager or artist. Again, these expenditures are all recoupable out of the artist's earnings.

Almost every Los Angeles– and New York–based label uses the funds approach, while Nashville labels almost exclusively use the cost plus method. The reason lies in the ability of a label to predict and control costs. In rock, alternative, and urban music, costs are much more difficult to predict and control, primarily because so many of the artists write and produce their own material with minimal record label oversight and involvement. In Nashville, there is much greater predictability of costs because of the use of pre-production techniques and closer label involvement with the record producer. Certainly, the cost plus method is a more realistic alternative for a cost-conscious label. Unfortunately, it just isn't always a workable option for the reasons mentioned previously.

THE ADVANCE AGAINST ROYALTIES

Regardless of the approach employed, the bottom line is the same. The record company is only making an interest-free loan that will be recouped from the artist's royalties, provided there is revenue earned from record sales. Only when the advance is recouped in full is the artist going to pocket any money in the form of royalties. In the unfortunate, but all too frequent event that the royalty revenue fails to "earn out" or to exceed the advance, the artist will not be expected to make up the deficit;

the label takes a risk on that amount when it decides to sign the artist. The same is true of video production expenses and other recoupable amounts advanced by the label to the artist. While an interest-free loan has value, it still must be repaid if and when the artist is successful. Responsible managers and artists would do well to remember that fact when negotiating their deal, asking only for advances that are necessary to help launch the artist. Doing so definitely makes getting royalty statements a much more rewarding experience.

CROSS-COLLATERALIZATION

Efforts should be made to specifically define and track recording costs and other recoupable advances. If at all possible, the artist will want to avoid "cross collateralization" of the royalty recoupment of one record against royalties earned by other records. The record company will almost always insist on cross-collateralization, especially with a new artist, but it never hurts to ask.

THE PRODUCER'S ROYALTY

And one more thing before you start toting up your record royalties: In addition to all other costs, the artist is responsible for paying the *producer's* royalty. The producer's override royalty ranges from 2 percent to 5 percent in the case of a top name producer. These amounts also come out of the artist's royalty. In most cases, the producer will receive 3 to 4 percent, which is deducted from the artist's 11 to 14 percent. Not exactly a get-rich-quick proposition, is it?

For those artists and managers who feel the record company is taking unfair advantage of the artist through deductions and rate reductions like the ones just discussed, it should be pointed out that few first albums by new artists fully recoup the company's investment. The record company, engaged in a high-risk proposition which requires a substantial financial and personal commitment on their part to "break" an artist, is trying to protect itself as much as possible. Without many of these devices, the company could simply not afford to sign as many new artists as they do. It should also be noted that an artist can dramatically improve his or her bargaining position through sales performance, thus becoming more valuable to the label. This will help in gaining more concessions and higher royalties in the future, or even an early contract renegotiation in cases of extraordinary sudden success.

CONTRACT TERM

Another area of importance to the artist is the length, or term, of the contract. The old procedure was to make the term one year with a number of additional one-year options usually exercisable at the election of the record company. Depending on the particular state in which the contract is entered, there are often restrictions on the maximum number of option periods. For example, California limits any contract involving personal services to seven years. More stringent restrictions are involved when the artist is a minor.

Many of these problems are avoided by a new system, which measures an artist's obligations in terms of the number of albums he or she must deliver over the term of the agreement. Usually, the standard clause calls for delivery of one album with consecutive options for six to seven more, exercisable at the election of the company without regard to the time period involved.

From the artist's standpoint, the attorney should seek to limit the number of option periods as much as possible, unless there are substantial guarantees involved. If the artist is successful, a shorter term will allow renegotiation to happen sooner. If the artist's albums are unsuccessful, or should he or she become unhappy, a shorter term allows the artist the freedom to seek an alternate record affiliation. Obviously, the record company will resist this approach, arguing that it needs product guarantees to ensure that it recoups its investment, especially if early releases prove unsuccessful.

RECORDING AND RELEASE REQUIREMENTS

Recording and release requirements are another vital area of artist concern. Normally, the company is under no obligation to actually release any of the artist's recordings. The artist's negotiations should seek some type of release commitment from the company. Usually the requirement to release a specified number of records during any one year of the contract is a precondition to the exercising of the next option period by the company.

PROMOTIONAL AND TOUR SUPPORT

Another important element in contract negotiations, especially for the new artist, is promotional support. The artist will seek a financial commitment from the record company in the form of trade ads, media time buys, and other forms of advertising.

For tour support, the artist should request that the label help finance his or her personal appearances to enable him to promote the record releases. Tour support is usually in the form of direct cash subsidies, or label responsibility for any expense deficit incurred by the artist in connection with a particular tour. The strength and ability of the manager and booking agent, and the types and importance of dates the artist will play, will weigh heavily on the company's decision in this area. The company doesn't want to commit money to help promote a tour that will be mismanaged or ineffective.

ARTISTIC CONTROL

Artistic control of the material to be recorded is a point often considered vital to an artist. This right is often granted to established artists with a track record in sales. It's not granted as often to a new artist because of inexperience and lack of sales history. As a practical matter, the A&R department, the artist–manager team, and the producer will all work together in the selection of material, with the company reserving veto power in the event of a dispute.

ROYALTY ACCOUNTING

Royalty accounting procedures are extremely important to the artist. Most record companies account semiannually. The artist should always seek the right to audit the company's books of account at reasonable intervals. A procedure should be set up to enable the artist to terminate the agreement in the event of non-payment of royalties or other material breaches by the company. Record companies will often oppose this type of clause or seek to word it very narrowly.

CONTROLLED COMPOSITIONS

Another standard practice by record companies is to seek a reduction in "mechanical royalty" payments it makes to the writer-artists for copyrighted material controlled by the artist and released on any album produced under the agreement. The usual practice is to pay 75 percent of the prevailing statutory rate, which is currently .695 cents or 1.3 cents per minute of playing time, whichever is greater. This in effect represents a sharing of mechanical royalties between the writer-artist and the record label. The company's argument is that they are the vehicle that allows the artist's copyright to be launched in the first place; thus,

a share of that income should go to the company to help defray
the costs involved. Needless to say, music publishers and writers
object to this. However, because of the strength of the record
labels, use of the controlled composition clause persists.

REMEMBER: IT'S BUSINESS

These are just some of the major elements of the recording
contract from the artist's standpoint. There are many more fine
points that are far beyond the reach of this book. The best and
only advice here is to get a good entertainment lawyer involved
at the outset of the negotiation process. It's not just a good idea,
it's essential.

As mentioned earlier, the record contract is strictly a business
relationship. The company will, whenever possible, try to
negotiate terms favorable to itself. The artist and manager should
do the same. Often, the record company will be accommodating
on certain points and inflexible on others. The key point to
remember is that the label's negotiator won't offer concessions;
the artist's representative will have to ask. An experienced
attorney will know what to ask for. The more the label is
interested in the artist, the better the resulting deal.

When it comes to record deals, it makes no sense for the artist
to enter into a contract which makes it nearly impossible to make
any money. However, for a first-time artist, the reality of a record
deal is that little or no money will be made. But then, it will be
nearly impossible to have a career without a record deal. This is
the music business take on "Which came first, the chicken or the
egg?" Nobody said it would be easy.

13

Music Publishing

One of the most complex, least understood, yet most important aspects of the entertainment industry is music publishing. An in-depth treatment of this intricate subject could fill several volumes. We urge you to consult our recommended readings section in the Appendix in order to become more fully informed. Our purpose here is to survey music publishing only as it relates to career decisions that will confront the artist and manager when dealing with the essential building block of the music business—the song.

Confusion over the ins and outs of music publishing is not confined just to the beginner. Many experienced managers confess to knowing very little when it comes to the subject of music publishing. This isn't surprising. Publishing requires, among other things, a working knowledge of domestic and foreign copyright laws, experience in negotiating and administering detailed contracts, an understanding of how performing rights societies and mechanical collection agencies are structured, and experience in royalty accounting—and, of course, the ability to recognize and help develop a good song. No wonder so many people are in the dark.

Before discussing the interplay of management and publishing, it's first necessary to grasp a clear understanding of the basic function of the music publisher to gain an overview of this key segment of the business.

THE MUSIC PUBLISHER

The music publisher's world revolves around the song. Any publisher will invariably tell you that the song is the foundation of the music industry. Without it, there would be no artists, no managers, no record companies, and no booking agents. Undoubtedly, there's a great deal of truth in this statement.

Conceding the importance of the song, the more specific question is, "What exactly does a publisher do with a song?" The function of a music publisher is to locate and commercially develop songs (often referred to as "copyrights") in much the same way that a manager locates artists and develops their careers. In both cases, publisher and manager are working to transform artistic potential into commercial success.

The music publisher searches for songwriters with ability and songs with potential. The publisher who has found a song with commercial potential then acquires the copyright from the songwriter in return for a promise to pay the writer a royalty based on income earned from the commercial exploitation of the composition. Once the copyright is assigned and a publishing contract is signed, the publisher then takes steps to protect the song by obtaining a copyright registration on the words and music.

An active publisher will work with the writer to perfect the song or possibly help develop and improve the writing style. Tape demos will be produced and lead sheets will be made. Once the song is in final form, the music publisher will try to match it with a recording artist whose style fits the song, trying to persuade the artist to record it or incorporate it into a television or live performance. In essence, the publisher and writer become partners with regard to the writer's song. The writer is the creative element, while the publisher is in charge of the business side of the relationship.

The reason a publisher will expend the time and money to find and develop potential hits is simple. Every time an artist sells a record embodying the song, the music publisher and songwriter make money. Every time the song is performed on television or radio, the publisher and writer make money. Every time a copy of sheet music or a printed folio containing the song is sold, the publisher and writer make money. Every time the song is used in a motion picture soundtrack, a commercial, or in a concert performance, the publisher and writer make money. When income is realized, it's the responsibility of the publisher to collect it and account to the writer for the royalties while retaining the balance. The songwriter's royalties, or writer's share, is usually the same as the publisher's share—that is, a basic split of 50–50.

The foregoing is an oversimplified account of the publisher's role. The process involves endless hours of listening to tapes, changing lyrics, reassuring songwriters, and all the other things that go into finding and perfecting a hit song, or better yet, a standard. The creative side of publishing is paralleled by a seeming avalanche of contracts, licenses, memos, letters, forms, and phone calls.

From a management standpoint, the music publisher should first of all be viewed as a potential source of material for the artist. Many recording artists don't write their own material and therefore must depend totally on songs written by others. Other artists who do write are not consistently able to turn out quality songs suited to their own recording styles and thus find it necessary to supplement their own material with that of others. Even the great singer-songwriters like Garth Brooks or Paul Simon will on occasion record songs by others if they feel the material will help their careers. Because every artist needs good material to sustain a career, most are open to the possibility of recording someone else's song, provided that it fits their style and sound. This is particularly true in the country and pop formats, which are more lyric- and melody-driven.

A manager, artist, or record producer seeking material should realize that a music publisher is only too happy to submit songs for consideration by the artist. While this is especially true of an established artist with a recording contract, it also applies to a new artist trying to secure his or her first deal. For this reason, the manager or artist should not shy away from the major publishing houses when seeking material. Nor should the manager overlook the smaller companies trying to establish themselves. Often, a lesser-known company will expend more effort than a larger firm to find a newcomer the right song, for they hope to cultivate relationships that have potential.

When approaching a music publisher for songs, the manager, producer, or artist should speak with someone in the publisher's professional department, which is responsible for finding and developing new songs and matching them with artists. This part of a publisher's operation is very similar to the A&R department of a record company. The person in charge, called the *professional manager,* is also involved in adapting previously recorded songs to the styles of currently popular artists. When approaching a professional manager, the artist or manager should specify the type of material that the artist records or performs, such as country, adult contemporary, R&B, and the like. The professional manager should also be given a tape of two or three songs indicative of the artist's singing style and voice quality. This helps him or her identify songs that might be appropriate. If the artist has a certain tempo, instrumentation, or sound in mind, let the publisher know this also.

It's also helpful for the manager, artist, or producer to specify whether previously unrecorded material or proven copyrights that could be given a new arrangement are sought. The distinction can be important from a legal standpoint. The revised 1976 United States Copyright Act, which went into effect January 1, 1978, gives the copyright owner (usually the publisher) the right to determine the first artist to record a particular song commercially. But after the song has been recorded and distributed to the public for the first time, anyone has the right to re-record it without permission from the copyright owner, provided that they pay the owner a royalty. Under the 1976 Copyright Act, this royalty was set and periodically adjusted for inflation by the Copyright Royalty Tribunal, an administrative body set up by the Copyright Act. This practice is commonly referred to as "compulsory licensing."

Congress abolished the Copyright Royalty Tribunal in December, 1993. The compulsory license royalty is now adjusted by an ad hoc Copyright Royalty Arbitration Panel (CARP) under the jurisdiction of the Library of Congress. Because of the compulsory licensing provisions of the Copyright Act, an artist can't record a previously unrecorded work without the copyright owner's permission. The manager, producer, or record company should therefore make sure that permission to record the work is granted by the copyright owner before any money is spent in the studio. That permission is granted by a mechanical license issued by the copyright owner to the person or firm (usually the record company) that seeks to record the song.

Another consideration in recording new or unproven material controlled by a music publisher is to ensure that the song hasn't been recorded earlier by another artist who might release the record ahead of or at the same time as the artist's release, thereby creating a competitive relationship between records. If the artist is of sufficient stature or is seriously interested in recording a new copyright, the manager or producer might request the publisher grant an "exclusive" on the song. This means that the publisher won't grant a license to anyone else for a stated period of time, giving the artist and record company sufficient time to record and release the song.

Still another aspect of recording previously unrecorded material is the possibility of a participation by the artist in the publishing income from the song. This is a practice that is understandably unpopular with music publishers. However, an established recording artist with a large record-buying following can, in some instances, persuade a publisher to give up either part ownership of the copyright (publisher's share only) or a percentage of the income earned from the sale of the particular recorded version; the inducement to the publisher is a guaranteed level of sales and performances on radio and television. Many publishers have policies against such practices, arguing that the integrity of their copyrights should remain intact. Other publishers maintain that there's never any guarantee a particular recording will be a hit, so there's no justification for giving up part-ownership or a portion of the potential income. The final decision often comes down to bargaining strength. How much would you be willing to give up to have Celine Dion release one of your copyrights as her next single?

Besides providing an artist with quality material, many publishers contribute to the promotion of a recording of their copyrights or even help to open doors at record labels for exclusive writer-artists. In recent years in Nashville, which has always been a song-oriented town, the music publisher has become one of the primary points of access to record labels interested in signing singer-songwriters to record contracts. Assuming a new artist signs with a music publisher as an exclusive writer, the publisher becomes a member of the artist's development team. Often, a manager can persuade the publisher to either purchase or co-op a trade ad or employ independent radio promoters to push a recorded version of a song. Some of the larger publishing companies have their own promotion staffs to complement the efforts of the record company.

An active publisher is also an excellent source of information regarding radio airplay and sales activity of a particular record. A manager is well-advised to develop contacts with the top music publishers to ensure a steady flow of material for the artist. An experienced publisher will always be thinking of songs for the artist and won't waste a manager's time by submitting weak or inappropriate material.

In the event that the artist does record a song controlled by an active music publisher, especially in the case of an "A side" single release, the manager should keep the company informed of all pertinent developments in the artist's career. This will help ensure a maximum contribution by the publisher to the success of the record.

MUSIC PUBLISHING INCOME

Let's now examine music publishing as a source of income for the writer-artist. The ability of the artist not only to perform but also to write songs adds an important dimension to his or her career. First of all, a singer-songwriter is guaranteed a steady source of material geared to his or her vocal and musical style. This generally makes the artist more attractive to record companies, booking agents, and managers than an artist who must depend on the writing of others. Secondly, the writer-artist has a much greater income potential than the nonwriter—*much greater.* One of the best examples is the Beatles. John, Paul, George, and Ringo were an extremely successful group, with all four artists sharing equally in record royalties and personal appearances. However, John Lennon and Paul McCartney, who wrote the majority of the group's original songs, far surpassed the other members in earning power as a result of their songwriting royalties. More than twenty-five years after the legendary group played their last concert, those same songs are still generating huge annual amounts. This illustrates the oft-repeated observation that hit records and rock stars come and go, but the real money in the music business lies in owning copyrights.

SPECIFIC SOURCES OF INCOME

Before considering the artist's publishing alternatives, let's briefly review the sources of income that can be derived from the exploitation of copyrighted musical compositions. Income is realized from five main sources:

- Mechanical royalties derived from the sale of records and tape embodying the song
- Radio and television performances
- Movie synchronization fees
- Sale of printed music
- Miscellaneous uses

Most standard songwriter contracts call for mechanical, performance, synchronization, and miscellaneous income to be evenly divided—50 percent to the writer and 50 percent to the publisher. A lesser percentage or set amount is paid to the writer as a royalty on the sale of printed music. This reduced payment takes into consideration the publisher's expense in printing, distributing, and selling sheet music and folios.

MECHANICAL ROYALTIES

The Copyright Act of 1976 sets a statutory rate of compensation that must be paid to copyright owners by anyone who manufactures and distributes recordings embodying the owner's composition in lieu of a negotiated rate. The current statutory rate is 6.95 cents or 1.3 cents per minute or fraction thereof, whichever is greater, for each record manufactured and distributed. This rate for "mechanical royalties" is subject to periodic adjustment by the Copyright Royalty Arbitration Panel. Assuming a writer-artist writes ten compositions included on an album that sells 100,000 units at the statutory mechanical royalty rate, the total amount of mechanical royalties payable to the copyright owner would be $69,500, assuming there are no deductions for collection fees. Of this sum, $34,750 would represent the writer's share, and the remaining $34,750 would be retained by the publisher. Although payment is computed in pennies, they can mount up in a hurry if a hit record is involved.

PERFORMING RIGHTS

Income from the public performance of copyrighted musical compositions on radio and television, in concerts and clubs, and even in elevators and doctor's offices, represents the single most lucrative source of publishing income. The performing rights of publishers and writers in the United States are controlled by three performing-rights societies, ASCAP, BMI, and SESAC. ASCAP and BMI control the bulk of all compositions written in this country. SESAC is a much smaller, privately owned society concerned with specialty niche areas of music including gospel, country, and Latin music, to name a few.

These societies license radio and television broadcasters as well as concert halls, nightclubs, and other users of music. To give you an idea of how much money this represents, in 1995, ASCAP collected almost $437 million from users of its music. Aggregate ASCAP, BMI, and SESAC collections approached $800 million. This underscores how big the performing-rights slice of the pie is for

member writers and publishers. Each respective performing-rights
society has a complicated payment system whereby it distributes
the proceeds from these licenses to its members, based on the
number and type of performances of the respective copyrighted
musical compositions they represent. For more detailed
information on membership and distribution formulas, consult the
performing-rights societies.

MOVIE SYNCHRONIZATION FEES

Income from motion picture uses of songs is another substantial
source of musical copyright income. Songs are usually licensed
for use by the publisher on a negotiated-fee basis. Producers of
major motion pictures are willing to pay substantial amounts for a
license to use the "right" song in their productions. Think of some
of the hit movies of recent years, such as *Forrest Gump* and *Pulp
Fiction*. The music contributed to the overall success of each
picture. For that reason, motion picture producers and film studio
heads don't hesitate in budgeting large sums for the right to use
copyrighted musical compositions in their movies. This process is
known in the industry as obtaining a *synchronization,* or *synch
license,* whenever the song is synchronized with the on-screen
images. Because motion pictures are publicly performed, a
separate performance license is also required. Additional
permissions and negotiations relating to mechanical licensing
come into play when the songs used in the motion picture are
released on a soundtrack album.

It should be noted that for licensing purposes music videos are
considered to be motion pictures and the same considerations
apply.

SALE OF PRINTED MUSIC

Printed music consists of individual sheet music and song folios
containing multiple compositions. This has proven to be an
expanding source of revenue, especially with the popularity of
the "personality folio," which features in printed form songs made
popular by the recordings of a particular artist.

MISCELLANEOUS USES

Miscellaneous uses of material include the use of songs on
greeting cards and song quotes used in books and articles. The
particularly lucrative commercial or jingle market for songs has

aspects which relate to performing rights, synch licenses, and miscellaneous uses.

It's clear from this brief overview of potential income sources how much a successful writer-artist stands to gain from a hit song. The question facing the manager is how to realize maximum benefits while still allowing time for other career pursuits, such as recording, touring, commercials, television, and personal appearances.

FINDING A PUBLISHER

Finding an experienced music publisher to handle a writer-artist's songs is advisable, especially in the case of an unproven one without a recording contract who seeks an outlet for material. An active, experienced music publisher who believes in a writer can offer a variety of services otherwise unavailable. One of the most attractive features of the arrangement is that a reputable publisher's fee is based entirely on a percentage of earnings from the writer's songs. Consequently, the publisher has increased incentive to exploit the writer's songs. By choosing this option, the writer-artist and manager take advantage of the publisher's expertise in copyright law, publishing, administration, song development, promotion, and exploitation. There is also a cost savings for obtaining copyright protection, preparation of lead sheets, production of demos, and costs associated with submitting the songs to other recording artists. The major drawback is that the writer gives up approximately 50 percent of potential earnings in the form of the publisher's share.

The writer-artist has two alternate ways of working with a publisher to exploit his or her songs, depending on the strength of the writing and the desires of the parties. He or she can either publish on a song-by-song basis or can elect to sign an exclusive writer agreement, whereby all songs written during the term of the agreement will be submitted to the publisher. If the latter approach is chosen, the writer should usually expect to receive a sum of money as a signing bonus or a cash advance recoupable against future writer royalties.

Certainly, any type of unrecoupable payment should be sought. Too many young, impressionable writer-artists have been seduced by cash *advances,* thinking these to be free money with no strings attached. Any time such a payment that is subject to recoupment is made, manager and artist should recognize it for what it is—an interest-free loan. Since the publisher has the duty to collect and account for monies received, it will make sure the debt is paid back by deducting any outstanding advances from the writer's share. For this reason, an writer-artist might be better advised to refuse advances, where possible, or to trade offers of front money for a shorter contract term that would allow for renegotiation with the publisher on better terms if success is realized.

FINDING AN ACTIVE PUBLISHER

When selecting a music publisher, it's important that the artist and manager choose a legitimate concern that will take action to secure recordings of the writer's songs rather than merely act as a "copyright collector." The latter sort of publisher finds songs, signs songwriter contracts, and then deposits them in a filing cabinet hoping something will happen either through the efforts of the writer, or perhaps by luck. The writer should feel comfortable with the publisher and be able to relate to the company's staff on a personal level. This is important if the publisher really intends to help the writer develop his or her songwriting skills and techniques.

Even though writer-artists may be convinced of a publisher's sincerity, it's also important that the publisher devotes time to exploiting the writer's songs. There's nothing worse for a writer than to be lost in the shuffle, especially when he or she is writing commercial material.

Regardless of whether the writer-artist chooses to work with a publisher on a per-song or an exclusive basis, he or she should seek the help of an attorney experienced in music publishing to negotiate and draft contracts. While many contractual terms are more or less standard, many others are not. Important items to be considered include the scope of rights granted, duration of the contract, territory, royalty rates, deductions from writer's royalties, time and method of royalty payments, right to audit publisher's books, and royalty advances or guarantees. Foreign aspects of the publisher's contract will be dealt with in a later chapter.

The trap to avoid is granting publishing rights to a publisher who's either unwilling or unable to exploit the songwriter's songs. Depending on the bargaining strength of the parties and the importance of the writer and song, the writer-artist's negotiator may request a clause in the contract whereby all rights to a particular song will revert to the writer after a stated period of time if the publisher hasn't been successful in securing a commercial recording of the song. Many music publishers object to this type of clause, maintaining it may take an investment of considerable money and time to commercially exploit a writer's songs; such a recapture clause, they argue, would undermine the total commitment necessary to achieve success. This argument is particularly valid if the publisher has advanced unrecouped monies to the writer. But certain companies won't object, provided that they're given a reasonable time to secure a recording and the writer agrees to repay any unrecouped advances against his or her royalties.

THE REALITIES OF MUSIC PUBLISHING

Before leaving the subject of finding a publisher, we should point out several realities of the music business which could have a significant impact on writer-artists. Almost every record company will have an affiliated music publishing firm to take advantage of its capacity to generate publishing income through the commercial release of its records. It is standard procedure for record companies to package the offer of a record deal with a co-terminus publishing contract. Because of antitrust laws, they can't compel the artist to sign with their publishing affiliate but, from a practical standpoint, they will have considerable leverage. The legal and practical advice from an experienced attorney on how to handle this likelihood can be of great value, especially where the artist and management have reservations about such an arrangement.

A point worth alerting new artists and managers to is the trend toward concentration in the music publishing field. A pattern of consolidation and acquisitions over the last several years has created international publishing giants: Warner/Chappell, Sony Music, BMG Music, EMI Music, and others. The continuing trend toward concentration in the industry could well change the face of music publishing in the coming years. The implications are not at all clear, but it would be in the interest of writer-artists to monitor potential changes in the structure and practices of music publishing. Your music lawyer will be able to advise you of these developments and offer sound advice on how to respond.

SELF-PUBLISHING AND OTHER CHOICES

An alternative available to the writer-artist who doesn't want to work with an established publisher is to self-publish or to let the manager or another employee administer his or her catalog. This is common in the case of an established recording artist who writes all or substantially all of his or her own material. This type of undertaking requires sufficient financial resources to hire people with publishing experience or a manager with sufficient time and experience to handle this additional responsibility.

The advantage of this arrangement is obvious. The artist retains not only the writer's share but the music publisher's share of the income.

The disadvantages are numerous, however. First, the writer-artist must bear all the expenses that would otherwise be borne by the publisher. Because of the lack of an organized staff, the artist-publisher may not be as effective as a regular publisher in obtaining cover recordings of his or her material by other artists. Finally, unless the artist or someone on staff has experience in the field of publishing administration, the artist could jeopardize his or her entire catalog.

There are other drawbacks. Normally, publishing administration doesn't come within the normal scope of management duties. Many managers simply aren't qualified to undertake this very complex and multifaceted job. Even if qualified, a manager may not have sufficient time to devote to matters of publishing as well as to the management of the artist's career. But if the manager does decide to undertake these duties, a separate agreement covering the scope of such publishing duties and compensation is advisable. In this event, and provided that the manager is receiving separate compensation for the publishing activities, the manager and artist may want to modify the management agreement to exempt publishing income realized by the artist's publishing firm from the income base on which the manager's fee or percentage is computed.

The structure and operation of the artist's self-publishing venture is beyond the scope of this book. However, the artist and manager are advised to consult an attorney thoroughly knowledgeable in the area of music publishing, someone who can provide counsel on the advisability of such an enterprise and can help organize and structure the artist's publishing operations. The respective performing rights organizations and mechanical collection agencies should also be consulted regarding their rules and procedures.

ALTERNATIVES

For many writer-artists, especially those with record company affiliations and established followings, there may be alternatives that a manager might consider: these are arrangements that fall between writing for an established publisher, and acting as a self-contained publisher.

The first of these arrangements is a joint copyright-ownership agreement with an established publisher. Often, a name recording writer-artist with a guaranteed outlet for recorded product has sufficient leverage to enter into an agreement whereby a music publishing company owned by him or her and a full-time, active publisher can jointly own the song copyrights. This allows the artist to take advantage of the active publisher's administrative, exploitative, and promotional capabilities while still collecting his or her writer's share and a portion of the publisher's share of income. Although the artist gives up part of the copyright owner-ship, he or she still derives greater income from, and maximizes the long-term development of, his or her copyrights.

Another approach is an agency representation agreement with an active publisher. This is similar to joint ownership, except that full copyright ownership remains vested in the writer-artist's com-pany. The established publisher is paid a percentage of the total publisher's share of income, but only from monies earned or accruing during the term of the agency agreement. Obviously, the inducement to a major publisher to enter into this type of arrangement is not nearly as attractive as a full or joint copyright-ownership arrangement.

A third alternative is an administration or collection agreement with a major publisher or a publishing administration service company. Here, the artist's publishing company retains an admin-istrative specialist to render specific services—such as copyright registration, performing-rights clearance, and administration and/or royalty collection and accounting—in return for a negotiat-ed fee or percentage of publishing income.

One last alternative that must be considered is the possibility of the artist publishing material through a company owned or con-trolled by the artist's manager or jointly owned by artist and man-ager. This raises possible conflict-of-interest problems with the manager: Will a manager in this situation be tempted to make a publishing decision that might be good for him or her personally but detrimental to his client's career? What happens to ownership of copyrights in the event of a breakup between the artist and manager? Finally, should the manager's fee be calculated on a percentage of the writer's share of income derived from material published by the manager's company? These are all potential problem areas. This isn't to say that such an arrangement isn't advisable. There's nothing wrong with it as long as there's full disclosure by the manager and artist of their positions, understood and agreed to by all respective parties. The best advice here is for artist and manager to consult their attorneys as to the structure of any such arrangement.

PUBLISHING-RELATED RESPONSIBILITIES

Regardless of the publishing alternatives selected, both artist and manager should be aware that in relation to songwriting and music publishing there are responsibilities that belong solely to the writer and his or her representative. The most notable of these is selection and affiliation with a performing-rights society. Performance royalties are paid directly by the societies to publisher and writer members on a separate basis. A writer can be affiliated with one society only and must select one, judging which society is best for him or her. As mentioned before, ASCAP and BMI are the leading societies in terms of license fees collected and royalties paid. SESAC has a smaller, more specialized membership. These highly competitive societies each offer certain advantages over the others. Their membership departments will be glad to talk to writers and managers concerning the relative merits of their respective organizations. The writer-artist and manager should be cautioned that failure to affiliate may result in losses of writer performance credits even though a song is copyrighted and published.

Once the writer has affiliated with the performing-rights society, he or she and the manager must deal with the society directly in the area of writer-related affairs. Although the publisher may offer guidance in this area, it's not mandatory. The manager is well-advised to contact a representative of the artist-client's society as to writers' duties and responsibilities.

There is no one "right" answer as to which publishing alternative or performing-rights society an artist and manager should select. The decision should hinge on what's right for the artist at a given stage of his or her career. Publishing and songwriting royalties are important long-term sources of income that can continue to accrue long after record royalties and personal appearance income have diminished or come to an end. As a result, decisions in this area should not be made hastily, especially in the early, breaking-in stage of a career where the temptation is often the greatest to compromise potentially valuable copyrights for some ego-warming praise and immediate cash. As in every other career area, it's much better to make publishing decisions with an eye to the future, when stardom has had its run. Awareness and knowledge of music publishing by both manager and artist, accompanied by careful planning and intelligent decision-making, can result in long-term financial security. Just ask Paul McCartney.

14

Music Videos, TV, Radio, and Film

The 1980s saw the beginning of a technological and creative revolution that would change the face of the music business forever. Music videos fostered an entire new genre that had not existed before. Many music industry professionals credit this new art form with turning a badly depressed music business around in the early '80s.

Now, MTV, VH-1, BET, TNN, and a number of other developing cable formats have taken the basic three- to five-minute video and merged it with more traditional television programming aimed directly at music consumers. In the process, they have created an entertainment staple that will not soon disappear.

The hardware/software combination of the videocassette recorder (VCR) and music video is only one manifestation of how technology and imagination have changed the industry. As the video revolution was being felt, network and syndicated radio programming began enjoying similar unprecedented success, rather than the demise that many media experts had predicted. For the first time since its heyday in the 1930s and '40s, radio experienced a comeback in variety, concert, and interview programming centered around music acts. Led by an assortment of syndicaters and entrepreneurs, a wide range of music-based programming for radio, beyond the standard top-40 format, came into being.

Pay Per View (PPV) television programming is an innovation that has come of age relatively recently. Artists as diverse as the Rolling Stones, Wayne Newton, Bon Jovi, Elton John, and Hank

Williams, Jr. have either played or are planning PPV concerts with possible one-night grosses in the tens of millions of dollars. The coming of high-definition digital television could fuel an accelerated move to PPV and other audiovisual programming innovations.

While specific formats and configurations are nearly impossible to predict, it is a safe bet that entertainment in general and music in particular will never be the same. With the galloping pace of technological development, new delivery systems for musical entertainment will become the norm. The Internet and direct satellite TV are just two more examples of what the future holds for artists and their fans.

The management implications of all this are overwhelming. Failing to appreciate and understand the changes and opportunities brought about by new technology can spell the difference between enjoying a thriving career as an artist or manager and being left behind to dream of what might have been.

MUSIC VIDEOS

Thanks to the invention of the VCR, the growth of cable television, and the pioneering efforts of MTV, the music video is now an entertainment staple. Record company A&R departments have been forced to factor video potential into their decisions of whether to sign an artist. Because fans now expect to see their favorite artists on video as well as listen to them on records, most major labels have set up in-house video production departments. A whole new category of awards now recognizes video excellence and popularity. The music video is here to stay.

From a management standpoint, exactly what role do videos play in an artist's success?

The answers vary considerably and will probably be somewhat surprising. The majority of managers and record executives we surveyed harbored serious doubts about the ability of a music video to break a new artist or record or even to directly generate record sales. However, most agreed that a well-produced music video can have a significant *indirect* impact on solidifying and increasing sales. They were even stronger in their belief that the music video is an indispensable tool for creating name and identity recognition of an artist, which ultimately translates into long-term record and concert-ticket sales.

Music videos are always a potential source of conflict between artist and record label. As a rule, artists and their managers value the music video for any number of reasons. These include ego gratification and status within the industry and the promotion value the video has for concert bookings, merchandising, and record sales.

In recent years many labels have been cutting back on videos (or at least have threatened to), taking the position that money earmarked for video production would be better spent on alternative promotional vehicles. This conflict is fueled by the fact that it is almost always the record company that advances the money to produce a video. Because most videos do not have sufficient commercial appeal to recoup the rather substantial sums it takes to produce them, record labels are forced to deal with videos as expensive promotional tools. As a result, videos are often budgeted only after a record breaks, if at all.

There are of course, notable exceptions—artists who are viable in the home video market. One of the most successful is Michael Jackson, who has been able to compete with motion pictures, comedians, and popular exercise videos for sales and rentals. Videos represent another source of income in excess of their cost for an artist with the unique talents of a Michael Jackson. Not surprisingly, Jackson finances the productions himself and keeps the profits, but such an arrangement is clearly the exception.

At least for now, it is the record company that makes the decision to produce a video for promotional purposes, and usually they provide the funding. For that reason, the label will expect a substantial voice in the creative content of the video, along with control of its exploitation.

MUSIC VIDEO COSTS

Music videos aren't cheap. Even the most bare-bones production will cost $40,000. The average price range for a rock video produced in Los Angeles or New York is $100,000 to $250,000, depending on the stature of the act. Country and rap videos are generally less expensive, with the average cost running from $50,000 to $75,000. Of course, it's possible to spend just about as much as you can write a check for. There have been some videos that have run a million-dollar tab or more; a handful have cost several million or more. That's a lot to recoup. Nonetheless, such amounts are sometimes spent on videos with megastars, surely more for ego than for record sales.

That leads to the next question: How does the record company get its money back? This varies according to the label, but the standard approach is to deduct a portion of the cost from the artist's record royalties. This is usually a deduction of 50 to 75 percent, and sometimes it's higher. The balance comes from revenue generated by commercial sales, rentals, and licenses.

Because of their investment, the record company also demands extensive right of ownership and control over the video production. Any new artist should expect the record company to demand exclusive audiovisual rights, along with the right to own and license the copyright to any music video produced pursuant to the terms of the overall contract. Generally, record companies will offer artists a video royalty equal to 50 percent of net revenues after recoupment of all production costs, distribution fees, and other expenses. Finally, the label will regard a video as a controlled composition and will demand a free synchronization license as well as waivers of other applicable copyright fees on the video production.

Managers should be cautioned against an overly broad grant of exclusive rights to the record company. Such a grant might impair the artist's ability to pursue motion picture and television opportunities. Artists and their managers should also attempt to use any leverage they have to modify or limit the record company's standard recoupment policies and liberal definition of terms such as "recoupable distribution fees and other expenses." An experienced music lawyer is indispensable when it comes to negotiating the fine points of audiovisual rights with record labels and publishers. As mentioned previously, few artists have the money and bargaining power to finance and control their own productions; as of this writing, they are rare exceptions. If a substantial commercial market develops, that could change, but for now the record company is in the driver's seat when it comes to music videos.

TELEVISION

It's virtually impossible to be engaged in the entertainment industry and not be affected by the impact of commercial television. Network and cable TV have significantly changed the character of entertainment around the world. Prior to television, an artist could reach a mass audience primarily through live network radio, which had only a fraction of the programming alternatives available through television or personal appearances. Television has changed all this.

Today, an appearance by an artist on the right television show can be seen by tens of millions. Given the profusion of channels and formats which include music video programs, in-concert series, cable and network specials, talk and interview shows, documentaries, late-night and variety programming, and even game shows, made-for-TV movies, dramatic series, and sitcoms, an artist's name can be turned into a household word in a matter of weeks. There's almost limitless potential for instant career acceleration.

However, the prospects for career development offered by television must be balanced against the ever-present dangers inherent in the medium. The same mass exposure that can produce an instant success can just as quickly overexpose the artist, spawning an overnight has-been. The manager should be careful to choose only those types of appearances that will enhance the artist's career plan. Doing a game show might be fun, but it can quickly trivialize an artist unless handled correctly. By the same measure, an appearance on a Saturday morning kid's show might strike just the right chord by winning over a new following of kids and their parents. The same is true of charity events.

The amount and type of television exposure is always a judgment call and subject to second-guessing. Decisions should be made with care. One way to ensure that they are is to see that the career plan contains specific television goals and guidelines. There's nothing more potentially damaging to a career than indiscriminate, randomly selected television appearances. The manager with a make-it-up-as-you-go-along policy or no policy at all is flirting with disaster.

BASIC TELEVISION PLANNING CONSIDERATIONS

To help write an effective television policy, let's look at some basic considerations that should go into TV-appearance decision-making. Television producers, programmers, and sponsors are always looking for artists or celebrities with "name value" to enhance their programs. When evaluating name value or drawing power, they're generally looking for someone with wide national appeal rather than a regional or a localized following. As a rule, an artist's value is directly proportional to current activities, unless the artist has achieved living-legend or celebrity status. A hit record, recent award, or national concert tour will undoubtedly make the artist more attractive and give the producer and manager a hook on which to justify an appearance. Visual appeal and personality are also factors considered by television professionals. Overall name-identification value is yet another consideration.

The most common types of television appearances, aside from music videos, are network or cable specials, talk shows, in-concert series, and musical-variety or concept shows. The major multifaceted booking agencies maintain strong contacts with the producers and talent coordinators of these programs through in-house television departments. A strong agency contact is often instrumental in getting an artist the "right" slot on the "right" show. Many of the major record companies also maintain contacts in this area because of the impact such appearances can have on record sales. Many top-level managers also make it their business to maintain strong television contacts.

The guest appearance on a musical-variety, concept, or talk show should be viewed primarily as a promotional tool. Talk shows rarely pay guests above AFTRA scale, which is less than $1,000 for a network program. From a career-development standpoint, this fee should be the least of an artist's worries, for an appearance like this can be the one break the artist needs to enter into the national limelight.

The financial return for a musical-variety or concept show appearance can be more substantial, depending on the artist's name value and the budget of the particular show. However, just as with talk shows, money should not be the only factor considered. Again, a slot on a show can be of untold value to an artist in terms of promotion and exposure. A case in point is the first United States national television appearance of the Beatles on the Ed Sullivan Show in the early 1960s. This was the major push that helped launch the group in the United States. This exposure helped them to achieve superstar status in relatively short order.

The TV special is probably the most attractive alternative to the established artist from a financial, promotional, and artistic standpoint. This is especially true if he or she is able to exercise a measure of creative control over the program and guest-selection process, which many do. Here, the procedure is somewhat different from that of the previous examples. Often the artist–manager team and/or an independent television producer will formulate a concept for a special and then sell it, either to a television network or to a sponsor. Naturally, the more name value and following the artist possesses, the easier it will be to sell the show.

In addition to hosting specials, established artists appear on such programs as guests, many times at the invitation of the show's artist-host. Some major artists limit their television appearances to this type of format to avoid the problems of overexposure and negative image projection.

MAKING THE RIGHT TELEVISION DECISIONS

As mentioned earlier, careful attention should he given to any television offer based on some of the following factors.

First, the manager and artist should consider the type of show. Is its format consistent with the artist's image, career plan, and goals? For instance, a serious singer-songwriter would stand to gain little by a guest appearance on a TV quiz show or situation comedy. Such a format would be more consistent with a comedian's image and career objectives.

Second, consider the show's ratings. This will determine the exposure value of the particular program for the artist and may indicate the quality of the program and how it's perceived by the viewing public.

Then there is another consideration: Who are the other guest stars? The artist wants to be presented in the best possible light. The stature of other performers, billing, time slots, and so forth will have a bearing on whether the artist will want to appear on the show.

Potential for overexposure is also a major consideration. Once the artist is too accessible on television, the concertgoer and record buyer won't be nearly as interested in paying to hear or see the artist when they can get the same thing free on television. There's also the danger that too many appearances will cause the audience to tire of the performer. Their adulation can quickly turn to indifference. This has ended the career of more than one artist. Making the right decision here isn't easy. It requires a great deal of judgment on the part of the manager to say "no" to lucrative offers for the sake of preserving the artist's career.

While most of this discussion has been couched in terms of the established artist, the same guidelines are generally applicable to a new artist. The major difference is that the artist without established name value will find it much more difficult to get television exposure, especially the "right" exposure. The new artist should be encouraged to develop strong management, booking agency, and record company connections to help break the national TV-exposure barrier. Alternative formats, such as regionally syndicated shows and specialized cable television, may serve as a means of gaining experience and exposure. For example, an excellent option available to new country artists is The Nashville Network (TNN), which is dedicated to programming country music in multiple formats. Programmers maintain close contact with Music Row labels, managers, and agents as they constantly look for up-and-coming artists. Due to the popularity of country music, and because TNN is available on a high percentage of the country's 800 cable television systems, a new artist can be exposed to tens of millions of potential new record buyers and concertgoers.

Based on the success of MTV, VH-1, TNN, and other music-oriented cable networks, as well as the promise of other new and exciting possibilities offered by the Internet, the video and television segment of the music business represents unlimited opportunity for resourceful and forward-looking artists and their managers.

RADIO

Another important aspect of an artist's career, especially a recording artist, is radio. In the early 1950s, television succeeded in replacing radio as the primary vehicle for reaching the mass audience with the live performance. Almost simultaneous with this change came the increased importance of the phonograph record. As the radio networks dropped their variety-oriented entertainment and stations became more independent, there was a need for new programming ideas and concepts. Likewise, the record companies needed new promotional avenues to help boost sales. The result was a shift to the programming of records on radio stations.

This development has continued to the point where AM and FM radio airplay is probably the most important promotional vehicle available to the record companies. Record airplay is the lifeblood of radio programming.

It's essential that recording artists and managers realize and understand the crucial importance of radio airplay to their careers. Without it, the mass record-buying public will generally remain unaware of both the artist and his or her recordings. The strategic role that radio plays is demonstrated by the significant sums of money the record companies budget to promote radio airplay of their products. The artist and manager should be aware of the promotion department's job and the radio station's needs and objectives. This understanding will contribute greatly to the overall success of the artist's records.

The primary rule every artist and record company should keep in mind regarding airplay is that radio stations are in business to make a profit. They can only make a profit if they attract advertisers. Since advertisers are attracted by a station's ratings, the station's record playlist is formulated to obtain the best possible ratings. In other words, programming is *not* designed to help either a record company or an artist sell records. Many artists and managers are unwilling to accept this reality.

Because ratings are all-important, stations will program only those records it thinks will draw listeners. To help them do this, almost all major and secondary market stations retain consultants who advise them on developing the most listener-luring playlist possible. In many instances, the consultant has replaced the radio station director when it comes to playlist content. Playlists are usually restricted to between twenty and thirty current records. Depending on the station, this list may be supplemented by six- to nine-month hits, as well as "golden records" that go back as far as five years. This means that most additions to playlists are going to be hits or have been recorded by hit artists with past track records.

Very few new artists get added to these already tight playlists. Those that are must have a record with super-commercial appeal that's not too long, not too short, and fits into the station's format. Like it or not (and many do not), it's a reality of the business.

While some progressive, R&B, and adult contemporary stations may be a little less restrictive in their programming, the same general rules apply. There are certainly much less restrictive listener-supported, college, and alternative stations, but their influence is generally limited.

We urge artists and managers to become familiar with primary and secondary radio stations in various markets around the country that have formats consistent with the artist's recordings. Getting to know the radio consultants, program directors, and on-the-air personalities can often be helpful.

Besides the radio people, the manager should also get to know the record company's promotion staff, for unless they believe in an artist's record, there's little chance he or she can convince a program director or programming service to program it.

Learning about radio is a major educational project, but it's well worth the effort. The learning curve is higher than ever before, due not only to increased sophistication but also to the increasing trend toward more and different formats and subformats. To give you an idea of how radio categorizes records in today's market, the following is a recent listing of chart formats and subformats in *Radio and Records* (*R&R*), one of the leading industry trade magazines for radio:

CHR (contemporary hit radio)

CHR pop	CHR alternative
CHR rhythmic	hip hop

AC (adult contemporary)

NAC (new adult contemporary)

NAC tracks	NAC albums

Urban

urban	urban AC

Country

Rock

active rock	rock

Alternative

alternative	alternative tracks
alternative specialty shows	adult alternative albums

If you are not confused enough, by these groupings, compare *R&R*'s formats to the *Billboard* charts:

Albums

the Billboard 200	jazz/contemporary
classical	kid audio
classical crossover	new age
country	pop catalog
heatseekers	R&B
jazz	

Singles

the Billboard Hot 100	Latin
adult contemporary	R&B

adult top 40	rap
country	rock/mainstream tracks
dance/club play	rock/modern rock tracks
dance/maxi-singles sales	

It's not just the top-40 anymore, is it? The importance of radio exposure to a recording artist cannot be overemphasized; it's an essential rung in the career ladder.

RADIO SYNDICATION

Besides traditional radio programming, the last decade has seen a dramatic increase in radio syndications, reminiscent of the pre-television era, when radio was the dominant entertainment medium in the nation. The artist and manager should factor in the increasing opportunities for nationally syndicated radio programming that focuses on talk and music formats. This is simply one more promotional tool available to an artist seeking to break or sustain a career.

LAW AND TECHNOLOGY

Before leaving our brief discussion of radio, it is important to note the changes law and technology have brought and will bring to radio.

LAW

With regard to law, the Telecommunications Act of 1996 was a major step in deregulating the communications industry. As a result of the bill, ownership restrictions were lifted, which most likely means that fewer entities will control more stations. It could also mean that there will be more start-up stations, more formats, and more choices for consumers.

TECHNOLOGY

Technological advances—SoundScan, BDS, the Internet, and beyond, will continue to play a major role in how music is delivered, sold, and tracked. In 1991 SoundScan was introduced to the worlds of radio and record retailing. SoundScan is a tracking system which uses the bar-code data of participating record retailers to determine exactly what people are buying in exact quanities. This information is used by *Billboard* in calculating its charts and by major record companies in structuring their promotion and marketing campaigns. Currently, SoundScan covers more than 80 percent of all retail record sales. The impact on radio playlists is significant.

Of perhaps even more far-reaching impact is BDS, or Broadcast Data Systems, which is owned by *Billboard*. BDS is a computerized tracking system for radio. The system listens to radio broadcasts to calculate exactly what songs are played at what times. This data is then used to calculate the airplay various records are actually receiving. Again, the implications of this information-gathering for radio programming, not to mention the performing-rights societies (ASCAP, BMI, and SESAC) are staggering.

And then there is the Internet, which could completely change the face of radio and the music business. Who knows? All this is just one more indication of the new level of sophistication in every aspect of the music business. The managers and artists who can recognize the opportunities and challenges presented by the quickly changing legal and technological landscape will be the ones to prosper in the coming years. For those who can't keep up—well, we all know what happened to the piano roll, silent movies, and the eight-track tape player.

MOTION PICTURES

Motion pictures, clearly a big part of the entertainment industry, has its own peculiar rules and complexities. As with television, the motion picture industry offers the opportunity for long-term career maintenance to those artists who have acting ability. Just because a person is a successful recording artist doesn't necessarily mean that he or she will be a hit on the big screen. There have been successful recording artists and songwriters who have possessed acting ability and screen appeal, allowing them to add an extra dimension to their careers. Frank Sinatra, Bette Midler, and Cher come immediately to mind. Other singers who tried a crossover from music to movies are better left unmentioned.

Acting, while having similarities with performing for a recording, requires a different talent and discipline. Those versatile enough to master both can reap tremendous rewards, not the least of which is career longevity. For these reasons, a manager is well advised to think in terms of possible involvement of his or her client in motion pictures as a career supplement or eventual alternative.

The ins and outs of breaking into and succeeding in motion pictures could easily fill a separate volume. Here are just a couple of words of advice for managers looking for an entry into Hollywood. While most major motion picture studios are also active in the production of television programming, movie people and TV people tend to live in separate worlds; they rarely talk to each other. And, as a rule, movie and TV people never talk to record people, and vice versa. However, they *all* talk to agents and lawyers. For that reason, your best bet for gaining an entry is through your attorney or a responsible agent at a major, full-service booking agency.

The second point deals with the dangers of bad roles and overexposure. The rules applicable to television appearances are generally the same for movies. Our advice is to be careful. A movie is fine if an artist can act, but it is a potential catastrophe if he or she can't. Late-night cable movie reruns will make sure your client's deficiencies are forever remembered. Even if you get a top money offer, the best decision is to pass if the screen role doesn't fit into the career plan, or if the stretch from singer to actor is just too far. If a movie is part of the career plan, manager and artist are advised to get a good lawyer and a well-connected agent. Whatever you do, don't plan on giving up the singing career until after the second Oscar.

Personal Appearances

One of the most potentially lucrative aspects of the music business is the personal appearance. A hot artist with a hit record and an explosive stage show can command six figures for a single appearance, while grossing millions over the span of a successful concert tour. In addition to the live gate, the personal appearance remains one of the best vehicles for boosting record sales and capturing valuable media attention. The ability to turn on an audience can be a valuable negotiating asset when dealing with record companies, booking agents, and promoters. From a long-term career standpoint, an artist's live performance has the potential to outlive and out-carn his or her recording career. Many artists who have been moderately successful as recording artists have maintained lucrative careers for years strictly on the basis of their in-person performances.

But before you assume that the personal appearance is a certain path to riches, stop and consider the changes over the past decade that have made it more difficult than ever before for an artist to make a living on the road. Much of the difficulty relates to the dramatic rise in tour costs, which has made the personal appearance a much trickier proposition than ever before. High-tech special effects, increased transportation costs, lighting, sound, and ever-expanding entourages of the support personnel needed to bring a live show together have all combined to drive up the price of going on the road. This is especially true for hard rock and heavy metal acts and established superstars, whose fans demand a lot in exchange for the $18 to $30 they pay for their tickets. The manager of several headlining concert attractions estimated that an artist who could net 25 percent of a six-figure gross after expenses would be doing well.

Besides costs, artists are confronted with a national trend of top club venues going out of business. Much of this results from a change in attitudes about alcohol in this country. In the 1980s almost all fifty of the nation's state legislatures raised the legal drinking age to 21 and passed stern measures against driving and drinking. As a result, a number of high-profile clubs that proliferated in the late '70s and early '80s are gone. Fairs and outdoor festivals have, in many instances, replaced the nightclub. Unfortunately for many new acts, these venues demand established artists to satisfy larger numbers of concertgoers, who are drawn by known commodities they have heard on the radio or seen on music videos. Consequently, while the potential rewards connected with the live performance are probably greater than they were ten years ago, so are the challenges. This underscores the need for strong management to make the personal appearance a worthwhile part of an artist's career.

Regardless of the spiraling costs and other problems inherent in live performances, the personal appearance remains the lifeblood of an artist's career. The excitement generated by a tight, well-produced concert remains a unique and necessary experience for both the artist and fan. The record-breaking attendance figures at concert halls, stadiums, and festivals across the country make it abundantly clear that there is no acceptable substitute for live music. The challenge is to provide a terrific show as efficiently and as inexpensively as possible, without sacrificing quality. That task falls on the shoulders of management.

When it comes to live performance, there are many different alternatives available to the artist. Depending on the client's career goals, track record as a recording artist, and style of performance, the manager can select the most favorable type of personal appearance. Basically, the alternatives available to the manager fall into three categories: clubs, private parties, and concerts. These broad categories can be divided into many levels, or what we refer to as venues.

CLUBS

In many cities across the United States, the 1980s and early '90s saw a demise of the club scene. Fortunately, that trend has started to reverse itself. Part of the explanation lies in the unprecedented growth of casino gambling. Where there is gambling, there are show rooms and lounges which require live music. Most of this growth is centered in the three top gaming states of Nevada, New Jersey, and Mississippi. However, the club scene is being revitalized nationally. Destination cities like Nashville, Orlando, and others are seeing a resurgence of clubs that attract visitors with money to spend on travel and entertainment. Regardless of trends, the nightclub is a venue that comprises a substantial segment of the demand for live music. That is not about to change anytime soon.

Clubs can be divided into lounges; rock and show clubs; showcase clubs, or listening rooms; performance theaters; and large hotels and national chains.

LOUNGES

For the sake of our discussion, let's define a *lounge* as a restaurant or bar that usually employs four artists or less. This type of engagement normally requires soft music to facilitate the sale of cocktails or enhance the atmosphere in a restaurant. The broad heading of lounge entertainers would include everything from a solo pianist at an exclusive dinner club to a quartet of country or rock performers playing at a Saturday night watering hole. There will obviously be exceptions; some lounges may employ a group larger than four. Normally, however, a lounge will attempt to keep the number it employs to a minimum. Another characteristic of a lounge engagement is that the audiences are small. Generally this venue is not conducive to the performance of original material.

The lounge market employs thousands of artists, providing jobs for many individuals in the entertainment business on a part-time basis and/or artists in the early stages of their careers. Moreover, many artists who have become weary of the concert circuit or of larger clubs prefer the low-key environment and relaxed atmosphere of lounge engagements.

ROCK CLUBS AND SHOW ROOMS

Traditionally, rock clubs and show rooms have more of a music or dance orientation than do lounges. Because of the emphasis on music and dancing, rock clubs and show rooms are livelier than lounges and more conducive to the performance of original material. They usually employ groups of artists ranging from four to ten members. Because emphasis is placed on popular entertainers from the local or regional area, these clubs' budgets are larger than lounges'. While showcase rooms (see below) and lounges are staples in resort and gaming destinations, almost every city of moderate size has at least one rock club or show room. Surprisingly, many smaller cities have show rooms with high budgets.

We've purposely omitted discos and dance clubs from this survey because they emphasize recorded music as opposed to live entertainment. Discos and dance clubs that do utilize live music would otherwise be included in this category.

SHOWCASE CLUBS AND LISTENING ROOMS

The showcase club or listening room is another important category of club, especially from the standpoint of the artist's career development. In the major cities, especially in entertainment centers like New York, Los Angeles, and Nashville, there are key clubs that have a policy of only booking recording artists. The format and atmosphere is listening-oriented and is perfectly suited to the presentation of original material. These clubs are usually well covered by reviewers from publications such as *Billboard, Variety,* and *The Hollywood Reporter.* They are also frequented by the general press, industry figures, and record buyers. The potential for exposure and the concert-like atmosphere make rock clubs and show rooms extremely important for breaking in a new recording artist.

Because of the importance of showcase clubs, booking an artist into them can often be difficult. The competition is stiff, and the money is usually minimal. One example of the bargaining power that owners of important showcase clubs possess is what is known as a "pay-to-play" policy. Some of the important hard rock clubs in Los Angeles have instituted a policy whereby a band must guarantee the sale of a minimum number of tickets before they will be permitted to perform. Because many of these groups regard exposure in these clubs as an essential step to a record label affiliation, they do what is necessary to get their fans to show up at these venues.

Certainly, not all showcase clubs have a pay-to-play policy, but they do want only the best up-and-coming talents to attract and hold their clientele. As a result, clubs look to those with connections in the industry to help supply them with talent. This is why a manager seeking to position an act in one of these venues should seek out influential booking agents and record companies to help secure dates. If an act is already signed to a record company, they will often help subsidize the artist's appearances in showcase rooms through tour support, radio and print advertising, or purchase of a block of tickets for radio program directors, the trade press, and others the label regards as helpful in selling records. This support is often necessary because the showcase club usually doesn't have to pay top dollar to artists competing with each other for dates.

THE ARTIST-SPONSORED SHOWCASE

A common technique for an unsigned artist trying to create some excitement is to sponsor his or her own showcase, much in the way a record company would for a newly signed artist. The first step is to perfect original material and a tight show in rehearsal and later in lounges or showrooms. Once the act is ready, the manager uses professional connections to attract record executives, agents, publishers, and anyone else who could help boost the artist to the next career level. Because industry pros are a tough audience, it's also advisable to pack the club with as many enthusiastic fans as can fit through the door.

While such a showcase performance is obviously staged, it is perfectly acceptable to all concerned. It not only gives potential career partners a chance to see a new artist in action, but it also provides an opportunity for a manager to showcase his or her organizational ability and resourcefulness. Because artists seldom rate a second chance for such concentrated exposure, everything must be right before the manager gives the go-ahead for such a showcase.

PERFORMANCE THEATERS

With the surge of popularity of Branson, Missouri, a town in the Ozark mountains, a new genre of venue has come into its own. This is the performance theater, which is a hybrid of a showroom and a concert hall. These facilities, usually located in resort towns, seat between 1,000 and 3,500 fans and offer family entertainment by name acts who are no longer active recording artists. In fact, most such artists *own* these venues, so the expenses and aggravations of the road are eliminated, and because they are based in resorts, promoters and agent fees are avoided. Album and tee-shirt sales come from gift stores on the premises, and other items, ranging from books to key chains are promoted right from the stage instead of on the radio.

The artist's shows can be seen twice a night with matinees on Wednesdays and Saturdays. Artists such as Andy Williams, Boxcar Willie, Roy Clark, and Ray Stevens led the way in Branson. Recently, other resort destinations such as Myrtle Beach, South Carolina, and Pigeon Forge, Tennessee, have followed suit. This is a great way for a name artist with a great stage show to earn a very nice living even when his or her recording career is largely a thing of the past. Loyal fans are eager to buy an artists' backlog of albums and tapes while getting a chance to shake hands and get an autograph in the process.

LARGE HOTELS AND NATIONAL CLUB CHAINS

The final venue available to the artist in the club market is found in the large hotels and in the national club chains. This category includes hotels in large cities or in Las Vegas, Atlantic City, Miami and other resorts. Many of these hotels are part of chains such as Hilton and Hyatt.

An example of a franchised national club chain that has done well in recent years is The House of Blues. Because the budgets are usually substantial in this segment of the market, these clubs are capable of attracting top-caliber talent. There are no restrictions on the number of artists employed. The hotels and chains have the resources to buy the best, from single performers to extravagant productions. At this level, the artist's fees are high, and so is the standard of excellence.

These types of rooms serve several functions. Performers who may not have been tremendously successful as record sellers, but who are nonetheless superb entertainers, find this level appealing and financially rewarding. Singers such as Wayne Newton and Johnny Mathis are examples of those who sustain stellar careers while rarely releasing records. This is also an attractive career alternative for artists who have built names through record sales, but who are no longer considered chart toppers. Tom Jones is an excellent example of a performer who can do a first-rate live show, having made the transition from million-selling recording artist and television star to sought-after, highly paid showroom headliner.

Another attractive aspect of this segment of the club market is its international scope. Artists with the ability to connect on a global level can expand their career options in direct proportion to the number of markets they can appeal to around the world.

PRIVATE PARTIES

A second major category of live appearance is private parties. This level includes high school proms and dances, college fraternity parties, corporate parties, military-base functions, and other private engagements utilizing live entertainment. This level of personal appearance offers the young artist numerous opportunities to develop and perfect his or her talent. Many national artists have come directly from this circuit. College parties especially offer young artists the chance to build an extensive following long before a record affiliation is established. This following can be translated into future record sales.

Most of these engagements are dance-oriented. The audiences are generally receptive and lively, providing the young artist a chance to make reasonably good money that will help finance the move up the career ladder.

CONCERTS

The last broad area in live appearances is the concert. This segment can be broken down into three parts: college concerts; festivals and fairs; and promotions.

COLLEGE CONCERTS

Almost every college, regardless of its size, presents concerts of some kind for its students during the school year. The college concert is a good way to popularize or introduce new recording artists as well as to maintain and expand the following of established acts. College audiences represent an important source for record sales. One of the most attractive features of the college audience is the acceptance of a wide range of performers and styles of music.

Because of the enrollment base of most colleges and universities, these institutions are able to allocate high budgets for concert entertainment. This makes the market both attractive and competitive to artists who have become established through hit records. College venues can range from 1,000-seat auditoriums to 20,000-seat coliseums.

FESTIVALS AND FAIRS

The decline of clubs has been accompanied by the popularity of the outdoor festival and the increased use of talent by state fairs.

Today, almost every major- and secondary-market city in the country has its own event, which is usually held in the spring and summer months. State fairs usually follow in late summer and fall. Other specialty events focusing on specific types of music, such as the New Orleans Jazz and Heritage Festival or the Concord Jazz Festival, as well as numerous blues, country, and bluegrass festivals held throughout the United States and Canada, also provide numerous opportunities that didn't exist even ten years ago. The major full-service booking agencies have separate departments that concentrate on these lucrative venues.

PROMOTIONS

The final concert category is promotions, some of which involve independent promoters and promotion companies whose bookings for artists range from isolated concerts to multicity tours. Whereas the college concert and festival buyer isn't motivated to book an act based solely on profit potential, the promoter is. Normally, the veteran promoter has established a relationship with various booking agencies and managers of national artists. Once a promoter has proven to be financially sound and reliable, agents and managers entrust him or her with the promotion of more dates and, subsequently, entire tours.

The promoter is a purchaser of entertainment who signs the artist performance contract as the employer who guarantees the artist's fee, arranges the location for the concert, promotes the event, and coordinates the actual performance the night of the show. The promoter must also make sure that the artist and all who participate in producing the show are paid and is responsible for applicable taxes associated with the production of the concert. He or she takes all the risk for a potential profit.

With the rising prices of artists, arenas, radio spots, printing, and amusement taxes, the promoter must select the artist to be promoted cautiously. For this reason, the professional promoter will attempt to book complete tours in order to protect against a fatal loss on a one-night promotion.

Veteran promoters are primarily interested in headliner acts and tour packages. The novice promoter usually gets the lesser-known acts, but that is how he or she begins to develop a reputation. By promoting a tour that will help an agent, manager, or record company develop the market potential of a new artist, the promoter will have gained their respect—especially if the artist subsequently becomes successful. As a result, he or she is likely to get additional dates for that artist.

Many college students who serve as entertainment buyers for their schools establish friendships with booking agents and managers. These students often prove themselves trustworthy and capable promoters. Consequently, the agents will sell them dates during the summer for their own entrepreneurial promotions.

It must be emphasized that both booking agents and managers of national artists should exercise the utmost caution when dealing with unknown promoters. The financial repercussions to agent, manager, and artist are simply too great to entrust a tour or a string of dates to a beginner. If a particular promotion isn't successful and the promoter doesn't have the financial capacity to cover the loss, who'll pay the artist? Take this isolated situation and multiply the loss times eight, ten, or fifteen cities on a tour. The artist could conceivably play a multicity tour, and after paying hotel, transportation, and equipment rentals, actually lose money.

Even if the artist is protected by a contract, the cost and time to litigate may make the collection process economically unfeasible. For these reasons, booking agents normally require substantial deposits from promoters. The economic consequences to the artist are simply too serious not to exercise extreme care in this area.

Sometimes, well-known artists retain their own promoters to set an entire tour. This is possible when artists are so popular and in such demand that normal promotional efforts to ensure profitable shows aren't needed. Despite this popularity, local contacts will still be used in most cases to coordinate necessary details. Artist who want to set their own tours usually have their own promoters or coordinators contact local promoters whom they will pay a flat fee for helping make arrangements in certain cities. Under this approach, the local promoters don't risk any money but just perform a task for a fee.

Promotions vary in size, but the more expensive attraction forces the promoter into a larger arena to make the show economically feasible. Generally, the professional promoter is concerned with concerts that have the capability of filling 10,000 seats and up. The optimum promotion obviously depends on the artist, size of the city, arena, and overall cost considerations.

Naturally, recording artists and record companies utilize concert appearances to promote record sales. A successful performance in an arena seating 20,000 to 50,000 people can translate into significant record sales. For this reason, the major record companies feel that well promoted concert appearances by their artists are a must in their overall marketing program. The experienced manager, artist, and promoter recognize this and work closely with the record company when promoting a concert tour.

LIVE PERFORMANCE CONTRACTS

The contracts used in booking artists for live appearances overlap in their terms and conditions, depending on the type of engagement involved. The name of employer, engagement location and address, date and time of engagement, rehearsal hours, and wage terms are all standard information contained in any artist performance contract. Also found in most contracts are clauses regarding the inability of the artist to perform due to sickness, accident, strikes, civil turmoil, epidemics, mechanical malfunctions, acts of God, or conditions totally beyond the control of the artist.

The American Federation of Musicians has a standard contract used by all licensed, affiliated booking agents. The beginning manager is well advised to become familiar with its terms.

The artist performing in the club market will frequently encounter clauses providing for hotel accommodations and discounts for food and beverages. These gratuities are sometimes essential in order to make some engagements economically feasible for the artist. The manager should ensure that all the terms are contained in the performance contract, both to avoid any dispute during the engagement and to facilitate financial planning of the artist's tour. In the club market, it's often necessary to set forth the exact hours of rehearsal time during the day in venues that have constant customer traffic.

The basic performance contract for concerts, promotions, and private parties is very similar to the club contract, but unusual features do occur. Many artists performing in these markets have certain additional requirements for successful presentations of their shows, and these are spelled out in an attachment to the performance contract called a *rider*. Some riders are quite extensive and contain costly provisions for the employer. For instance, many artists require the employer to furnish a specific type of sound system that can cost several thousand dollars. In addition, musical equipment, accommodations, special transportation, and food and beverages often appear as requirements in riders. The artist and manager must be cautious when preparing a rider so that it does not take on the appearance of a scavenger-hunt list. On the other hand, the employer should review the rider requirements carefully so as to be totally aware of all cost considerations relative to the engaging of a specific artist. An experienced booking agent will normally advise the employer of the requirements contained on the artist rider *before* a date is booked. The performance contract for promotions will require that the price of tickets and number of available seats be included. Furthermore, the number of *gratis,* or complementary, tickets is normally restricted, especially when the artist is to receive a guaranteed amount against a percentage of the total proceeds from ticket sales. Other clauses or terms are usually included that pertain to the artist's and promoter's percentage split of proceeds above a certain amount.

THE BOOKING AGENCY

The most direct way for an artist to secure club, private party, or concert engagements is through a booking agency. In many instances, concert, festival, and top-line club dates are impossible to secure without an agent. Regardless of the type of date, the booking agency serves as a meeting place for artists and purchasers of entertainment. Some agencies represent certain artists exclusively, thus requiring other agents to purchase from them if they have an engagement for that artist.

Booking agencies come in all sizes. There are a few that are international, multidimensional firms, such as William Morris, International Creative Management (ICM), or Creative Artists Agency (CAA). These "superagencies" maintain offices in major cities throughout the world and have numerous departments representing entertainers, actors, authors, television personalities, athletes, and other types of celebrities.

The next strata of booking agencies are the ones working primarily in the area of musical entertainment. These companies often specialize in certain types of entertainment, such as country music or jazz. They may also specialize in certain markets, such as club attractions, dance music for private parties, and so forth. Besides the firms that operate on a national basis, there are hundreds of regional booking agencies throughout the United States.

The manager should select a booking agent or agents capable of securing the types of engagements best suited to the development of the artist's career. The first step is for manager and artist to determine in what venue the artist should appear. Once this determination has been made, there are hundreds of agents representing the entire entertainment spectrum.

Finding the best agent for an artist may turn into a trial-and-error process. The manager must be alert and cautiously watch over the artist–agent relationship.

BOOKING AGENT COMMISSIONS

Agent's fees generally range from 10 to 15 percent of the fee negotiated with the buyer. Normally an agent's fee for booking a club engagement is 10 percent, while the fee for a private party or concert ranges from 10 to 15 percent. The fees for booking are somewhat negotiable, depending on the strength of the artist and the services the artist requires. The American Federation of Musicians has an exclusive Agent Artist Agreement, which attempts to govern this relationship between its members and affiliated agents. While the agreement covers broad areas of an exclusive agent–artist relationship, there are usually certain specialized terms associated with each situation.

As with every other member of the artist's development team, the manager and artist should choose agents or firms not simply on the basis of their track record with other clients, but also on their dedication to and belief in the artist. Getting lost in the shuffle at a booking agency can be disastrous, especially if the personal appearance figures prominently in an artist's career plan.

Once the right agency is in place, the artist and manager should cultivate their relationship with their agents, encouraging comments and criticisms and working closely with them to shape a realistic and effective career plan. While it might be fashionable to gripe about agents, the way most people do about lawyers, experienced managers know they can be one of your surest links to long-term success in the music business.

16

Merchandising, Commercials, and Corporate Sponsorships

Ten years ago, income from merchandising, commercials, and corporate sponsorships was, for the most part, icing on the cake for artists in the entertainment industry. Recordings, songwriting royalties, and personal appearance income comprised the bulk of most artists' earnings. Not any more. A maturing baby-boom generation, coupled with an ever more affluent younger generation, has become the target market for consumer products in every industrialized nation of the world. This phenomenon has created a worldwide mass-marketing explosion, driven in large part by the two essentials of the music industry: songs and celebrities. The result has been the formation of powerful new alliances between corporate marketers and the music business.

In the past, certain celebrities commanded fees or royalties totaling more than a million dollars from merchandising, commercials, and endorsements. Those activities have accelerated, in terms of both the number of celebrities selling products and the types of imaginative arrangements that resourceful artists and managers have been able to set up. Yesterday's million-dollar endorsement contract has been eclipsed by multifaceted corporate marketing programs that net artists millions of dollars, not only in fees but in tour support, artist advertising, and merchandising. The continued refinement of mass-marketing techniques, combined with the increasing influence and effectiveness of entertainment figures as corporate salespersons, will no doubt play an ongoing and powerful role in the career of an artist. An astute manager, aware of the possibilities in these fields, can help raise an artist's income level substantially while making good use of corporate involvement for promotion and image-projection purposes.

MERCHANDISING

Merchandising is one area of ancillary income and name projection of critical importance to an artist's bottom line. "Merchandising" generally refers to the marketing of products to the public on the strength of the artist's name or likeness. These products can include tee shirts, souvenir photograph books, posters, dolls, toys, and games. The range of artist-driven products is limited only by one's imagination.

The key to effective merchandising is to give the public a product they want and to present it so as to enhance the artist's popularity rather than to diminish it. This is not always an easy task. Good taste and thoughtful planning should serve as primary guidelines for any merchandising campaign.

The new artist negotiating a first record contract should be especially conscious of the potential value of his or her name and likeness. Many record companies will try to secure exclusive merchandising rights from the artist in return for a royalty based on the net sums they receive. The amount is usually 50 percent. The manager should try to retain these rights, at least in areas not bearing on the promotion of the records. For instance, it might be advantageous for the artist to give nonexclusive merchandising rights to the label in specific areas that could be used to promote record sales, such as tee shirts and posters. However, toys, dolls, and games would generally be outside the scope of legitimate record-promotion tools. If rights are granted, the artist and manager should retain all rights of approval mentioned earlier.

As with record companies, the artist should not give merchandising rights to specialists in the field until the artist's career merits such an arrangement. There's always the danger that a premature granting of rights could result in less favorable contract terms for the artist who lacks bargaining strength. When the artist's career has reached the appropriate level, the artist and manager should carefully consider the consequences before committing themselves to a campaign.

There are two primary types of merchandising: tour merchandising and general merchandising.

TOUR MERCHANDISING

There is no better place to sell tee shirts, hats, and posters to fans than at a packed concert hall where the artist is headlining. The frenzy and hype of a live show goes hand in hand with selling truckloads of stuff with the artist's name and picture prominently displayed. Under the usual deal, the artist licenses his or her identity to a tour merchandiser to coincide with an upcoming tour and a reasonable sell-off period that will allow the merchandiser to sell unsold inventory. The typical royalty payable to the artist is 25 to 35 percent of gross sales receipts. Foreign royalties are approximately 80 percent of U.S. and Canadian rates. Because of the risk involved, a tour merchandiser is going to be interested in dealing only with proven headliners and will require certain minimum performance guarantees from the artist to make sure there are enough dates and tickets sold to merit the investment. Depending on the drawing power of the artist, an astute manager may be able to negotiate a sizable advance chargeable against royalties to help finance the costs of the tour.

GENERAL MERCHANDISING

This takes in everything else not specifically connected to point-of-purchase sales in connection with the artist's tour. It includes mail-order, retail, fan-club, and even flea market merchandising, and so on. In most cases, the artist's general merchandising deal will be a separate contract. In effect, the artist is licensing his or her identity to a merchandising specialist who will manufacture and sell items embodying the artist's likeness. Royalties differ according to the item and marketing channel, with the range being 10 to 15 percent of the wholesale price of the item marketed at retail. Mail-order royalties usually run in the 25-percent range.

In certain instances the merchandiser may issue sublicenses to specialty merchandisers who have special expertise in and access to submarkets such as clothing, posters, and buttons. In a sub-license situation, the primary merchandiser is acting as an agent for the artist, keeping a commission in the range of 20 to 30 per-cent of income received from the sublicensee before remitting the balance to the artist.

COMMERCIALS

Commercials comprise another important source of income and provide the artist with a vehicle for exposure. Entertainment personalities of star caliber can command seven-figure fees for a national advertising campaign. They can also be expected to be seen by millions through television, radio, and magazine exposure. However, as with everything else, there's the potential for damage to an artist's career if the manager's dealings with the "commercial" market are not handled properly.

The word "commercial" may encompass any means by which an artist is used to promote, advertise, and sell a product. It may take the form of an on-camera television spot or a radio voice-over. In other instances, the commercial may be a printed advertisement in a national magazine or may even involve using the artist's picture on outdoor billboards or in connection with in-store product displays. In the case of a comprehensive national campaign, all these different formats may be used.

Just as a commercial can take many forms, so too may it be aimed at specific markets. It can be targeted at national, regional, or local markets. All these are variables that affect the desirability of the particular commercial and the money the artist can hope to make in return for his or her services.

Most major national advertisers retain ad agencies who have the responsibility for developing and producing their advertising campaigns. When developing a campaign that will call for the use of an entertainment personality, the agency will usually contact the major, multifaceted booking or talent agencies and other agents with access to important national acts. As a general rule, these agencies are based either in New York or on the West Coast. Since the advertising agencies' area of expertise is not entertainment, they depend on agents' knowledge and experience in the field. In some instances, an agency will have an in-house music department that might have contacts directly with artists, managers, producers, and record companies. In this case, the advertising agency might choose to deal directly with the artist or the artist's personal representative. The best way for a manager who does not have advertising contacts to get an artist commercial work is to develop a relationship with an agent who regularly works in the commercial field. It may often be possible, depending on bargaining position, for the manager to work with one agent for personal appearances and another for commercial work.

Basically, there are two approaches to advertising. One is *product sell*: Using the artist to make a direct appeal to the consumer to buy the sponsor's product. The other approach is known as *image advertising,* a more indirect concept. Here, there is no effort to make a direct sale. The advertising agency appeals to the buyer by suggesting that the product is a desirable commodity that should be a part of the consumer's life-style. Many national advertisers use this form of advertising in their national campaigns to supplement a local product-sell approach. Image advertising is generally a good fit with entertainers because of their mass appeal. The key here is to tie the product to the artist, thereby taking advantage of the artist's popularity.

When a campaign calls for use of an entertainer, the agency will usually come up with a type of person who would fit what they're doing. For example, let's suppose the agency wants to do an image-advertising television commercial for a soft-drink manufacturer. The largest target group of buyers of this product consists of pre-teens, teenagers, and young adults. The commercial is designed to center around an energetic pop/rock male artist with a high approval rating with the target-age group. The agency will draw up a list of five or six singers who fit this description and the general budget range they have to work with. The advertising agency will then contact agents to inquire about an artist's interest and availability.

Generally speaking, advertising agencies don't work with much lead time. Often, an artist's unavailability will end any chance of doing the commercial because air dates, once they're set, are usually inflexible. Once the agency finds an artist who fits their requirements, a contract is negotiated and a production schedule is set.

PROS AND CONS OF DOING COMMERCIALS

There are a number of factors bearing on the decision to accept or reject a commercial. Naturally, the money involved must be sufficient to warrant involvement by the artist. There's also the consideration of how a commercial will affect the artist's image and career development. What product is being advertised? It must be consistent with the artist's image. For instance, an artist with a reputation for an unorthodox life-style would probably not want to do a bank commercial. A beer commercial wouldn't be appropriate for an artist sporting a wholesome image. The terms of the contract to be negotiated with the advertising agency will also bear on whether the artist should accept the commercial. For instance, an artist should avoid a long-term commitment unless the financial return is sufficient. The artist may not want to grant unlimited rights to use his or her likeness in things such as in-store displays, posters, and billboards; this could have a cheapening effect on both image and career.

Another point to consider is the effect a commercial will have on the artist's future worth in the commercial market. Every time an artist does a commercial, there is a danger that his or her value will be diminished, especially if the ad campaigns are national in scope. Eventually, the artist will no longer be considered fresh or unique. Therefore, a manager hoping for a more lucrative contract may want to defer accepting a commercial offer until later in the artist's career or think about a regionally limited commercial for the sake of gaining experience and some financial return without running a risk of lessening the artist's value.

As in numerous facets of the business, the manager should be wary of the danger of overexposure in commercials. Too many TV guest shots, along with an extensive national ad campaign, could result in saturation and a drop in demand for the artist's concert performances and records, causing severe career damage. No commercial is worth taking if it will have an extreme negative effect on a developing career. On the other side of the ledger, a well-produced national television commercial for a good product can give an artist's career a significant boost.

The proper degree of exposure is a question of judgment. The manager must make a calculated projection of a commercial's effect based on all the relevant information available.

ENDORSEMENTS

A related area of ancillary income is the endorsement, which has many of the attributes of merchandising and commercials. It involves the artist's name and likeness being directly connected with a specially manufactured product line. Professional athletes serve as a frequent example of endorsements, such as Michael Jordan and Shaquille O'Neal, both of whom are paid millions of dollars to endorse a wide range of sporting goods and other athletic products.

The same basic considerations discussed in merchandising and commercials also apply to endorsements.

CORPORATE SPONSORSHIP

Probably the most significant development over the last decade in the area of commercials and endorsements has been the increased involvement of corporations in the careers of music artists. In the late 1980s, the appeal of recording artists to corporations eager to tap into expanding markets grew substantially. This paralleled skyrocketing costs affecting almost every aspect of an artist's professional life. Artists who once toured the country in station wagons and panel vans suddenly found it necessary to use jets and tractor trailers. Crowds demanded state-of-the-art sound, lights, staging, and special effects. Fewer opportunities in clubs and more at outdoor festivals and promotions ushered in a new era of personal appearances. It all added up to more people and more money. Acts that once depended on personal appearance income were going in the hole just to promote their records. Increasing costs along with growing corporate interest in music artists set the stage for new alliances with the corporate world.

Today, imaginative managers and corporate marketers are entering into a new era of corporate sponsorships which include packaged tours; multiyear corporate spokesmanship arrangements; television, radio, and print-ad combinations; and a host of other complex joint ventures. One of the most successful of these arrangements involved Michael Jackson and Pepsi Cola in the early 1990s. This relationship went well beyond the traditional one-shot product commercial, allowing Pepsi to tap into Jackson's huge following. It reputedly cost the soft-drink manufacturer millions of dollars to attract hundreds of millions in sales. Obviously, Jackson and Pepsi thought the arrangement was mutually beneficial. In the wake of this deal, the area of corporate involvement entered a new dimension.

CORPORATE TOUR SUPPORT AND PRODUCT TIE-INS

A recent trend that should be of special interest to managers and artists is the concept of corporate tour support. Aside from radio, the most effective way to sell records is a personal appearance tour. While this has always been true, touring is more expensive than ever before. Fans demand more of everything before they will lay out their $18 to $30 and more for a concert ticket. This means state-of-the-art lights and sound, special effects, custom designed staging and a road crew capable of producing and transporting the show from town to town. It is not uncommon for an artist to have four or five tour buses and several tractor trailers on the road to transport a small army of people and equipment. The current Reba McEntire–Brooks & Dunn tour requires a convoy of eighteen trucks and buses. That spells huge overhead. The costs associated with producing such a show can make such a tour counter-productive unless supplemental income sources can be found.

Luckily for artists, sophisticated product-marketing programs sponsored by major corporations have provided much of this badly needed income. In recent years, corporations such as Budweiser, Crown Royal, and Fruit of the Loom, to name just a few, have gotten involved in the concert sponsorship business. These programs underwrite many of the expenses of a major tour while including product tie-in, special-product CD and cassette premiums, and in-store appearances by artists—all backed up by nationwide print, TV, and radio campaigns. Depending on the relationship between company and artist and the specifics of the deal, an artist can reap all the benefits of touring and commercial endorsements in one sophisticated package arrangement.

All these new options have created a host of decisions for artists and their managers. Should an artist take advantage of lucrative commercial offers, or would it be more advisable to hold out for a more lucrative spokesmanship package at a later stage of the artist's career? The choice is always a gamble because a manager can never be sure that more attractive offers will ever materialize or that the artist will be able to sustain a career over a long period. There is also the matter of an artist appearing to sell out for corporate money or sponsorship. And then, how much money is enough? What other benefits can be derived? What are the potential risks? How will fans react?

The right strategy clearly depends on the artist and the opportunities that present themselves. The following is a list of considerations that the manager and artist should appreciate in order to get the most out of any corporate relationship.

1. The overall worth of the deal in both hard dollars and in-kind corporate contributions
2. Advertising and marketing potential for the artist
3. A clear understanding of the corporation's objectives
4. The prospects for renewal of the relationship

While it would be logical to think that corporate tie-ins are only available to established headliners, that is fortunately not the case. Product marketers such as Miller Genuine Draft and Justin Boots, to name only two, are open to relationships with developing artists and popular club bands around the country. A typical deal provides the group with everything from equipment, posters, and merchandise, in exchange for the right to associate their product with the artist's live performances.

CONTRACTUAL ARRANGEMENTS

Merchandising, commercial, and endorsement contracts, including corporate sponsorship arrangements, are legally based on the artist's commitment to provide his or her unique personal services, along with the grant of a license to use the artist's identity for the sale and promotion of products or a company. The personal services aspect is similar to commitments in which artists promise to use their talents to make records or concert appearances. As with any other contractual arrangement, the scope and term of the commitment, along with creative input into the final product, are critically important factors.

Licensing one's name, likeness, or any other aspect of personal identity, such as a distinctive voice, is a separate right belonging to the artist. It is protected by the developing legal doctrine known as the *Right of Publicity*. When negotiating with product-related companies, merchandisers, and corporate sponsors, the artist's manager should make every effort to place a value on the attributes that make the client unique and thus incapable of being replicated by some other personality.

Obviously, the more versatile and distinctive the artist is, the more value can be attached to him or her for ancillary income purposes. Michael Jackson's management did an effective job when it came to convincing Pepsico executives that "Thriller" and Pepsi had enough in common to merit opening up the corporate change purse.

Some of the more important factors to be considered in the contract negotiation process are the length of the contract and the date from which the term will be measured. For example, assume a television commercial is to run for one year. Should the year begin running from the date the contract is signed, or from the date of the first production of the commercial, or from the date of the first airing? This is a negotiable point. Other key terms include territory, which can be national, regional, or local airing. Another issue to settle is scope of rights, such as television rights only, television and radio, print, outdoor advertising, and point of purchase (which includes in-store displays and posters). In addition, advances, guarantees or flat fee, and creative control of production are other points that must be negotiated.

Normally, an artist is paid an advance against residuals or is given a guarantee of residual remuneration based on a negotiated percentage of applicable American Federation of Television and Radio Artists or Screen Actors Guild scales. Depending on his or her bargaining position, an artist's manager may negotiate a contract that pays the artist at the rate of scale, double scale, or higher. This rate is then multiplied by the number of radio and/or television airings the commercial receives according to AFTRA and/or SAG rate schedules, and is paid to the artist in much the same way a songwriter is paid by performing-rights societies. The manager should become familiar with AFTRA and SAG rates and procedures. Representatives of these organizations will be glad to talk to managers about their organizations.

THE "NO COMMERCIALS" POLICY

To illustrate some of the various legal and practical considerations that go into placing a value on a given artist's unique characteristics, consider the real-life example of singer–actress Bette Midler. Over the span of her career, Bette Midler has proven to be one of the most versatile entertainers working. She parlayed early success as a cabaret singer in the 1970s into a string of top-selling records and film soundtracks. She also became a headlining concert act and a successful motion picture actress and film producer. Her greatest assets were an outrageous personality, distinctive voice, and versatility. Midler and her management were also shrewd enough to recognize that the substantial sums she could earn from commercials could potentially offset demand and her popularity in other ventures. Consequently, she adopted a policy of not doing commercials.

Later, Ford Motor Company tried to persuade her to do a voice-over of one of her well-known songs for a commercial they planned to shoot. When she refused, they enlisted a singer from her backup group and instructed her to imitate the famous singer's voice as closely as possible. The soundtrack was played over a commercial without Midler's permission, giving the target audience the impression that the famous singer was endorsing the product. She brought a lawsuit against Ford (*Midler vs. Ford Motor Co.*) and won, even though her name or face were never connected with the commercial.

An analysis of this case demonstrates several valuable lessons for managers confronting possible commercials and endorsements. First is the question of whether to do commercials at all, and if so, what kind. At least part of Midler's decision rested on an assessment of how such work would impact on her demand in other areas. After weighing the options, she chose to pass up the potential income in favor of other considerations. So she passed on all commercials. Some artists in this situation might well pass up a car commercial, but have no trouble doing a soft-drink promo. Robert Palmer and George Michael, like Michael Jackson, have done just that, apparently suffering none of the repercussions Midler feared. From a long-term standpoint, because Midler has yet to do a commercial while still in the prime of her career, her asking price at a later date—if she chooses to reverse or modify her policy—will more than likely be higher than it would be at present. In fact, her no-commercials stance combined with her recognizable, one-of-a-kind personality were most likely the very things that attracted Ford's interest in Midler in the first place.

This example also demonstrates that artists who choose not to license others to use their name or likeness for commercial purposes have legal recourse. It should be noted here, however, that while the Right of Publicity is a generally accepted legal doctrine, it is not uniformly interpreted by the states. This is why an attorney should be consulted before any decision is made in this lucrative area.

NO EASY ANSWERS

The fields of merchandising, commercials, endorsements, and corporate sponsorships provide the artist with additional avenues to financial fulfillment and career development. But they can also present some very tricky decisions for the artist and manager. The rule in this area is to think twice before making a commitment.

Once a basic direction is determined that complements the overall career plan, make sure your attorney is involved. Making the right decision about ancillary exposure of the artist can be a crucial plus or minus in realizing career goals. Artists and managers who merely view this as an isolated opportunity to make a little extra, quick cash could be making a serious miscalculation over the span of a career.

17

Thinking Globally

Starting with the decade of the 1980s, the entertainment industry witnessed the beginning of unprecedented growth of international markets. With the recent advances in technology such as the Internet, international economic accords like GATT and NAFTA, and the worldwide dissemination of American pop culture, the global marketplace has become a potential gold mine for United States–based artists and their managers. More than ever before, artists' managers must think globally if they are to completely realize their clients' career potential.

The new emphasis on global career exploitation is driven by America's leading export, entertainment. Demand has never been stronger for American films, television, and music. This has had a significant and beneficial impact on the earnings of U.S.–based record companies, music publishers, and artists. Foreign markets now account for about 60 percent of all gross income earned by these various entertainment entities. Some sectors account for more, some less, but the future trend is clear. The share of foreign dollars spent on American-based artists and entertainers is sure to increase as more nations of the world achieve a higher standard of living, acquire more leisure time, and continue to be served by the rapidly developing international communications network.

Given potentially lucrative overseas markets, it is no surprise that more artists and managers than ever before are thinking in international terms. The popularity of American entertainment presents them with the opportunity to broaden their appeal and increase their incomes substantially.

Worldwide acceptance of artists' records or songs can make a big difference in a record company or music publisher's annual balance sheet. Artists such as Elton John and Celine Dion are top draws throughout the world, enjoying popularity everywhere that many artists receive only in their own country. Their increased record and live performance revenue is in direct proportion to increased international appeal.

It should be emphasized that few artists have this universal appeal. Because of differing cultures and tastes, an artist may be a major star in France but be ignored in neighboring Germany. This divergence in national appeal, along with the fact that these smaller markets can't come close to matching the U.S. in box-office or record sales potential, helps explain why many artists and managers consider the international market too much of an uphill challenge to merit the time, money, and effort it takes to make inroads. However, in light of the projected growth of the international marketplace over the next decade, these managers and artists would do well to reconsider.

FOREIGN RECORD SALES

The last five years have seen an unprecedented consolidation in the ownership of record distribution networks. Of the six big entertainment conglomerates, all are foreign-owned except Time-Warner—a further sign that the recording industry has become an international enterprise. Because of the huge investment a major label makes when signing a new artist—between $500,000 and $1 million to record and market a first album—the record companies are increasingly interested in recouping their costs from sales outside the United States. But while more major record companies might be controlled by corporate entities outside the United States, American artists are still the staple of the business.

Generally, when an artist signs with a major record company, the latter will demand world rights to the artist's recordings. In the case of a few major artists, certain territories may be exempted.

Foreign record sales are usually achieved in one of two ways. In the first of these, the conglomerates BMG, EMI, Time-Warner, MCA, Polygram, and SONY use their affiliated companies in the world's major developed nations to distribute and sell products that originate in the U.S. For a truly international star, such as Michael Jackson, the marketing and distribution muscle of these companies makes a simultaneous global release possible. Certainly, this is a decided advantage to an artist who has international appeal and a manager with a global vision. Because of the tendency of companies to think beyond national boundaries, you will likely receive a warm welcome from such labels, provided that the talent and appeal is there.

In the second approach to achieving foreign record sales, American companies that have no branch affiliates enter into licensing agreements with foreign record labels. These agreements can take the form of a blanket worldwide foreign agreement with a major overseas company that has its own branch affiliates, such as the London-based EMI; or the deal can be made on a country-by-country basis through independent foreign companies.

As a rule, an artist is paid a royalty calculated at 50 percent of the rate normally paid for American sales. This rate may be negotiated upward, to as much as 75 percent of the domestic rate, depending on your bargaining position and whether or not the American record company is dealing with its affiliated branches or unaffiliated independent licensees. This lower-than-domestic rate is justified by the record company on the grounds that they receive substantially less on foreign sales than on domestic.

Most recording contracts make no guarantees as to the release of an artist's records in foreign markets. Depending on your bargaining position, you should try to negotiate a guaranteed release in key countries of the world, especially if the record company has insisted on securing world rights. But be prepared for the record company's reply to this type of proposal. They may say that they don't always have control over what will be released in a given country, especially if independent licensees are employed. Another frequent response is that the foreign record company won't want to release a record in their territory unless it's a hit in the United States or unless the artist has a previous track record in the particular foreign country.

The status of foreign record deals may be somewhat different where the artist is signed to an independent producer who, in turn, deals with the U.S. record company. An established producer may succeed in exempting certain foreign territories from a contract with the American label. In this event, the producer would be free to make independent licensing agreements on a country-by-country basis in return for an aggregate producer–artist royalty.

The manager interested in expanding the artist's career into international markets should investigate the overseas capabilities of various foreign record labels as one consideration in choosing a label—assuming that option is available. Despite ownership, some record companies are more conscious of international sales than others. As a rule, companies with foreign affiliates are in a better position to release and promote records in foreign territories. However, as with any large organization, it is always possible to get lost in the shuffle, unless you are selling huge numbers in the U.S.

An artist's international ambitions can also be limited by musical genre. For instance, companies are geared up to push artists like Alanis Morissette, Celine Dion, and Sting, while country or rap artists are commonly considered to have less appeal in foreign markets. (There are notable exceptions.) Record labels may not be willing to underwrite the costs to realize overseas sales. It is possible a smaller company with strong independent licensees may be able to devote more time to help the artist promote record sales in foreign territories.

But, again, because foreign markets have their own tastes in music, careful consideration should also be given to the type of material the artist records. If having an international presence is part of an artist's career plan, the manager, artist, and producer should seek songs with cross-cultural appeal whenever possible.

And yet they should be careful not to think internationally at the expense of the American market. This would be self-defeating, especially since most foreign countries look to the success of a record in the U.S. as an indicator of its potential in a foreign market. The goal here is to strike a balance between domestic and foreign appeal.

FOREIGN TERRITORIES

The industrialized world is rapidly changing. At this writing, the fastest-growing nations are in Asia. Nonetheless, for record distribution and music publishing purposes, the major territories are generally defined as follows:

Major Territories

Canada, United Kingdom (Great Britain, Scotland, and Ireland), Germany, Japan, Italy, Australia, The Netherlands, France

Minor Territories

The Scandinavian countries, Switzerland, Belgium, Spain, Brazil, Argentina, Chile, Mexico, Hong Kong, Thailand, New Zealand

Emerging Territories

Though they account for minimal sales now, over the next ten to twenty years, markets such as China, India, and the Eastern European countries will become increasingly important. As a result, many of the majors are currently working to gain a foothold in these potentially gigantic markets in anticipation of the future.

ROYALTIES

As to foreign royalty rates, an artist can expect to receive about 50 percent of the rate normally paid for American sales, except for sales in Canada, for which the number is approximately 85 percent of the U.S. rate. The foreign 50 percent rate may be negotiated upward, to as much as 75 percent of the domestic rate, depending on your bargaining position and whether or not the American record company is dealing with its affiliated branches or unaffiliated independent licensees. This lower-than-domestic rate is justified by the record company on the grounds that they receive substantially less on foreign sales than on domestic.

FOREIGN MUSIC PUBLISHING

Foreign music publishing works a lot like foreign record distribution. Domestic publishers seeking to exploit their copyrights on a global basis with the help of agents called *subpublishers,* whose job it is to manage the publisher's copyrights in the licensed territory. The subpublisher seeks to exploit the copyright, collects the income, and remits a negotiated share of the money to the American publisher while retaining the balance. The arrangement somewhat mirrors that of the American record company's foreign record-licensing agreement. As with foreign record distribution, a U.S. publisher may have affiliated offices in foreign territories to do this, while smaller companies will use independent overseas licensees on a territory-by-territory basis. The typical split in subpublishing agreements can range from collection deals where the foreign subpublisher retains 10 percent of the income earned, to deals where the foreign publisher is active in securing foreign cover recordings in exchange for 50 percent of income generated by the new foreign recording. (Cover refers to a second recording of a song originally made famous by someone else's recorded version.) Most of the deals today allow for the subpublisher to retain 15 to 25 percent on the release of original recordings first released in the United States, and 40 to 50 percent for foreign covers it procures.

Typically, an American publisher will grant rights on either a song-by-song or a catalog basis to foreign music publishers for a negotiated term. Depending on the commercial potential of a particular composition or catalog, the foreign subpublisher may pay the copyright owner an advance against royalties to obtain rights to the material.

SONGWRITER'S ROYALTIES IN SUBPUBLISHING AGREEMENTS

Generally, no provision is made in the songwriter's contract for a reduced royalty on foreign income to the writer. However, as a practical matter, a writer's income will be diminished because the royalty is based on a percentage of income actually received by the publisher. Since foreign subpublishers deduct a percentage of the gross income they collect, there'll be less money to divide between the publisher and writer. For instance, let's assume $100 in mechanical royalties is earned in France. Assuming the French publisher by contract is entitled to 50 percent of all mechanicals earned in the territory, it will retain $50 and remit the remaining $50 to the U.S. publisher, who will, in turn, normally be obligated to pay the writer 50 percent of the mechanical income actually received by the U.S. publisher. Consequently, $25 is payable to the writer and $25 is retained by the publisher.

It should be noted here that most subpublishing agreements grant the foreign licensee the right to collect all mechanical, synchronization, and miscellaneous income. However, with regard to performances, the subpublisher either collects the total publisher's share or just the foreign publisher's share from performances directly from the foreign performing-rights society. Generally, the foreign society will collect the writer's share of performance income as a result of reciprocal agreements with ASCAP, BMI, and SESAC. The writer's share is paid directly to the respective American performing-rights society after the deduction of a small collection fee. The American society will then pay the applicable amount directly to the writer.

AT-SOURCE PAYMENTS

A major consideration of the writer-artist when signing with an American publisher is a determination of whether royalties paid to the company by foreign subpublishers, and ultimately to the writer, are computed at the source and are not diminished on account of any sublicense granted by the subpublisher. For instance, let's assume that the American publisher enters into a subpublishing agreement with a French publisher for the territories of France and Switzerland. The subpublisher negotiates a clause whereby it agrees to pay the original publisher 50 percent of the income actually received by it in France. The French publisher doesn't have an office in Switzerland and thus finds it necessary to enter into a subpublishing agreement of its own with a Swiss publisher on a 50-percent royalty basis. The money earned by the Swiss publisher is $100. The division of income in this situation would be as follows: $50 is retained by the Swiss publisher, with the balance being remitted to the French publisher. The French publisher in turn retains 50 percent, or $25, and remits the balance to the original American publisher. Out of this $25, $12.50 is remitted to the writer, and the balance is retained by the American publisher.

Sometimes, these types of sublicenses are unavoidable, especially in order to ensure representation in smaller countries, or when the original publisher is in a disadvantageous bargaining position. However, whenever possible, the writer should determine the American publisher's foreign subpublishing structure and learn whether payments are computed at the source from the important foreign territories.

Usually, the American publisher will have absolute discretion as to the terms it negotiates with regard to foreign licensing or subpublishing agreements. This right will, of course, be subject to any limitations in the agreement with the writer. The writer can protect him- or herself from improvident foreign agreements in one of two ways: The first is through a restriction in the original writer's contract, which may be difficult to obtain; and the second is by the choice of a domestic publisher with an active and successful subpublishing situation in major foreign territories.

TRANSLATIONS, ADAPTATIONS, AND ARRANGEMENTS

Another aspect of foreign publishing that can affect the songwriter is the right of the subpublisher to make translations, adaptations, and arrangements of compositions, including the right to have new lyrics written. Without this right, it would be extremely difficult to exploit the writer's songs in certain territories.

Royalties payable to a local lyric writer will vary depending on local industry practice and the strength of the lyricist. It's customary for the subpublisher to pay the lyric writer royalties out of its share of the income; these are based on the mechanical and synchronization uses and sales of printed editions. The local lyric writer's share of performing rights income will come from the American writer's share. Similarly, in some cases foreign arrangers may be entitled to receive a small portion of the American composer's performance share.

As with records, the writer-artist should be aware of the appeal his or her songs will have in foreign territories. Subject to the terms of the subpublishing agreement, it is usually always the responsibility of the foreign subpublisher to get artists in the territories it controls to make recordings of the songs. In order to do this, the subpublisher must have material that will be acceptable to these artists. Because of language differences in non–English speaking countries, melody becomes a key consideration in adaptability. The writer interested in international acceptance of his or her material should become acquainted with the musical tastes of some of the key foreign markets, such as the United Kingdom, France, Germany, and Japan.

Often a writer writes with a certain artist in mind. As we have seen earlier in the chapter, a successful recording by an artist with an international following can account for considerable income from the foreign territories and can also help develop the composition into an international standard that will be recorded hundreds of times over the life of the copyright.

The foregoing represents a brief overview of what is involved in foreign music publishing. Beyond the legal complexities is the problem of identifying honest and active subpublishers to represent the artist's copyrights. The assistance of a music attorney specializing in foreign subpublishing is essential for avoiding potential traps that await the unwary. However, when done properly, the writer-artist's and publisher's income potential is more than doubled. In short, it is worth the effort.

PERSONAL APPEARANCES

A third potentially lucrative area of international concern is the personal appearance. As in the United States, concert, nightclub, radio, and television appearances provide an additional source of income, while also serving as an effective record promotion tool.

The rules regarding coordination of personal appearances and record company promotion in the U.S. apply equally to the foreign market. The large booking agencies, such as William Morris,

ICM, and CAA, have foreign offices to handle the booking of an overseas tour. Smaller companies often maintain reciprocal working agreements with separate foreign agencies. If the artist is not affiliated with an agency that has international connections, the manager can contact reputable foreign agents or consultants who specialize in arranging overseas tours.

A popular American artist can command substantial fees in those foreign markets where he or she has name value and commercial appeal while also boosting record sales and music publishing income. Once dates have been set, the same general principles of personal appearances and "the road" apply to foreign tours. The manager and road manager should place special emphasis on each country's laws and regulations concerning passports, visas, work permits, and other potential travel restrictions.

If the artist is to travel to non–English speaking countries, thought should be given to hiring interpreters or guides to help ensure that the tour goes smoothly. It's helpful for the manager and artist to have at least some familiarity with the geography and customs of the countries they'll be visiting. This will not only contribute to a more successful tour but will add to the enjoyment of the experience by the artist and traveling contingent. The local agent or contact can provide the artist with help in this area.

Apart from expanding the artist's markets, the foreign tour is an excellent device for avoiding domestic overexposure. An absence of several months from an artist's home country can help create a renewed demand for the artist once he or she resumes domestic touring.

PART FOUR

Career Maintenance and Control

The Manager's Juggling Act

What does a manager do? Or better yet, what doesn't a manager do? Generally speaking, a manager's job description covers anything necessary to further the career of the artist-client. He or she is a coordinator, adviser, negotiator, psychologist, planner, promoter, and a friend to the artist. We believe the term "juggler" aptly describes a manager's diverse functions and responsibilities. Just as one problem is solved, new ones requiring immediate attention usually appear. This is what makes personal management an ongoing process with no real stopping-point short of termination of the artist–manager relationship. That means the manager must be on-call 24 hours a day and aware of what is going on in the artist's professional and (sometimes) personal life as much as in his or her own. The manager is the focal point of hundreds of decisions that must be made daily. The manager's judgment and ability to make the right decision at the right time can spell the difference between stardom and what might have been. It all goes to illustrate the critical role imaginative, intelligent, steady management plays in the success of an artist's career.

We thought it would be useful for aspiring managers, artists, and others who play a role in the artist's professional life to develop a feel for the job beyond the previous discussion of the various business and creative components that go into being a great manager. The best way to do this is by constructing a typical day in the life of an artist's manager. This composite profile is based on interviews with a number of top-flight managers we talked to in Los Angeles, New York, and Nashville. We have purposely omitted mentioning any names or focusing on any one manager in our profile, though all of it is based on fact.

What follows, then, is a composite picture of what it is like to fill the shoes of an artist manager for a day.

We'll call our manager Mark. His top client is a Nashville-based country artist who records and performs under the stage name Michelle. She has charted two albums for a major record company and is considered one of Nashville's hot new recording artists.

Mark also represents an up-and-coming and eclectic singer-songwriter named Jeff James, who records for a small boutique label in New York. Mark feels that Jeff is destined to be an important artist in the vein of Lyle Lovett or John Prine, both in terms of recording and songwriting.

Hoping to diversify his client base, Mark is also thinking of signing an established gospel artist from Memphis named Derian Williams. Derian, at the age of 25, is already considered by many to be the next star in the gospel world. He wants to expand his horizons in Los Angeles and is trying to make a transition to pop and R&B. Derian has just recorded a promising pop album for a major West Coast label and is looking for an experienced manager who can guide his career into new areas without sacrificing his gospel fan base. Mark knows that what Derian wants to do is both risky and tricky. But he also knows that if he decides to take on Derian as a client, it will be the kind of challenge that makes him love his work.

MORNING

Today is Friday. As a manager Mark is unlike other business people accustomed to a routine; his day will potentially be quite different from the day before. Earlier in the week, Mark's day started at a breakfast meeting in Los Angeles, where he was exploring some possible television opportunities for Derian. Later that night, he was on the "red eye" flight from LAX to New York for meetings with Jeff's record label and the primary corporate sponsor for Michelle's first national tour as a headliner, scheduled to begin in two weeks. After spending Tuesday and Wednesday in New York, Mark took an early flight back to Nashville on Thursday so he could spend a full day in the office catching up on work he couldn't take on his trip. Even with a lap-top computer, fax, and cellular phone, there is just so much you can do on the road.

Next week Mark is scheduled to spend a few days traveling on the tour bus with Jeff, who is on the road doing a round of college concerts in Texas and New Mexico. Given Mark's hectic travel schedule, he's glad to be back home in Nashville. He has just arrived at his Music Row office from an early Friday morning workout at the gym, where he has been making mental notes on a possible career plan for Derian. As Mark sips his first cup of coffee, he digs through a stack of morning mail. Among the bills and junk mail are copies of *Billboard* and *Music Row*. The latest copies of *The Gavin Report* and *CMA Closeup* lay on his desk. He quickly checks the chart positions for Michelle's CD and single on the *Billboard* country charts before turning to the gospel charts to see how Derian is doing. He then quickly scans *Gavin*'s Americana charts to find Jeff's CD holding at 18. Mark then turns his attention to *Music Row* to see what's going on in Nashville. He is pleased to see a favorable article spotlighting Michelle as a fast-rising female artist in Music City. He makes a note to call the magazine to compliment them on the story.

Having quickly scanned the trades, he returns to the stack of mail before him. In addition to a monthly financial report from Michelle's business manager, tickets to an industry fund-raising gala, and an assortment of invitations to showcases and writer's nights, he discovers several performance contracts that are late additions to Michelle's upcoming national headliner tour. He carefully reviews each contract, giving special attention to the date, time, and place of engagement and to the compensation clauses. He also makes sure there have been no modifications to the rider provisions. Some sizable deposit checks are enclosed with the contracts. Mark instructs his secretary to forward the checks to the business manager to be deposited in Michelle's account.

He returns to the contracts, which he scrutinizes with an eye for detail. Though he has never practiced, his law degree serves him well. If Mark finds anything in the contracts that doesn't meet his approval, he'll contact the booking agent regarding the appropriate modifications. However, on this particular morning all the contracts received are in order, so he promptly signs each one and instructs his secretary to return the remaining copies to the booking agent.

Also included in the mail are several new offers for concert performances next summer for Michelle; these have been forwarded to Mark for his approval by her agency. Each offer must be examined in view of its economic and exposure value. Mark will normally contact his artists if any offer has unusual features. Mark notices one of the engagement offers is for an amount twice Michelle's normal asking price. However, the engagement is to be held outdoors. The artist and manager had previously formulated several live-performance guidelines, one being that she would do no outdoor engagements unless billed as the headliner. Since the money offered is extremely high, and several other name attractions have already agreed to perform at this engagement, she might want to consider making an exception for this offer.

After the mail has been processed, Mark begins making and returning telephone calls. Representatives from his artists' record labels, publishing companies, and booking agencies have all called requesting information. These people receive top priority. Upon returning the record companies' calls, Mark is surprised to learn that Michelle's album is extremely successful in four new markets in the Midwest. Excited by this information, Mark calls the booking agent to share the news. He informs the agent of his desire to add these new markets to the headliner tour. The agent replies that she'll check with buyers in the markets and will call back toward the end of the day.

Before making any other telephone calls, Mark is interrupted by an unexpected visitor, Michelle. In short order, Mark learns she is very upset with one of the members of her backup group. There is something going on with the bass player who also does some backup singing, but she can't put her finger on it. Both she and Mark know that the bass player will play a key role in the success of the tour. If there are problems, they need to be addressed now. Mark attempts to get all the facts so he can define the real problem. Is the musician's playing or singing ability affected? Is the real problem his attitude or a personality conflict? After an in-depth discussion, Mark feels he knows what the trouble is and how to remedy it. He reassures Michelle that the problem will be solved one way or another, and he encourages her to make the most of today's rehearsal. An appointment is set with the musician for later that day.

That settled, Mark takes the opportunity to run the outdoor concert offer by Michelle. Her answer is "no!" Mark doesn't push it, although he thinks it would be good to make an exception in light of the money and exposure value. But now is not the time to push the issue. Before the artist leaves, he makes a copy of the

Music Row article for Michelle. She thanks him and is out the door, relieved that he will take on the problem with the bass player.

After Michelle leaves, Mark is informed that he has an emergency telephone call from her public relations firm. Trouble: The firm can't have the publicity campaign ready in time for the tour. Mark and the public relations contact have a rather heated discussion regarding the firm's inefficient handling of the artist's affairs. Mark has had enough excuses and delays. He threatens to terminate the relationship with the publicity firm. Immediately following this unfortunate encounter, Mark instructs his secretary to arrange appointments with representatives of three other PR firms for the next day. Time is running out. The artist's publicity campaign must be planned and activated immediately in order to coincide with the efforts of the record company to promote the tour. Mark wants to see if it is feasible to switch firms at this late date, or possibly after the tour.

Next Mark receives a call from the booking agent he spoke to earlier. She informs him she has secured a firm offer from a promoter for all those new markets where Michelle is making sales inroads. However, the promoter wants to block-book the dates for several thousand dollars less than the normal price. Mark instructs the booking agent to have the buyer submit this offer in written form. The agent says she'll call back when a fax is received.

Immediately, Mark contacts the promotion department at the record company to inquire about the feasibility of the label providing extra tour support in the new markets to help offset the lower live-performance fee, in the event that he accepts the dates as offered. The record company representative tells Mark that he'll check and be back in touch.

As the morning quickly dissolves, Mark remembers that he needs to call Jeff on the road to give him a full report on his New York meeting with his record label. Mark swivels to his desktop computer and calls up Jeff's schedule. It shows that Jeff is in Lawrence, Kansas, for a concert that night at the University of Kansas. Even though it is nearly 11 A.M., Mark is sure Jeff is still asleep after the previous night's concert in Kansas City. He decides to contact him later on in the afternoon.

LUNCH

Today Mark has a luncheon appointment scheduled with Michelle's attorney. During the meeting, the attorney advises that all the employment agreements with the road crew now in effect should be modified to include several new clauses. Moreover, the lease agreements for the tour vehicles have been approved and are ready for the artist's signature. In addition, the attorney, who also represents Jeff James, explains the legal ramifications of an incident involving the artist and an irate auditorium manager at a concert performance earlier in the year. It seems that Jeff became angry at the way the auditorium manager's staff was handling the lighting effects and made some derogatory comments to the audience regarding the intellectual capacity of the crew. As a result, the auditorium manager is suing Jeff for slander.

The attorney next presents Mark with the proceeds of a recent collection suit, which was successfully concluded, involving an overdue concert fee. Finally, Mark tells the attorney that Jeff wants to form his own music publishing company. He wants the attorney to look into what will be necessary to get the new venture up and running. All in all, the meeting wasn't too bad. Mark has experienced far worse.

EARLY AFTERNOON

Mark hurries back to the office to meet with Jeff's record producer. They're scheduled to review the artist's latest recordings. Both Mark and Jeff agree that the mixes on the recordings are not acceptable.

Unfortunately, Mark must relay this information to the producer so as not to upset him. Mark calls him and conveys the negative news as tactfully as possible. After a lengthy session, the producer hangs up, convinced that Mark is an idiot when it comes to recording. However, Mark has gotten him to agree to remix the recordings anyway.

Following this small victory, the booking agent calls again with several new offers for Michelle's tour. After listening carefully, Mark accepts two of them that are consistent with the tour's routing. Several of the offers merit consideration if the price can be increased or the dates changed. The remaining offers don't make sense from a routing or financial standpoint and are refused.

As the afternoon draws on, the road manager for Michelle's tour arrives to begin finalizing hotel and travel accommodations. After discussing the budget limitations for various expense items, the road manager begins making the necessary arrangements.

Mark instructs him to contact the program directors at the important radio stations in the cities where engagements have been set. Perhaps an increase in airplay for the artist's latest record is possible. Mark sends the road manager into the adjoining office to start accumulating the necessary information to start the in-house promotion campaign for the tour.

Mark next speaks with Michelle's business manager regarding the bookkeeping procedure for the tour. The same system that she has previously employed will be used. Mark arranges a meeting between the business manager and the road manager so they can discuss any questions he might have about the system.

The meeting is interrupted by an emergency call from Michelle, who is at rehearsal and in a rage. The monitors of the sound system aren't working. The rehearsal must be cancelled and the system fixed. Mark immediately locates a technician with replacement equipment and has the road manager personally direct him to the rehearsal location. Mark notes that Michelle's outburst over this equipment failure is out of character. It is obvious to him that Michelle is feeling the pressure of success. Her second album recently entered the Top Ten in the country charts, and her first national headliner tour is only a couple of weeks away. The problems with the bass player are not helping. He has to get that straightened out before doing anything else. Mark makes a note to take Michelle to brunch over the weekend to bolster her confidence and reassure her.

The rehearsal cancelled, Mark meets with the musician with whom Michelle is experiencing problems. Mark learns that bass player is having some serious domestic difficulties. After a candid conversation, Mark becomes sympathetic to the musician's situation. He explains the great pressure the artist is under because of the upcoming tour and the amount of rehearsal still needed. The musician promises Mark he will pull things together before the tour. Mark assures him that he'll explain the situation to Michelle and encourage her to be understanding. Since the musician is quite concerned about several legal aspects of his domestic crisis, Mark recommends an attorney that specializes in such matters.

Mark immediately calls Michelle and tells her the results of the meeting with the bass player. This is the first she has heard of domestic problems, though she suspected that such might be the case. Michelle is understanding and also relieved to learn that the problem isn't being caused by a personality clash between her and the musician.

Still, she is concerned about the sound system, which hasn't been repaired. Mark assures her that the road manager will take care of it.

LATE AFTERNOON

Half an hour later, after helping resolve the minor catastrophe with the sound system, the road manager returns and begins contacting radio-station program directors. Mark joins him in talking to these people about the artist's upcoming appearance in their cities. He enjoys playing the role of radio promotion man, especially after two stations promise to add the record to their playlists.

At 4:15, Mark finally gets through to Jeff in Kansas and gives him a full report on his meetings with the record label and Jeff's lawyer. They spend another twenty minutes on the issue of Jeff's new publishing company. Unfortunately, Jeff has to do a sound check, and Mark has an urgent call on hold. Before saying hurried goodbyes, they promise each other to block out some time to talk on the bus in Texas and New Mexico.

The call on hold is Michelle's booking agent. She informs Mark that in the new market areas the promoter she'd spoken of earlier has received firm offers on the proposed engagements. Putting the agent on hold, Mark contacts the record company's promotion department to see if a decision has been made on extra tour-support money. The proposal is being considered by the business affairs department. Mark advises the agent to delay until a decision can be made by the record company. Maybe they'll get an answer tomorrow.

EVENING

With the evening approaching, Mark goes to Michelle's dress rehearsal to review a portion of the concert presentation being prepared for the upcoming tour. Watching and listening to the rehearsal stimulates Mark's thoughts about his client's creative direction. He has several comments and ideas to offer about the show. This is the area where Mark and Michelle excel as they feed off each other's ideas. Mark's thoughts provoke additional ideas from Michelle, who is astute when it comes to the details of her career. After an hour-long discussion, both Mark and Michelle are excited about several new approaches to the concert production they've agreed to try. They're both starting to feel excited about the upcoming tour.

Before leaving the rehearsal, Mark again mentions the offer for the outdoor engagement. He asks Michelle to reconsider because of the money involved and the positive exposure value. Mark also adds that several other name recording artists will be performing at the same concert. She agrees this time to think about it and give Mark an answer over the weekend. He suggests brunch on Saturday. Confiding to Mark that the pressure is taking its toll, she gladly accepts, welcoming the brief break.

Mark starts to leave when he's cornered by two members of the artist's backup band who inquire about the itinerary for the tour. Mark briefs them of the general tour schedule and promises to give them an exact itinerary as soon as the details have been finalized.

Finally on his way home, Mark can't help but think about the problems involved with finding a new public relations firm and activating a campaign in time for the tour. He'll probably be forced to stay with the current firm, but he vows to get rid of them after the tour if they can't pull things together. He also makes a mental note to make a follow-up call to the record company tomorrow morning about his tour-support proposal.

The conversation with the producer also pops into his mind. Mark smiles to himself, knowing that the tapes are going to be remixed even though the producer thinks Mark has a tin ear. To Mark, taking an occasional bullet for the artist is just part of the job.

All the problems of the day are balanced out by the excitement generated by the rehearsal. The creative give and take with the artist make all the problems worth putting up with.

Mark arrives home for a late dinner with his wife. He has a meeting scheduled with Derian over the weekend before he flies to El Paso to catch up with Jeff's college tour. He would like to put in an hour of concentrated time on his proposed career plan for Derian. The biggest potential challenge revolves around helping Derian expand from the gospel world to the pop R&B world without alienating his current fan base.

After dinner, Mark retires to his study to do some thinking. He checks his answering machine for any calls. There's an urgent message to call the booking agent at home. The message has the making of another emergency. The booking agent tells Mark that she's heard a rumor that Michelle will been nominated as Best Female Artist of the Year by an influential national fan magazine. The agent points out that this, coupled with the upcoming tour, could dramatically raise the artist's asking price for personal appearances.

After hanging up, Mark's mind begins to race, thinking of all the implications and repercussions such a lucky turn of events could have on Michelle's career. The excitement builds for the second time that evening. Mark must either confirm or deny the rumor that the booking agent has given him. He decides to call a friend on the West Coast who may know something about the report. It's almost midnight, but because of the time difference, it's only 10 P.M. in Los Angeles. He picks up the telephone for the fifty-fifth time since that morning and begins dialing a phone number scribbled on the back of one of his business cards. "Hello, Norma? I've just gotten a report that . . . ."

19

Helping the Record Company Help You

Once the artist and manager have succeeded in establishing an affiliation with a major record company, they've cleared a crucial hurdle. In one way, they've finally achieved the success they worked so hard to attain. Yet, in another way, the work has only begun. Signing a contract with a good record label and becoming an established recording artist are two entirely different matters. To bridge this gap takes the same type of hard work it did to interest the company in the first place. The only difference is that the record company is now a potent ally rather than a closed door that must be pried open. At this stage, the manager's role turns from salesperson to motivator and coordinator.

Where the record company is concerned, the manager is the artist's advocate, press secretary, adviser, planner, negotiator, decision-maker, protector, and spokesperson all rolled into one. Because of the record company's substantial financial investment in a new artist, combined with the increasingly sophisticated and complex requirements for selling big numbers to a mass audience, a proactive, experienced manager is an essential help to the label in allocating its resources and making the most effective use of its assets. By contrast, an unrealistic, uncooperative manager can be a thorn in the side of a record company. Sometimes, that is necessary to protect the artist, but not all the time.

The most common complaint against managers voiced by the record company executives we surveyed is that many of them don't fully understand or appreciate the functioning and inner workings of the record business in general and the record company in particular. Managers should have a thorough understanding of the organizational structure and procedures of the label. The executives, however, were quick to praise those managers who made it a point to understand what a record company could and could not do for an artist. Effective management is impossible unless the manager is able to relate to the record company on its own terms. This means having the same level of knowledge and skill as those he or she will be working with at the label on a daily basis.

UNDERSTANDING THE RECORD COMPANY

The record company has only one objective—to sell records. Record companies in the United States don't receive performance royalties from broadcasters, as do some in Europe and other foreign territories. They don't share in income from the artist's concerts, television appearances, commercials, endorsements, or songwriting royalties. The only way they can make a profit and stay in business is by selling compact discs and cassette tapes. The manager should always keep this basic truth in mind.

Any suggestions and requests you make as a manager should in some way be designed to help the record company succeed in their objective. The fact that your plans and requests will directly benefit the artist's career is of no real concern if it will not help sell records.

Major record companies in the United States, based mainly in the recording centers of Los Angeles, New York and Nashville, usually have branch offices in other cities to deal with specific or specialized functions. For obvious reasons, many maintain self-contained offices in Nashville that specialize in country music. Others maintain branches in key markets around the country to handle regional marketing, promotion, and distribution.

Record companies are no different from other businesses. Most are divided into departments charged with certain phases of the company's activities. Each department has a supervisor who reports to the president or other upper-echelon executive. The president, in turn, reports to the board of directors or the parent company, which is concerned with the overall direction and profitability of the company.

Although no two companies are structured exactly alike, most are organized along the same lines with regard to division of responsibility according to subject matter. Each label has a chief executive officer and an executive staff responsible for the overall operation and management of the label. Individual areas of responsibility are usually divided into the following departmental areas: business affairs; legal; accounting; artist and repertoire; marketing and sales; promotion; press, publicity, and advertising; artist relations; and career development.

BUSINESS AFFAIRS DEPARTMENT

The business affairs department, as its name implies, is responsible for controlling the company's business direction. It's often staffed by attorneys and other business-oriented people. This department is historically a training ground for top label executives. Among other broad business-related duties, this department negotiates and administers artists' contracts. Once a decision is made to sign the artist, you as the manager will be in contact with the business affairs department. This department also has input into decisions involving tour support, promotion budgets, and the like.

It's valuable for the manager to get to know the people in the business affairs department. Because of their background and responsibilities, they'll be much more likely to appreciate a manager with a businesslike and professional approach to his job. A favorable impression never hurts.

LEGAL DEPARTMENT

The legal department at most companies is involved in drafting contracts, licenses, and other legal documents negotiated by the business affairs department. They're also called upon to render legal opinions concerning various aspects of the label's operations.

ACCOUNTING DEPARTMENT

The accounting department rounds out the business and financial components of the company. The artist should have a special interest in this department because it's responsible for computing and mailing his or her royalty checks.

ARTIST AND REPERTOIRE DEPARTMENT

The Artist and Repertoire (A&R) department is concerned with the artistic development of a record company. As discussed earlier, the A&R staff is responsible for bringing new talent to the label. In addition, it's their responsibility to serve as the creative contact point between the artist, producer, manager, and the record company. They're involved in helping the artist select material, a studio, and a producer. Often, the A&R contact acts as the production supervisor as well as artist's liaison within the structure of the record company.

Many A&R people also fill the role of record producer. The A&R department will generally have input into any decision having to do with the creative matters affecting the label.

MARKETING, SALES, AND DISTRIBUTION DEPARTMENT

The marketing, sales, and distribution department is the lifeblood of the company. This department is concerned with selling records that have been developed through the efforts of the artist and the A&R department. It's very important that the marketing specialists be excited about the artist's record. Without this enthusiasm, it's difficult for them to convince distributors, rack jobbers, and one-stops of the selling potential of the product. The A&R person often plays a newly submitted tape by an unsigned artist, or the preliminary mix of one of the label's current artists, for marketing personnel to get their opinion of the record's commercial viability.

Once an artist is signed and a record completed, the marketing and sales staff will structure a marketing approach with the help of other departments such as A&R; promotion; press, publicity, and advertising; artist relations; and career development. Once the record is released, this department makes sure that the product is available to retailers to fill demand. It closely monitors sales and reports to other key departments at the label, as well as the manager. It's important for the manager to know the people in this department also. An experienced manager can make a significant contribution to formulation of the marketing plan and can help the company make it work.

PROMOTION DEPARTMENT

Promotion goes hand in hand with marketing and sales. Once the record to be released is selected and the marketing approach is set, the promotion department will be involved in exposing that record in whatever manner the marketing plan dictates. This can mean getting radio airplay, setting up promotion parties, in-store displays, and so on. Most labels have field promotion people assigned to a specific territory. The home office coordinates their efforts on a daily basis, and, in much the same manner that marketing tracks sales progress, the promotion department reports to the department head on their progress in terms of airplay. The department head, in turn, analyzes and distributes this information to others in the company, as well as to the artist's manager. This information is important in helping the label, manager, and artist know which move to make next.

PRESS, PUBLICITY, AND ADVERTISING DEPARTMENT

Another department key to an effective marketing campaign, as well as to the artist's overall long-range career, is the press, publicity, and advertising department. This component of the record company helps keep the artist's name before the public through press releases, trade and consumer stories, print ads, time buys, and other exposure through the media. Thus press, publicity, and advertising is a tremendous asset to an artist. The manager can help ensure that these marketing tools are used to their maximum effectiveness by constantly keeping the department informed of every aspect of the artist's career and by cooperating in arranging interviews, press conferences, and other publicity activities.

ARTIST RELATIONS DEPARTMENT

The artist relations department can be very helpful to the manager in areas of scheduling, routing, and attending to the numerous activities of a busy artist. This department serves as a contact point between the artist and label. The manager should strive to keep artist relations people informed of the artist's schedule and plans.

CAREER DEVELOPMENT DEPARTMENT

Some of the larger labels have a separate department devoted to the artist's career development. This is a strong indication of the contemporary record company's commitment to the principle of career longevity, as opposed to the hit-and-miss approach that the one-shot hit record represents. Career development acts much like an in-house manager, attending to many of the management-oriented functions discussed in this book. The record company feels this is necessary in order to protect its investment, especially in the case of young, inexperienced artists or artists with weak management. An experienced and conscientious manager can often accelerate the growth and development of the artist's career by working closely with this department.

PRODUCT MANAGERS

Coordination is obviously a problem in large, departmentalized, multioffice record companies. Certain labels, such as CBS, use *product managers* to help solve this problem. The product manager is assigned to certain specified projects and instructed to guide a particular artist's record through every phase of the process we've just discussed. The artist's manager, obviously, can greatly assist the product manager in making the record a financial as well as an artistic success. Other labels may use the career development or A&R department as the coordination and contact point for a specific artist or product.

WORKING WITH THE RECORD COMPANY

With the record company's various functions and division of responsibilities outlined, let's turn to some specific things that you as manager can do to help the record company help the artist.

Once the recording contract has been negotiated with the business affairs department, you should waste no time in meeting with the label executives to discuss the company's plans for the artist and his or her records. Most likely, this will have already been done prior to signing. An artist should never sign with a label until at least a basic understanding of the company's intentions is clearly established. However, even assuming that this phase has been completed, it's a good idea to reconfirm the previous discussions at the level of the president, if possible.

Next, you as manager should spend whatever time necessary to meet everyone you possibly can who is connected with the label. This means going from department to department establishing one-to-one personal relationships with the various record company personnel. As pointed out in Chapter 11, "The Artist's Development Team," this does not mean department heads only. Everyone at the label, regardless of responsibility, has a contribution to make to the artist's career. For this reason, you should take time to meet the individual promotion people, the press and publicity staff members, the secretaries, even the mail room personnel. When you meet these people, tell them about the artist and his or her music and where the artist is trying to go with his or her career. Make yourself accessible and ask for their thoughts and opinions. The more people there are with a personal stake in the artist's career, the greater the chances for success.

After getting to know the record company personnel, you may want to introduce the artist to them. This tends to reinforce the collaborative spirit or personal investment the manager is trying to create. These preliminary meetings are the first round in helping create and build enthusiasm at the record company and the commitment needed to break an artist with the public.

INVOLVEMENT IN THE PROCESS

The business of selling records begins with the A&R department. You as the artist's manager should meet regularly with A&R to discuss your client's material and production release schedule. Even though, by contract, the A&R department may have final say as to material selection and release decisions, most often they'll take into consideration any recommendations and suggestions you make, provided that you are realistic and have thought things through.

The same holds true of almost any other contact you have with the record company. It's just human nature that a positive, cooperative approach will result in more satisfactory results for your artist-client. Enthusiasm is infectious. It is the manager's job to spread that enthusiasm throughout the hallways of the artist's record company.

Once a collective decision has been made regarding the product that will be released, you should turn your attention to the marketing scheme. Talk to the marketing and sales, promotion and press, and publicity and advertising departments about the artist's objectives and strategies. The emphasis here should be on arriving at a coordinated, unified approach that is consistent not only with the artist's image and goals but also the company's assessment of how best to market the artist and his recordings.

Prior to these discussions, of course, the artist and manager should have carefully worked out which route to take in maximizing the marketing and promotional efforts. We encourage you as the manager to work out and present to the record company a set of general proposals that are flexible enough to conform to their views and circumstances. By making such suggestions, you are at least assured of having some input into the final decision by the company. And even if yours and the artist's ideas aren't adopted, you have demonstrated competency and ability to the company. Respect for your work as manager among the various department heads is extremely important.

When making proposals, it's very important for the manager to keep in mind that no one likes to be told how to do his or her job, though some people are more sensitive about this than others. The manager should always appreciate the other person's psychological makeup and act accordingly. There's always the danger of appearing to take over rather than merely give suggestions. The rule of thumb here is: Use tact when dealing with record company personnel.

Once a marketing plan has been conceived, the manager's function turns to that of coordination. You must work with various label personnel and other members of the artist's development team to adequately prepare for the record's release. This will include coordinating with booking agents, promoters, publicity firms, television producers, and anyone else who will affect the record marketing process. If a promotional tour is contemplated, tour support must be finalized.

Once the record is released, the manager becomes the record company's point of contact with the artist. You should keep the various departments informed of the artist's schedule as well as any relevant developments pertaining to him or her. You should also be available to deal with any problem or new development that might arise. You'll want especially to maintain close contact with marketing and promotion concerning sales and radio airplay. Heavy sales or airplay in particular markets will affect decisions such as which dates to accept and which interviews to grant.

If the artist is touring, arrangements must be made for press conferences, interviews, and in-store promotions. This will necessitate coordination with the artist relations, press, publicity, and advertising and promotion departments. You'll want to talk with the career development department to review the audience reaction to the artist's live performances and determine the impact the appearances are having on sales and airplay.

During the entire process, the manager and thre label must always be thinking about the artist's next recording session, next record release, and next tour. It's a never-ending process requiring almost daily contact and communication with the various departments of the record company. However, it can be enormously rewarding if done effectively.

THE END RESULT

There will be nothing more exciting for you as a manager than watching your artist-client's first record start to gain wide airplay and to break in terms of sales, for you'll know that you've been in great measure responsible for making it happen. This is a reward that can't be measured in terms of dollars and cents. It's the end result of months of planning, communication, and follow-up with the record company. Major record labels have the resources and expertise available to achieve these results. It's up to the manager to make sure that these assets are put to best use.

20

Managing the Road

The traveling and touring aspect of an artist's career is commonly referred to in the entertainment business as "the road" or "roadwork." To some entertainers, the road offers many exciting opportunities: the chance to meet new people, see new sights, and visit new cities or foreign countries. However, to others, especially the veteran artist, the road is anything but exciting. These performers view it as a boring, monotonous existence that takes them away from family, home, and a normal way of life. Regardless of the artist's viewpoint, the road is an essential element in the careers of most artists.

WHY TOUR?

Touring has a direct and significant effect on an artist's popularity and audience appeal. The personal appearance is absolutely essential to the new artist trying to become known and develop a following. This is one of the few ways new recording artists have to display their talent and create a demand for their records.

The road is equally important to the established artist from a career-maintenance standpoint. To ensure continued popularity, he or she must maintain visibility and contact with fans. Although records and videos are effective promotional devices, there's no substitute for the personal appearance. This allows the audience to establish a closer relationship with the artist while permitting someone who has been around to win new fans. With the competition for the entertainment dollar being so intense, no one in the industry today can afford to take anything for granted, especially their fans. For those who do, there's the probability that the people who buy the records and concert tickets will shift their loyalties and dollars to other, more active and visible artists who haven't lost sight of what it takes to get to the top and stay there.

Beyond developing and maintaining popularity, there's another very important reason why artists find the road a necessary part of their career: money. While its true that most new artists usually run a deficit as they promote a record and try to build a following on the road, many established artists whose concert, one-nighter, and club appearances account for a large portion of their incomes do make money on tour. This is especially true for artists in the country, R&B, and gospel worlds.

Because a successful personal appearance tour is an excellent record-promotion device, record companies frequently insist that an artist be a working act before they'll even consider offering a recording contract. Several record company presidents told us flatly that they would never sign artists without seeing them perform. There are certainly exceptions, such as Shania Twain, who sold six million albums in the country and pop markets without touring. However, most recording artists have yet to find a suitable substitute for selling their records to fans one concert at a time.

Despite the many dramatic changes in the music business in recent years, one thing that hasn't been altered is the link between artists and their fans. The road offers an artist the chance to win over thousands of potential buyers in a single evening, while renewing and strengthening ties with existing fans. Besides direct sales, word of mouth created by an artist's visit to a city attracts the curiosity of others. All this, coupled with good recordings, exciting performances, and a positive public image, translates into a hot artist. This is precisely why Garth Brooks recently signed autographs at Nashville's Fan Fair for twenty-three hours without a break. With all the new artists and radio genres, there is more reason than ever to not take for granted the fans and the record sales they represent. The road is the most effective way of doing that.

Since the road is critically important to so many careers, the manager must do everything possible to make sure that every aspect of an artist's personal appearances is successful. This is why a manager will often travel with the artist or be present at key engagements. When the manager is unable to travel with the artist, he or she usually employs a road manager. For all practical purposes an extension of the manager, the road manager coordinates the numerous aspects of a personal appearance or tour, making hundreds of decisions daily. In this chapter, we'll discuss the various functions of the manager and road manager relative to touring. While the following discussion assumes the artist has chart activity at the time of the tour, many of these basic principles are still applicable to the artist without a record.

PREPARING FOR THE TOUR

The manager's first order of business is setting an objective for each tour. (The word "tour" is used throughout to refer not only to a series of dates but also to isolated engagements.) What is the artist trying to accomplish? Is the objective solely to promote a new record release? Or is the goal perhaps to capture a specific market or region? Often the artist is trying to make as much money as possible within a particular time frame. The underlying objective will influence many of the manager's decisions when formulating the tour. Artist and manager must know exactly what objectives the tour is to achieve, which in turn should be compatible with the artist's career goals and career plan.

Before accepting any dates, the manager must ensure that the artist's act is ready for the road. That means working to develop a stage presentation that is both entertaining to the public and compatible with the artist's image. The show must be smoothly running, tight, and professionally produced. This requires adequate planning and rehearsal time, during which a great many decisions regarding material, arrangements, sequence, dramatic effects, lighting, sound, wardrobe, equipment, sidemen, choreography, background singers, and conductors should be made. On the basis of the tour objectives and the artist's image, the presentation should be formulated and refined until both artist and manager are satisfied that the show is more than just good—it has to be drop-dead great.

Once the artist and manager agree on the format of the show, musicians and background vocalists must be located and rehearsed. At the same time, the manager must employ offstage support personnel such as sound technicians, lighting crew, equipment handlers, drivers, and a road manager.

Early in the planning stage of the tour, the manager should meet with the artist's booking agent to discuss the objectives and structure of the tour and set a realistic high and low asking price for the act. An experienced agent can provide valuable information concerning the marketability and price range of the artist, based on the target markets, arena capacities, style of show, rider requirements, and current popularity of the artist. If the objectives of the artist are unrealistic, it's best to find out at this stage, before the support people are employed. The manager will project the artist's overhead and the costs associated with the production of the tour on the basis of the per-date asking price of the act. If the general price limits are lower than previously estimated by the manager, modifications may have to be implemented to reduce the cost of producing the show.

Assuming that the booking agent is confident that the artist's asking price can be obtained without difficulty, the next consideration is availability. This will depend on the artist's existing schedule and the type of engagements he or she seeks to undertake.

Once the manager and booking agent have thoroughly discussed the scope of the tour, the manager will need to know how long it will take to set the tour. Here's where an artist's popularity pays dividends. If the artist has a hot record on the charts and a reputation for a high-energy stage show, the agent should be able to set the tour easily, provided that the price is not out of line. It should be noted that, in the case of a touring superstar, price is usually a lesser consideration because the talent buyer knows that the concert will most likely be an automatic sellout. Conversely, if the artist doesn't have a current record release and isn't known for his or her performing ability, the agent's job will be much more difficult.

Artists often become upset if a booking agent can't deliver the type of dates for the desired amount of money. Although booking agents do have some influence on the marketing process of the artist, they don't control every aspect of it. They must work with the product as it exists. Once the artist has expended the resources available through the development team members—the record company, publicist, booking agent, manager, and so on— the decision to book the artist is up to the buyer. That decision is based upon his or her perception of the commercial potential of the artist to sell concert tickets. The agent can do a great sales job and still not achieve the desired results for the artist because many of the factors influencing the buyer's decision are beyond the booking agent's control.

Of course, in some instances, the agent *may* be the deciding factor that influences the customer's decision. Therefore, it's important that the manager maintain a close working relationship with the booking agent, whose confidence, belief, and excitement about the artist can definitely influence customers' buying habits. Still, it would be unrealistic to think that the booking agent can control the talent buyer's decision-making process. The act must be able to stand on its own merits.

As the preceding chapter made clear, the artist relations, marketing, publicity, and promotion departments of the record company should be advised of the tour arrangements. The various departments of the record company will require a certain amount of lead time to activate their promotional machinery. For the artist, booking agent, and record company to achieve maximum benefit, they must all move in a carefully coordinated manner. The record company, therefore, should also have input in setting tour objectives and target areas. This is especially true when the record company is providing the artist with tour support money.

As the booking agent receives offers from buyers, these are communicated to the manager, who may accept or reject them at his or her discretion. If the offer is in a desired market and within the price range previously established with the booking agent, the manager will probably accept it. However, supporting dates, routing, travel factors, and overall tour developments could force a negative decision. If the offer is beyond the designated market area or the price is under the minimum agreed on, it will probably be rejected. In some instances, the financial or promotional value of a supporting date will force the manager to depart from the original tour plan. Submitting each offer to the manager offers him or her an opportunity to follow the development of the tour.

Usually, as each date is booked, the agent will send a press kit to the employer containing the artist's latest record, photographs, biography, and other promotional material. Often the artist's publicist, record company, and manager will send additional promotional material so that the employer receives adequate publicity.

The booking agent will issue performance contracts to the employer and will also forward a signed copy of each contract to the local office of the American Federation of Musicians or other applicable labor organization in the city where the engagement will take place.

While the booking agent and record company prepare for the upcoming dates, the manager will be busy finalizing the tour personnel, acquiring needed equipment, and making transportation arrangements. Here, a road manager must be employed, if one is not already on staff, to work very closely with the manager on all the tour preparations yet to be discussed.

The next phase of tour preparation involves three important areas: travel, public relations, and protective functions.

TRAVEL ARRANGEMENTS

After the tour dates have been set, the road manager will usually make the hotel and travel arrangements, including ground transportation needed when the artist or support team plans to travel by air. Otherwise, the road manager should inspect any vehicles that will be used—buses, automobiles, and equipment trucks—to be certain that they're safe and efficient. A travel agent is often used to make hotel and travel arrangements. When this is done, the road manager acts as liaison between the travel agent and artist's tour personnel.

The road manager must also make sure that all members of the tour have valid passports when traveling abroad and that they're affiliated with the necessary labor organizations. While many travel arrangements can (and must) be made in advance of the tour, there will always be problems or changes in schedule which will necessitate the road manager making modifications in advance plans.

PUBLIC RELATIONS

The public relations functions of the road manager are often overlooked because of more pressing duties associated with the tour. Public relations awareness on the part of the road manager can prove to be a real asset to the overall career development of the artist.

A substantial part of the road manager's public relations work can be done before the tour begins. A list should be compiled of the names and addresses of key radio stations, program directors and on-air personalities; television stations and newspapers; music equipment stores; local union representatives; record promoters and distributors and record stores in the cities where the artist will perform. The road manager should make an effort to develop a friendly relationship with all these people by contacting them in advance of the engagements. It's also a good idea to send them press kits and invite them to the engagement. As a follow-up to these initial contacts, the record company should be instructed to send complimentary records and other information about the artist.

All key record-company personnel should be kept current on all tour developments with an itinerary of the artist's tour, including the exact dates, places, and performance times. This will allow the company to make sure that the product is in the stores and that promotional efforts are being coordinated.

The road manager should also contact the employer (or promoter) to verify that adequate publicity material was received. At this time, any questions regarding contractual rider requirements of the artist's, the location of the engagement, or other matters relative to the performance can be discussed. Again, we must stress the importance of the road manager establishing a personal relationship with the employer prior to the arrival of the artist. Once in a tour-date city, the road manager should attempt to meet personally all these contacts. If this is impossible, and it often is, he or she should call and invite them to the performance.

PROTECTIVE FUNCTIONS

The last general area of a road manager's duties involves precautionary measures to ensure the successful completion of the tour. The first step is to know where to reach the manager at all times during the tour. It's absolutely imperative that the road manager have, and always hold onto, the following items:

- A route sheet with all pertinent engagement information.
- In the event a problem occurs with an employer, photocopies of the artist performance contracts, including all riders and special attachments.
- A file containing names, addresses, telephone numbers, social security numbers, local affiliations, and emergency contacts for all members in the tour.
- If foreign travel is involved, the passports of everyone going on the tour.
- All vehicle ownership and registration documents.

• If the artist's personnel are covered under a hospitalization insurance policy, all the necessary identification forms. If each member maintains his own medical insurance coverage, the road manager should have a photocopy of the individual policy and identification card.

Moreover, a duplicate set of all these items should be kept at the manager's office in the event that the road manager's file is lost or destroyed.

Advance plans should be made with the manager or artist's accountant regarding the bookkeeping procedure to be used during the tour. The road manager should fully understand the procedure and have an ample supply of accounting forms. If possible, all payments from employers for artist's services should be in the form of cashier's or certified checks. When the road manager does receive cash, interbank deposits should be used to transfer the money quickly, thus avoiding accumulation of substantial amounts of cash.

In addition, the road manager should have at least two major credit cards and an adequate amount of cash. Carrying large sums of money on the road should be avoided.

Contacting the local musicians' union representative in advance of the tour can be helpful if it's necessary for the road manager to replace a musician for an engagement due to accident, sickness, or other unforeseen emergency. When personnel problems arise during a tour, the road manager must act decisively. Substantial income could be lost unless the problem is solved quickly. The local union representative is a good starting point, especially if the road manager is on a first-name basis with him or her.

If the artist will be traveling by automobile and the equipment will be transported by truck, it's wise for the road manager to know in advance the names of local dealerships representing the brand of vehicle being used. A telephone call and an autographed picture to a dealer in the city in which the artist is performing not only helps if extraordinary service is needed, but may even create another fan.

Another precautionary measure regarding ground transportation is to maintain a good relationship with a major rental car company. Again, the personal touch, or simply knowing who to contact at three in the morning, can help tremendously when the group needs a vehicle to make it to the next date.

ON THE ROAD

Once the tour has begun, the road manager's responsibilities increase and the amount of time to make decisions decreases. The road manager's primary function during the tour is to oversee the artist's timely arrival at the place of the engagement. Whether traveling by air or land, the problem of coordinating departure, arrival, and alternate modes of transportation in the event of schedule changes is ever-present.

Once the artist and support crew arrive at a performance site, the road manager should focus on the stage set-up. Through advance communication with the employer, the road manager can arrange for the arena to be open for the road crew at the desired time. An efficient road crew is not only advantageous to the artist, but also economically helpful to a promoter when unionized stage hands are being paid on an hourly rate.

While the stage is being set up, the road manager should inspect the dressing rooms, to make sure that they're adequate, and should determine their proximity to the artist's entry and exit points. If the artist requires food and beverage in the dressing room, this should be arranged.

Following the stage set-up, the road manager should supervise the sound check and a brief rehearsal, if desired by the artist. The arena should be closed to the public during this phase of activity. Once the road manager leaves the arena, security people should be present until the equipment is dismantled.

The road manager should attempt to structure the artist's daily schedule to allow sufficient time for rest prior to each performance. While this can be an extremely difficult task, every effort should be made to see that the artist is well rested before each performance.

On the day of the show, the road manager is responsible for all last-minute details, ensuring that the show begins on time and runs smoothly and acting generally as a field general for the lights, stage crew, sound technicians, and all other support personnel. Depending on the type of engagement, it may be necessary for him or her to review the ticket manifest and receipts to determine if percentage fees have been earned and properly paid.

The road manager should evaluate all aspects of the artist's show. Was the performance too long? Was audience reaction enthusiastic? Did the lighting effects dramatize the performance? A written report of each performance should be forwarded to the manager immediately after each engagement. These reports serve as a diary of the tour and as a directory of all the people involved in the production of each show. After the tour, these people should be contacted by telephone or letter that thanks them for their help.

Once an engagement has been successfully completed, the road manager begins focussing on the next date, until the tour is concluded.

While the foregoing outlines the many functions of a road manager during an extended tour, to cover them all is impossible. Whatever problem may occur, it's the road manager's duty to deal with it, while insulating the artist from as much unnecessary distraction during the tour as possible.

AFTER THE TOUR

The manager must make the final determination of the success of the tour. The reports filed by the road manager serve not only as a good control device but also as a reference in evaluating results. The record company can provide the manager with sales figures of the artist's product after the tour; this is a good way to measure the degree of the artist's impact on a particular market after the concert.

The booking agent will be directly in contact with the employer or promoter after the event. Here, too, is a reliable source of feedback concerning the artist's performance.

After the tour, the road manager and artist should sit down together to review every aspect of the just-concluded dates as a way to get ready for the next round of personal appearances. The artist and manager shouldn't be satisfied with success that is limited to markets that were a pushover or with a tour that elicited mixed reactions or audience indifference. Staying on top means constantly refining and improving the artist's live act. As with every other area of the artist's career, planning, hard work, and follow-through will add up to success.

21

Career Review and Evaluation

It's extremely difficult for highly successful artists to remain objective about their careers. Yet, to ensure continuing success, they must always be willing to strive to maintain an edge on their competition. That means keeping the creative side of the career fresh and innovative and the business running smoothly. While big royalty checks from record labels and publishers, lucrative performance contracts, and thunderous applause are all evidence that the artist has made it, a realistic perspective must be maintained. The same goes for a new artist who has finally begun to break through with radio airplay, record sales, and live performance bookings. In show business, today's victories guarantee nothing tomorrow.

The primary responsibility for career review and evaluation falls to the manager. While the management process requires constant scrutiny and adjustment, a major formal review should take place at least once a year. Most major corporations do it, so why should an artist's career be any different?

THE IMPORTANCE OF A GOOD ATTITUDE

It's human nature for anyone, especially an artist, to find criticism distasteful and ego-deflating. A positive self-image is reinforced by the acclaim heaped upon the artist by the public and press. In the face of negative reviews the common response is, "If I'm no good, why are my concerts still packed and record sales soaring?"

There is an element of truth in that kind of response, assuming ticket and record sales are indeed soaring or at least holding their own. Unfortunately, it's not always the whole truth. An artist who can't accept any constructive criticism has begun to lose perspective, which means the life expectancy of his or her career is at risk. By contrast, the mature professional capable of acknowledging the need for ongoing reassessment can breathe new life into a career whether it's soaring or beginning to fade. It's common sense that the manager, record company, producer, and booking agent all want the artist's career to flourish. When the artist succeeds, they succeed. The advice they offer is motivated by a common economic bond, as well as by personal concern. Though it's not always the case, an astute artist should realize this and welcome ongoing reevaluation of his or her work. Failure to do it is a sure danger signal.

RE-EVALUATING ARTIST AND ACT

The manager should review and scrutinize all facets of the artist-client's public and professional life. Has the artist become complacent? Been overexposed or underexposed? Developed bad stage habits? What has audience reaction been to the artist's live performance? Once the manager has assessed the positive and negative points of the artist's work, both should discuss ways to improve the weak areas without sacrificing the strong points. While the artist and manager always make the final decision on matters affecting the artist's career, their willingness to consider the opinions of others can help keep their perspective clear.

At this point, any artist who has retained a "yes man" for a manager is probably going to be in trouble. It's unlikely that a manager who can only maintain his or her job by constantly agreeing with the artist can offer any constructive comments if they conflict with the artist's viewpoint. Instead of having an adviser, the artist has retained nothing more than a puppet who knows the right lines to say—someone who could have been obtained for much less than the percentage the artist is paying. In this all-too-common situation, trouble can't be too far away.

THE BUSINESS REVIEW

The business structure and operation of the artist should be re-evaluated periodically, usually on an annual basis. All legal documents should be reviewed, insurance coverages updated if necessary, and accounting records audited. The artist's budget should be carefully studied to determine if any breakdowns or excesses have occurred during the year. Often, the annual summary reflects the accumulation of various expenses that have previously gone unnoticed but prove to be significant at year's end. Once these are detected, adjustments for such expenditures can be made in the new budget.

All reports to governmental authorities relative to the artist's business should be prepared, explained to the artist, and filed with the proper authority. Since many of the business matters may not be fully understood or appreciated by the artist, the manager would be well advised to request a letter from the accountant, attorney, and insurance agent reviewing their particular areas of the artist's business for the year. The manager can then wrap up the review of the business operation at a meeting specifically for that purpose. If the artist has questions or desires additional information, the manager can offer the summary letters to help clarify his or her business status. In some instances, it may be best for the accountant, attorney, and other advisers to be the annual business meeting to personally answer any inquiries from the artist. Regardless of procedure, at least one meeting a year should be devoted to an evaluation and review of all aspects of the artist's business.

THE CREATIVE REVIEW

The creative evaluation cannot be forced into a predetermined time frame as easily as the business review. Since styles and trends in the entertainment industry change so rapidly, this dimension must be constantly under scrutiny. The guiding principle is the maintenance and projection of the artist's image. If a major change in image is desired, the artist and manager should consult all members of the development team before embarking on such a far-reaching move. A total departure from an established image could be professional suicide for the artist.

Let's assume that the artist and manager are satisfied with the artist's current image. Their primary concern, then, is the proper maintenance of that image. Several factors must be reviewed in assessing the efficiency of team members in projecting and enhancing the artist's image.

THE ARTIST'S MATERIAL

The first important factor is the selection of material for recording and live performances. Where is the material coming from—the artist or other songwriters? The material must be compatible with the artist's voice, style, and abilities. Most importantly, is the material becoming dated or below par? Just because the artist has been a past success is no guarantee of what will happen in the future. Usually an artist who writes his or her own material has a common thread running through most of it. The artist must take care not to confuse a recognizable sound or successful formula with a recycling of the same song with new words and different titles. On the other end of the scale, care should be taken not to overreact during a creative lull and embark on a radical departure in recording or performing style that will alienate long-time fans.

THE RECORD PRODUCER

Another key influence affecting artist's image that should be evaluated periodically is the record producer. The artist and manager must review the producer's work and product in view of the artist's evolving goals, not the producer's.

For instance, let's suppose an artist and producer have been working together for several years, finally achieving some degree of success on their most recent album. The record company wants the follow-up album to be in the same artistic vein to take advantage of the sales and excitement generated by the last. However, because the success of the previous album has afforded the producer a new-found degree of financial security, when he's not pleased with the overall sound of the artist's material, he demands a radical change in direction despite the commercial success of the recent album. The artist believes in the producer's ability as a result of the success of the last album. But the artist also agrees with the direction suggested by the record company.

The manager must resolve the dilemma without compromising the direction and image of the artist. If the producer is diverting the artist from a strategic course, then a new producer may be in order, unless a solution can be found through other means. The manager can't let the producer satisfy his artistic aspirations at the expense of the artist. To guard against this situation, the artist–producer relationship should be examined at certain intervals.

EVALUATING THE OTHER PLAYERS

The review should encompass not just the record producer, of course, but also other major players who influence and enhance the artist's career.

THE RECORD COMPANY

The effectiveness of the record company should also be assessed at various stages. The manager must be aware of personnel and organizational changes occurring within the company that could be detrimental to the artist. The resignation or firing of key record-company executives, mergers or acquisitions, and shifts in company policies all could have some effect on the artist's relationship with the record company. It is also vital that the artist get his or her share of the resources and attention from the label. If it becomes apparent that the artist does not figure in the long-term future of the company, it's time to look elsewhere.

Rest assured that all record labels conduct periodic reviews of their artist rosters with the view of cutting the least productive artists to make way for new blood. The examples of artists and labels parting company after long, successful relationships are many. While this is sometimes sad, its also a reminder that the music profession at this level is very much a business.

THE BOOKING AGENT

The artist and booking-agent relationship also requires periodic evaluation. The first measure of whether the relationship should continue centers around the results the agency has gotten for the artist. How many dates? What kind of money? Have new markets been developed, or is the artist just playing the same venues? All of this should be considered and analyzed.

Assuming the relationship has been mutually beneficial, the role of personalities should also be considered. The artist may become affiliated with a certain agency because of a particular individual. The artist may be affected if that individual leaves the agency or is transferred into another department.

Changing goals and objectives are certainly another consideration when re-evaluating the artist's agency affiliation. As mentioned previously, many booking agencies specialize in specific types of performances or are confined to certain geographic regions. While one agency may be ideal for an artist at an early career stage, a shift in direction or a new level of career success may render the agency incapable of helping the artist.

For instance, let's assume that an artist has been performing her songs quite successfully in the club market for a number of years. While interested in recording, she has never stressed this aspect of her career, since her club dates provide her with a substantial income. The infrequent recordings submitted to various record companies are impressive, and the artist is eventually signed by a major label. Within six months, an album and single are released. The response is overwhelming; both the single and album soar up the charts. The record company, astonished with this new-found success, releases another single, and it too climbs the charts. Eagerly, the record company encourages the artist to set a tour to capitalize on the market acceptance. But the booking agency that has been so successful in securing the artist her club engagements isn't capable of arranging the concert dates. As a result, the agency attempts to keep the artist in club markets. Asked for a partial release so the artist can retain another agent for concert dates, the agency reacts negatively. A problem ensues.

Such situations are not uncommon in the entertainment business. The manager must scrutinize the booking-agent relationship to make sure that this aspect of the artist's business is deriving maximum economic benefit.

OTHER SUPPORT PEOPLE

As emphasized above, everything affecting the artist's image must be inspected to complete the re-evaluation process. This critique should apply to the sound and lighting crews, the music director, backup musicians, and all other personnel used by the artist. The publicist and road manager should also come under the magnifying glass. Their activities are vital to the proper maintenance and projection of the artist's image.

REVIEWING THE ARTIST-MANAGER MATCH

Being as objective as possible, the artist and manager should evaluate their own relationship. Has it been a successful match? Has the manager been good for the artist's career? Are both moving toward the accomplishment of predetermined career goals? This is also the point when the artist's career goals and strategies should be reviewed in order to keep them current. The artist may wish to change career direction or set new goals. Whatever the case, a periodic re-evaluation will ensure that career goals, strategies, and tactics will always be effective tools.

In conclusion, the manager should attempt to give the artist an overview of his or her entire operation, including a concise review of the business machinery and an in-depth discussion of all the creative factors influencing the artist's image. Critical comments from the artist's development team members should be considered and discussed, as should the contributions of all the people who play a role in the artist's career. Every phase of the artist's career should be reviewed, from the selection of musical material to the color of his or her shoes onstage.

The manager should recap the year in terms of goals achieved and milestones accomplished, as well as those objectives that have failed to materialize. The career plan should be measured against these success and failures. Is the plan still a good one? Are last year's goals still relevant to changed circumstances? Are there new opportunities or obstacles that require a change in direction? If the career plan should be modified, now is the time to do it.

After an objective analysis, the best-case outcome is that all is well, as manager and artist toast to bigger and better things. However, on the other hand, both parties may agree that a termination of the relationship is best for artist and manager. If either party disagrees about prematurely ending the relationship, then their differences should be compromised or attempts made to settle them. If this can't be done, both parties must consider a release as a possible solution to their problem.

The key to making this process work is a shared openness to valid, constructive criticism. If the manager and artist don't stay in touch with current reality through periodic career assessment and re-evaluation, you can be certain that the music industry and the fans will, at some point, do it for them.

PART FIVE

Mastering Success

22

Coping with the Stress of Success

Many who aspire to a career as a recording artist equate their goal with the ultimate dream job that will make them rich and famous. Unlike most jobs, getting paid to sing and play music isn't work at all, it's fun. Instead of punching a clock, stars travel, attend awards shows, sign autographs, and live a life-style full of fancy hotels, limousines, adoring fans—all on the way to becoming millionaires. What's not to like?

That vision of the pot of gold at the end of the rainbow, intertwined with life as a celebrity, has, for decades, lured countless would-be stars to Broadway, Hollywood, and Music Row to take their shot at the big time. That quest for the elusive dream of stardom has written countless stories of struggle and sacrifice, and it will write countless more. For a fortunate and talented few, the dream comes true beyond anything in their wildest imaginations. But tens of thousands more fall short of their dream and are forced to settle for something less. Of these, many go on to lead happy and productive lives out of the spotlight. Others retreat into bitterness and disillusionment. Life sometimes isn't fair, but everyone who tries for the gold ring knows or at least should know that there are no guarantees, especially when it comes to something as fleeting and fickle as a career in show business.

Up to now, this book has dealt primarily with making the most out of that elusive break that leads to record contracts, agents, and all the rest. To most people, getting a record deal with a major label would be the ultimate. But what happens after the public starts to say "yes" in a big way and keeps on saying it with every new record release and every new concert tour?

That is when the work *really* starts. While getting there presents familiar problems and obstacles, staying there presents a much more subtle range of pressures and challenges.

Scott Hendricks, who has produced hit records for Brooks & Dunn, Faith Hill, and Alan Jackson, and is currently president and CEO of Capitol Nashville Records, put it like this, "An artist has absolutely no idea of the work and pressures involved in stardom until it happens." This was echoed by every manager and every record company executive we talked to. Everybody is familiar with the sad, yet true stories of artists who were overwhelmed by too much, too fast. For those not adequately prepared, the dream can quickly become a nightmare. For others able to take their new-found fortune and celebrity in stride, the gift of stardom can be a positive life-changing experience.

Those few who have experienced the white-hot exhilaration of managing an artist who is a nobody one day and a household name the next are the only ones who fully appreciate the reality of coping with the stress of success. Although you can never adequately prepare for that roller-coaster ride, you can try. That is why we offer this vicarious peak at what coping with major success is like from the inside. By way of a warning, some of you may change your minds about wanting stardom when you see what comes with it. Others of you will file the information away and brace yourselves for the ride.

As with the manager's juggling act described in Chapter 18, we have taken great pains to avoid focusing on the managers or stars who have sketched for us what it's like to hit a home run in the music business. In what follows, their experiences serve only as the background, which we have melded with our own observations and experiences to create a purely fictional (yet based on hard fact) account of the good, the bad, and always fascinating sides of stardom.

Therefore, let's pick up our "day in the life" story of Mark, from Chapter 18. Mark, as you remember, is our Nashville-based artist's manager, whose most promising artist is Michelle. The time is one year later, and Michelle has gone from being an up-and-coming Nashville artist to a worldwide phenomenon whose latest CD has sold over four million copies thus far. The last three singles went to number one on the *Billboard* Hot 100 as well as the country charts. The CD topped the *Billboard* Hot 200 Albums chart for four weeks in a row and is still comfortably entrenched in the top

10 after nine months. Offers for concert dates have tripled, and the money that Michelle is now able to command has gone through the roof. To the outside world, Michelle has the world by the tail, and from all appearances, so does her manager, Mark.

MORNING

Mark has just arrived at his Music Row office from his usual early Friday morning workout at the gym. Since Michelle's career really took off a year ago, he has found it more and more difficult to have time to himself, but he knows that staying in shape is a must if he is to have the stamina and balance he needs to cope with his new status. Now that Michelle is the music industry's newest star, Mark is the industry's newest star manager.

As is his custom, Mark sips his first cup of coffee and goes through the morning mail. Mark has five times the volume of mail he had a year ago, not to mention twenty-three faxes on his desk, all requesting an immediate reply. Because of the volume of offers, requests, and inquiries, Mark has hired Ross, a recent graduate of Belmont University's Commercial Music Program, which is offered through the university's business school. Mark's original plan was to have Ross serve as a developmental manager for several new acts he has intended to sign, but as a result of Michelle's success, those plans have been put on hold. Ross spends most of his time helping Mark just keep up with Michelle's career.

As Mark reviews the mail and faxes and quickly scans the trades, Ross arrives for their usual 9 A.M. morning meeting with a coffee cup in one hand and a dozen or so phone-call slips in the other. Mark and Ross immediately begin to plow through the faxes, which include everything from new concert and television offers to a well-known Nashville songwriter's inquiry about collaborating with Michelle on songs for her new album. Because Mark and Ross will be meeting with Michelle later in the morning, they want to review and prioritize new offers to present for her consideration. Meanwhile, in the outer office, Mark's secretary is fielding a flood of phone calls and collecting this morning's round of new faxes. The office has never been busier. As far as the three of them are concerned, it's a mixed blessing.

After the meeting, Mark leaves the office to run errands. Actually, he wants to get away from the phones to do a little thinking prior to a lunchtime meeting with Michelle. Despite the dramatic increase in income and interest generated by Michelle's career, all is not well. Mark feels pushed. There don't seem to be enough hours in the day to handle the demands of Michelle's career adequately and also give the necessary time to Jeff and Derian, his other clients. They have both had good years too, though nothing approaching Michelle's success. If things keep going like this, he is going to need even more help.

In his car, Mark reflects on the combination of talent, preparation, and luck that has brought Michelle to this amazing point. It all started with the release of Michelle's third album last year, several key television appearances, and what would go on to be MTV and CMT's "Video of the Year," which in combination catapulted her into the national limelight. While country audiences were aware of her rising star, the wider rock and pop markets had little idea who she was. That changed with the third album, which had a more distinct rock and pop feel and knockout songs that Michelle wrote or co-wrote. On David Letterman's "Late Night" show on CBS, the rapport between Michelle and Letterman was memorable; she was not only attractive but quick, with the ability to more than hold her own with the comedian-host. That same show featured a clip of her video, which was both sexy and beautifully produced, as well as the national debut of the first commercial, up-tempo pop single from the CD. That one appearance succeeded in captivating a national mass audience.

The next day's press coverage and talk-show buzz brought her several more network-TV opportunities, and within ten days, Michelle seemed to be everywhere. That concentrated exposure brought her millions of new fans. From there, pop radio picked up on the single from country radio. The crossover effect caused record stores to sell out across the country. Her label could not press CDs fast enough. Within a month, Michelle had become Big . . . Very Big.

Certainly, no one was more surprised than Michelle and her manager, Mark. She modestly told him in a phone call from New York the day after the Letterman appearance, "I was only being myself." Mark responded, "That's the whole point. That's what people like about you. By being yourself, you were able to reach millions of new fans in the space of ten minutes." Even at that point, Mark and Michelle had no idea how important "just being herself" with David Letterman had been for her career.

As Mark eases onto I-65 in Nashville, he realizes that all that has happened has been more than he had even thought possible.

But despite the money and his new-found power within the business, Mark is worried about the toll that career stress is taking on Michelle. The most immediate concern is the upcoming album, which is already two months behind schedule. Because of her increased concert schedule and the endless request for media interviews, television spots, and charity appearances, the time Michelle had usually allotted to songwriting has greatly diminished.

Michelle's hectic schedule has sapped her energy. She has found it increasingly difficult to write quality songs on the road. Yet the success of her previous album was due in large part to the signature songs she had written. From an artistic standpoint, it is impossible to write that caliber of song on demand and under pressure. Consequently, the album production schedule is off track.

To make matters worse, Mark and Michelle have committed to a European tour that is now less than two months away. The thought of it exhausts Michelle. To offset her anxiety, she has started drinking hard liquor every day for the first time in her life. This only further drains her energy. Though it isn't a problem yet, it could be.

The warning signs are everywhere. Mark knows that if something isn't done, Michelle and her career could flame out. To make matters worse, he is partially to blame and he knows it. When success started to come in buckets, both Mark and Michelle succumbed to "opportunity greed," and overloaded her schedule with a 75-city headliner tour. They conjectured that the initial blast of success might dry up as quickly as it had materialized. But it didn't, and by the time it was obvious that Michelle had staying power, her schedule was jammed.

Now that the overload is taking its toll, it's clear to Mark that something has to be done to allow his artist to better utilize her new-found clout while ensuring that her long-term career interests are being served. He also knows it must be done quickly.

LUNCH

Mark and Ross rendesvous at the restaurant, chosen for its relaxed setting. Michelle arrives a few minutes later. Mark offers his proposed solution to the problem. He'll take Michelle off the road to allow her to concentrate on the next album. This will require him to negotiate with agents and promoters to reschedule the upcoming international tour. His next call will be to the record company to postpone the release date of the album, thus buying more time. While anticipating the howls from the marketing department, his argument will be that it is more important to make the best record possible and avoid the risk of losing new crossover fans, while retaining Michelle's country base. Finally, Mark suggests that he and Michelle draw up very stringent guidelines regarding the granting of media interviews and television appearances. Michelle concurs with each suggestion.

AFTERNOON

After the lunch meeting, Mark and his client are alone on the terrace. For the first time in a year, they allow themselves time for a leisurely conversation. Mark eventually comments to Michelle about how tired she looks, as a way to gently broach the developing alcohol problem. Her eyes well up with tears.

"Now you've gone and done it good," Mark says to himself, thinking he's upset her with his remark. But after a moment, Michelle thanks him wholeheartedly.

"Mark, I'm so glad you saw it. I've wanted to talk to you about it—the pressure and the schedule and the drinking. I was afraid I was letting everyone down. I've got to get off the merry-go-round or there won't be anything left in another six months."

As the relieved superstar hugs him in gratitude, Mark sees how right his instincts had been. For the first time in months, both Mark and Michelle finally feel like they are regaining control of the career that has rocketed forward over the past year. Michelle stands back, takes a deep breath, and smiles for the first time in weeks.

AVOIDING A SUCCESS CRISIS

While the story of Mark and Michelle is fiction, it has been played out in reality time and again. Luckily, Mark had the good judgment to head off a "success crisis" before there were any lasting repercussions. Some artists and their managers aren't so lucky.

One of the primary causes of a success crisis is the sudden accumulation of substantial amounts of income in a short period of time. The developmental process for most artists takes many years. These are years of rejection and sacrifice with not a great deal to show for it. When success finally does come, things can change dramatically. Almost overnight, artists can find themselves with more money than they know what to do with. That rush of success seldom lasts, but it can be hard to believe it won't.

The initial shock of big money must be handled cautiously by artist and manager. At this point, priority should be devoted to the financial-planning aspect of the artist's career. This is certainly the time to turn to a top business manager or firm.

THE ARTIST'S EARNING PATTERN

The earnings for many successful artists tend to follow a pattern: Low income during the developmental phase, followed by a substantial jump once success is achieved. Earning will eventually rise to its highest point, followed by a gradual decline, to a point higher than where the artist began, but lower, obviously, than the peak. The artist's income cycle often will peak and fall several times during his or her career. The objective of the manager and/or business manager is to achieve the highest income level for the artist and sustain it as long as possible.

It's certainly understandable how an artist could lose perspective of financial reality. After starving and sacrificing for what seems like forever, it is difficult to start receiving checks for hundreds of thousands of dollars and more from record companies, publishers, and concert buyers and take it all in stride—it would distort anyone's view of the future. It's the manager's job to avoid getting caught up in it personally and to make the artist aware of the trap of believing that his or her bank balances are in any way a guarantee of what the future has in store. Instead, the manager should have already developed a plan for what to do when lightning strikes and it starts to rain hundred dollar bills. Although some would call this daydreaming, sudden stardom could well become reality. If you don't think so, just look around for the real-life Michelle stories. There are two or three every year.

WARNING SIGNALS

As in our story, success in large doses can often bring about physical abuses. An artist with enough money to buy anything he or she can dream up can be headed for disaster if not adequately prepared. Without a proper handle on life, the money earned by a successful artist may be funneled into material possessions, alcohol, drugs, cars, and houses—you name it. All people face this potential danger, but few have the economic capacity to truly indulge themselves. Stars do.

The manager must caution the artist to avoid a "materialistic rampage." Needless to say, this can be a very delicate area, but the manager must speak out if the artist's health or financial well-being is threatened—even if the artist becomes the adversary. It takes courage, but there are times the manager must say no and make it stick.

In situations where the artist absolutely refuses to listen and continues on a destructive course, the manager must exercise extreme caution. Often, another successful artist or close family member or friend may be able to talk some sense into the out-of-control artist. If advice and persuasion fail, the manager should leave a protective "paper trail" to support his or her objections to the artist's damaging behavior. If and when the inevitable crash does occur, the artist—especially the artist whose ego has obscured reality—may start looking for a scapegoat. Not being able to accept responsibility for his or her actions, the artist seeks a guilty party in order to protect an inflated, do-no-wrong self-image.

Some situations may become so unbearable that the artist not only refuses to take the manager's advice, but begins to see the manager as incompetent or as "the enemy," or both. For the experienced manager, this situation has only one solution—termination of the relationship with the artist.

While the economic consequences can be painful, the manager must think about his or her own future. If an artist has gotten totally out of control, canceling engagements, refusing to record, and taking the fans for granted, it reflects directly on the manager's reputation. When everything has been done to salvage the artist's career, it's best to let the artist suffer the consequences of his or her actions and avoid having two careers needlessly destroyed. Certainly, we're not suggesting that managers cut and run at the first sign of trouble. Loyalty and obligation come into play even in the worst of situations. However, if all else fails, the option of termination must be considered.

Another warning signal of a pending success crisis is complacency or laziness. The artist could be handling the emotional and financial aspects of a successful career but fall into a far different trap: the "I've made it" attitude. In the entertainment business, an artist is only as successful as his or her accomplishments today. Yesterday doesn't count. One of the characteristics of the music business is the constant change of styles and tastes, which lead to frequent star turnover. Unless the artist is ready for retirement, he or she must be prepared to work as hard, or even harder, once success has been achieved.

All too often an artist will have a hit record and believe there's no end to success. This is a fallacy as one look at the record charts confirms. How many new artists are included on the *Billboard* Hot 100 who weren't there a year ago? Yet, on the other side of the coin, consider the number of veteran artists who have sustained their careers, some for decades. This is proof that an artist can overcome change in styles and fads and retain and enhance his or her popularity and appeal.

Any artist who obtains a measure of success is well advised to be constantly aware of how to deal with the many dangers we've discussed. Whatever the fate of particular artists, the entertainment business will continue, with or without them. Over the years, the industry has lost gigantic superstars because of ego, neglect, death, or self-imposed retirement, yet there's always been someone to fill the void. Contrary to what any number of ego-driven artists have thought over the years, no one is that important or essential. Pop culture and life go on.

The financial rewards of a successful career, if handled properly, can provide lifelong recognition for a job well done along with a paycheck that will finance a good life. And then there is the applause from fans that provides great fulfillment. Effective management, a realistic approach to fame and fortune, and common sense are the qualities every artist must have or develop to make it to the top and stay there. Conversely, failure to adequately cope with sudden fame and unexpected fortune carries with it the seeds of professional and personal destruction.

23

Holding on to Your Money

Besides fame, money provides much of the motivation for those seeking a career in the music industry. The accumulation of money affords the opportunity to fulfill needs, both physical and psychological. But can we really ever have enough money to buy or obtain everything we may want in a lifetime?

What is enough is all relative to the earnings and aspirations of an individual. The typical up-and-coming artist wishes for enough money to make the monthly car loan and guitar payments. A moderately successful artist is paying for a home, a sports car, and three guitars. A star who's earning plenty of money still has problems. By the time he or she pays the band, bus driver, road crew, booking agent, lawyer, publicist, business manager, road manager, and personal manager—not to mention Uncle Sam—there's just enough money left to make the payments on two condos, forty acres of land, a house, two cars, a motorboat, a motorcycle, and that sixteenth guitar. No matter how much some people make, there will never be enough to satisfy an ever-increasing appetite, whether it be for more material possessions, financial security, or philanthropic and charitable causes.

There's an art to making money. But earning it is just part of the story. The greater challenge is holding on to the money a successful career has generated. The effective management of money requires at least as much talent as it took to make it in the first place.

MONEY MANAGEMENT

The art of money management can be divided into five areas:

1. Income/expense control
2. Investments

3. Tax planning
4. Retirement
5. Estate planning

INCOME/EXPENSE CONTROL

A well thought out *budget* is the first step in financial planning. It serves as a road map to one's financial future. Then, assuming that expense and income budgets have been carefully prepared, several control devices should be implemented. Of course, hand in hand with budgeting is the setting up of an *accounting system* on a weekly, monthly, or quarterly basis to accurately record the income and expense flow of the artist.

At the end of each accounting period (monthly, quarterly, semi-annual, or annual) the accountant or business manager should prepare a *profit-and-loss statement* and a *balance sheet*.

Whereas budgeting is analogous to drawing up a road map, the profit-and-loss statement is the traveler's log of what has happened during the trip and a description of the exact route taken. The balance sheet, a picture of the artist's economic condition, assets, and liabilities at a given time, is comparable to a photograph of the trip at a certain point.

These three financial tools provide the artist and manager with the information needed to maintain control over operating incomes and expenses. Of course, as the successful artist's income increases, the accountant may want to implement additional procedures to keep a closer watch over his or her financial well-being.

The manager's awareness of income and expenses becomes extremely valuable when modifications have to be made in revenue inflows or outflows. For example, if the artist's popularity starts to fade, causing his or her engagement price to fall, the manager may want to implement cost-reduction procedures to insulate the artist from personal loss of income. Conversely, if the artist's income is being gobbled up by taxes, he or she is making "too much" money, and the manager may recommend increasing some expenses to reduce net profit and put the artist in a lower tax bracket.

The same accounting procedures should be followed for the artist's personal earnings. Once the booking agent, manager, support crew, attorneys, publicist, travel costs, and other expenses have been paid, the artist will receive the balance. The amount of money earned by the artist should be controlled just as carefully as business earnings. The artist should maintain a personal budget, profit-and-loss statement, and balance sheet. This makes it much easier to spot any unnecessary economic drain and informs the artist of where the money is going. Remember, no matter how much an artist makes, there's never enough for everything. The successful artist must establish some priorities. Once this is done, his or her cash outflow can follow a logical pattern instead of resembling an irrational spending spree.

Another important aspect of income-expense control is the proper utilization of *credit*. Used wisely, credit is a valuable asset; uncontrolled, it can be the source of endless problems.

A hypothetical story will help illustrate this point. A group of young artists had just made the transition from "weekend warriors" to full-time professional entertainers. Faced with considerable travel commitments, the group leader procured credit cards from every major oil company. The cards were used indiscriminately, depending on which dealer was most convenient at the time fuel was needed. When the monthly statements arrived, it was easy to let them slide in favor of more pressing expenses such as salaries, motel bills, and equipment payments, for no one gas bill was that large. After eight months, even though the minimum monthly payment had been made, the group realized they had a major bill confronting them. Essentially, the group had been partially financing itself by using gas credit cards. After a short period of time, the oil companies started revoking their cards and began legal proceedings to collect the amounts due. This situation made it exceedingly difficult to get a bank loan to pay the accumulated debt.

Credit-card debt is acceptable for short-term financial help, but it's not a permanent or long-run solution. The artists could have avoided this embarrassing situation by seeking financial help from their banker in the beginning instead of waiting till their credit was nearly destroyed. Moral: Beware of credit-card debt.

The artist must also be cautious about the use of long-term bank debt or mortgage debt, both from a business and personal standpoint. The advice of an accountant, business adviser, or manager well-versed in business practices can be extremely useful in restraining the artist from overloading his or her debt position.

Usually the reverse is true for the young artist, who can't get enough financing to help develop his or her act because of the

risky nature of the business. Here, too, the advice of a professional can be useful in helping the artist acquire the financing necessary to develop a career.

INVESTMENTS

The next major area of money management is investments. Almost
all of us have an idea of what we'd do if we were suddenly
wealthy. It might be to buy land or put money into stocks and
bonds. The successful artist should realize that entertainment, by
its very nature, is a feast-or-famine business. Success won't last forever, so the artist would be wise to construct an investment portfolio to counteract the uncertainty of a career in entertainment. Of
course, these decisions depend on just how successful the artist
has been and the amount of wealth he or she has accumulated.

The assistance of an investment counselor is certainly worth
considering. There are investment firms specializing in stock and
bonds, real estate, and almost every other area of interest. The
large lending institutions and insurance companies offer investment counseling to their customers. Whatever the choice, the
artist should know what he or she wants from the investment:
Guaranteed short-term earnings? A solid retirement base? Is a high
degree of risk acceptable or anxiety-provoking? What kind of
diversity does the artist want in his or her investment portfolio?
Once those questions are answered, professional advice probably
should be sought, to ensure a balanced investment portfolio.

TAX PLANNING

Closely linked to investments is tax planning. The investment decisions of artists in the high-income brackets are greatly influenced
by their tax exposure. Investments that shelter income from taxes
may be more attractive to some artists, even though the rate of
return or potential profit margin is less than with other investments.

Probably the greatest adversary of the successful artist is the
Internal Revenue Service. However, the IRS's menace can be minimized by professional tax planning and money management.
Because most artists' income is concentrated in a limited time
period, their potential for tax exposure is much greater than that
of the normal individual. Therefore, as much of the artist's earnings as possible should be shielded from income-tax liability.
Such tax avoidance is not tax evasion, but to ensure that the artist
will stand on safe and solid ground with the IRS during all phases

of the artist's career, the advice of a certified public accountant or professional tax planner is imperative because of the ongoing and very technical changes in the tax laws.

One of the most unfortunate situations that can occur for an artist is to finally achieve success, only to receive a visit from the IRS for back taxes because improper income tax returns were filed. In some instances artists have failed to file any return. The artist and manager who bury their heads in the sand hoping that the IRS will go away are being foolhardy. No matter what amount of income is dribbling in, the artist should file the proper tax returns. All supporting documents necessary to substantiate the returns should be preserved. The importance of accurate record-keeping is magnified in a tax audit. The artist who maintains a good accounting system watched over by professionals is less likely to encounter problems with authorities than the artist who disregards record-keeping and accounting altogether.

PLANNING FOR RETIREMENT

Also linked with investments, but extremely specialized and serving a specific purpose, is a retirement plan for the artist. The investment portfolio can be constructed in such a way that certain investments will mature at a desired time, namely at retirement. On the other hand, investing with the primary purpose of retirement in mind would tend to limit investment opportunities. The artist should think of retirement as a specific part of his or her overall financial plan. Again, the advice of the accountant or investment counselor can be helpful in determining what can be expected from social security, union pension funds, or retirement investments. The artist's overall economic retirement needs should be analyzed, including his or her standard of living and that of any dependents. Based on these findings, a course of action can be devised that will provide the artist with an adequate retirement fund.

ESTATE PLANNING

The last major area of money management, estate planning, is concerned with the distribution of the artist's assets (after payment of all liabilities) to designated heirs. Unless an estate plan is implemented, the laws of the state in which the artist dies or owns property will dictate who will inherit the assets. The will is the legal instrument used to convey instructions regarding the distribution of the deceased party's assets. Failure to leave a will or write one properly can sometimes wreak terrible hardship on loved ones or have serious economic consequences. By the use of the marital deduction, trusts, and other legal devices, sizeable amounts of money can be diverted from federal and state taxing authorities to family and friends. In addition to economic provisions, a properly drawn will can make provisions for guardianship of minor children, specific bequests, and other extraordinary transactions, such as gifts to charities.

The attorney drafting the will should consult with the accountant and investment adviser in order to accumulate a complete set of facts about the artist's economic picture and any special bequests. The will should be reviewed annually to determine if any modifications should be made because of changed circumstances. If the artist is married, it's advisable that the spouse also execute a will.

Certain investments can influence the estate plan. For instance, life insurance is frequently used to add liquidity to an estate. Joint ownership of properties, charitable donations, and gifts are a few of the other avenues available to the financial planner in structuring the estate.

IT'S THE MONEY YOU KEEP THAT COUNTS

The artist and his or her manager or, in some cases, business manager, should approach the financial management of the artist's career with caution. This includes an awareness of the necessity of debt, its proper use and control, and keeping a watchful eye on the amount of debt and spending habits of the artist. The manager must maintain control over income and expense through budgets, profit-and-loss statements, and balance sheet. The manager's role in helping the artist accumulate wealth is aided by all these control devices.

Once there is success, there is going to be cash flow. But as any financial professional will tell you, it's not what you make that is important, it's what you keep. While tax planning and investments are important, the key to amassing wealth is a consistent ongoing program of controlling spending and developing the habit of regular saving. Odds are that, even for the most commercially popular artist, the years of earning the really big money will be limited. The artist who is ultimately most successful will be the one who has something to show for it, long after the heyday of performing is over.

24

Stardom
and Beyond

The objective of every aspiring artist is to make it to the top. There are plenty who are driven to be superstars, despite the mega-pressures and problems that ultimate status brings. As we have seen, stardom—a career of hit singles, streaks of hyper-popularity, and bursts of press and media attention—is a target that few ever actually hit. A multitude of traps and barriers, along with the unpredictability of public tastes, can suddenly stall a career despite the best efforts of an artist and manager to make the right moves up the career ladder. True stardom is reserved only for the fortunate few who possess the rare combination of unique talent, artistic and business vision, single-minded drive, willingness to adapt and grow, and most importantly, blind luck.

To illustrate these points, we have selected a handful of popular music stars who have put together careers that have spanned at least a decade. With each name, consider the early stages of their careers, the respective periods of dominance, the various phases their careers have gone through, their ability to diversify, adapt, and move into new areas, and their shared ability to sustain that most elusive quality in show business—longevity. Just as business schools and law schools teach by the case method, so should managers and artists study the careers of major stars for patterns and examples that can be adapted for their own benefit. What qualities do Bruce Springsteen, Diana Ross, Garth Brooks, Elton John, Reba McIntire, Paul McCartney, Tom Petty, Michael Jackson, Rod Stewart, Bob Seger, Aretha Franklin, and Madonna all share? Despite widely divergent styles and career paths, each has demonstrated the traits of vision, judgment, tenacity, and a willingness to change that matches the undeniable talent each possesses.

For those who have raw ability and choose to make a full-time commitment to reaching stardom and superstardom in the brutally competitive world of pop culture and commercial music, we offer words of encouragement tempered by blunt realism. Nobody has to be told that the failure rate is high. Nonetheless, too many people romanticize the business or underestimate the stress of irregular hours, constant traveling, and seemingly endless public scrutiny. Despite the increasing sophistication of artists, managers, and other industry players, too many talented people never come to terms with the cold, hard fact that entertainment is a mix of art and business, but mostly business. And just like every other business we know anything about, it is not a get-rich-quick proposition. Even for artists and managers who are grounded in reality and who have the talent and ability to do all the right things, there is still the fact of fierce competition for the scant available slots on record company and booking agency rosters and radio playlists.

Even after an artist convinces a record company, agent, publisher, and manager that his or her talents have the potential for being profitably marketed, success is still far from guaranteed. The artist and development team must still face the judgment of the public. A hit record today only makes it easier to get a fair hearing the next time out, but that's all. To stay on top, you must constantly and consistently produce results. Yesterdays seldom count. The stress created by that reality can sometimes be more than any single individual can handle while still retaining any semblance of a normal life.

And even for those who can meet the ongoing creative challenge, there are other barriers. While exceptions abound, age is still an ever-present adversary to the aspiring star, although as the baby-boom population grows older, this is less the case than it used to be. Still, the entertainment industry places a premium on youth: "You'd better make it today; tomorrow might be too late."

The changing taste of the public is another trap that has ended many a promising quest for stardom. And, as we've seen in earlier chapters, success itself can be an artist's undoing. Too much glamour, fame, and money too soon can destroy the artist unable to cope with these elements of a "success crisis."

Every successful artist should appreciate having achieved total financial security and fame, but not all do. Some are superachievers and want to scale new peaks. Yet, for those few fortunate artists who have achieved the artistic and financial fulfillment of true stardom while also holding their lives together, can there be any challenges remaining? This can be a troubling question to a superstar especially—one who, by definition, has "done it all." To hit the heights, that artist had to have a special drive that kept him or her going when others gave up. He or she must be a dreamer who seeks the unobtainable goal and is not afraid of attempting the impossible. But once the impossible *is* attained, there's a void for the artist who has never been programmed to slow down or lay back. So at this point, he or she needs new goals, new projects, and new challenges. The manager can play an important role in helping the artist begin a new journey.

While having done it all can potentially present problems, it doesn't have to. A star has all the money, contacts, and clout needed to take his or her life in any chosen direction, but the real test comes in the decisions the artist and manager make regarding how to put those resources to best use. The directions available to the star seem limitless. Of course, many choose to keep on performing, recording, and writing with the goal of expanding artistically, and their status gives them the freedom to try anything. They can choose the dates they want to play without worrying about the money involved. They have more freedom of choice in the records they'll record and release and the songs they'll write. These lucky few can pace their careers to get more enjoyment out of the things they do rather than be controlled by the pressures of having to make it.

Stardom affords the artist the capability of getting involved as an entertainment entrepreneur. Many stars have successfully launched new record labels, motion picture and recording studios, publishing firms, booking agencies, and management companies. Others have used their fame and fortune in non–show business ventures, including real estate investments. An artist's stature and financial stability also allow him or her to get involved in charities by giving benefit concerts or acting as a spokesperson for a particular cause.

Many stars use their financial security to develop themselves through other endeavors such as writing, lecturing, and travel. This also allows them the time to develop closer bonds with their families without the pressures of having to leave home for a tour or a recording date.

For those fortunate few, the best advice any manager could give to a client is simply, "Relax and enjoy whatever you decide to do." Believe it or not, such advice is not always so easy to take.

STAR MANAGERS

In Chapter 22, we saw how stardom affects an artist. We also saw how the artist's success affects another very important person, the manager. The enormous success of the artist-client also translates into star status for the manager within the power circles of the industry. When it comes to finding tomorrow's hit-makers, there is no better calling card for a manager than a client who's hot. Beyond financial rewards and respect for the manager from others in the entertainment industry, the star's manager finds a level of personal satisfaction in helping make his or her clients' hopes and dreams come true. Playing a starring role in helping your client realize his or her full potential, both as an artist and as a person, is itself an art form. No amount of money or acclaim can replace the satisfaction that comes from seeing your efforts succeed on a grand scale. That is a satisfaction not many in this world get to experience.

KNOW YOUR PRIORITIES

Now back to reality. Despite superior talent and textbook-perfect planning and execution, few artists and their managers ever achieve stardom, much less superstardom. And of those celebrities who do succeed in grabbing the gold ring, how many fall victim to the excesses and dangers created by their own success, or suddenly find their careers stuck in neutral or prematurely finished because of any number of circumstances, many of which they could not control?

Regardless of your level of success, the underlying lesson is clear. True success lies in having your priorities straight as a human being. There is no better formula for being a success as a person and an artist or manager than loving your work and giving a hundred percent to whatever you decide to pursue. Add the dimension of sharing your accomplishments with friends and family and giving back to those around you, and chances are, everything else will take care of itself. As with any other endeavor in life, the fun is in getting there.

Apart from the promise of financial reward and personal satisfaction that goes with achievement, the entertainment industry offers participants an almost undefinable feeling that causes people to do whatever is necessary just to be a part of it. The thrill of being up there onstage singing, playing, and entertaining has always been the intangible that pushes talented people to overcome obstacles and meet the challenges of making it in the music business. We hope that never changes, and we doubt it ever will. Call it "sawdust in your shoes" or the "smell of the greasepaint, the roar of the crowd"—whatever it is, it gets in your blood, quickens your pulse, and makes all the headaches seem bearable. As any artist or manager will undoubtedly tell you, "There's no business like show business."

APPENDIX 1

American Federation of Musicians (AF of M) Booking Agent Agreement

(A) **Purpose:** The American Federation of Musicians, hereinafter called "Federation," agrees to franchise the Booking Agency signatory to this Agreement, hereinafter called "Agent," to render services to members of the Federation, hereinafter called "Members," upon the terms and conditions set forth herein which are in conformity with the policy and objectives of the Federation to assure the availability to its Members of competent, fair, honest and scrupulous booking agents, to prevent unfair dealing by such agents with its Members, and to maintain wage scales for its members.

(B) **Application & Acceptance:** Agent has submitted to the Federation a completed application for a Booking Agent Agreement. Agent warrants and represents that the statements made therein are true and complete as of the date hereof.

Therefore, in consideration of the mutual covenants between them, the Federation and Agent agree as follows:

1. Federation hereby accepts the application of the Agent, and approves and franchises the Agent as qualified to act as an agent for its Members.

2. Agent shall represent and deal with Members in accordance with the terms and conditions of this Agreement.

3. Agent shall fully comply with all applicable State licensing requirements where such requirements are not in conflict with Federal law.

4. (a) **Reports to the Federation:** Agent shall promptly report to the Federation any change in the facts stated in the aforesaid application. Upon request, Agent shall promptly furnish to the Federation any information requested relating to Agent's performance of its duties hereunder and pursuant to agreements and arrangements with members.

 (b) **Agent's Responsibility**: Agent shall be responsible for any violation of this Agreement by any subsequent person, firm, partnership or corporation employed, retained or utilized by the Agent, or otherwise associated with the Agent, in representing or dealing with Members, as fully as if Agent had violated this Agreement.

5. **Agent Not Employer:** Agent shall not act as the employer of any Member for whom he or she is the agent.

6. (a) **No commissions, considerations in excess of stipulations in Schedule 1:** Agent will not charge, accept or receive from any Member any commission, including consideration in lieu of money, in excess of the commissions stipulated in Schedule 1, attached to and made a part of this Agreement, for the booking of any engagement.

(b) In no event shall the payment of any such commissions for the booking of any engagement result in the receipt of Agent commissions, including consideration in lieu of money, from any person or persons, including any Member, which in the aggregate are more than the commission stipulated in Schedule 1. Any commission, including consideration in lieu of money, received by Agent for furnishing the services of any such Member for any engagement from any source other than the Member for whom Agent renders services, shall be reported to such Member and the amount thereof shall be deducted from the commissions otherwise payable by such member.

(c) **Escrow:** Any money received by Agent as a deposit or advance from the purchaser of the services of a Member(s) shall be maintained by the Agent in a separate escrow account for the benefit of the Member(s) until completion of the engagement for which the money is received by the Agent.

(d) **Contracts must incorporate terms of this Agreement:** All agreements, contracts or arrangements between Agent and any Member for the booking of engagements for said Member shall incorporate therein each and every portion of this Agreement and, if not specifically incorporated therein, all said engagements, contracts or arrangements between Agent and any Member shall be deemed to incorporate by reference each and every provision of this Agreement. No said agreement, contract, or arrangement shall contain any provision which is in conflict with any provision of this Agreement. Any said agreement, contract, or arrangement which provides for the exclusive retaining of Agent by a Member shall not be effective until it has been submitted to and approved in writing, by the office of the President of the Federation, which approval shall not be unreasonably withheld. The provisions of this paragraph (d) shall not be applicable to said agreements, contracts or arrangements which were or are entered into between the agent and a musician while the musician was not or is not a Member of the Federation.

7. (a) **All Agreements in writing:** All engagement contracts procured by Agent providing for the performance of services by a Member for any purchaser of such services shall be in writing on the applicable, officially approved, Federation contract form, which shall be fully completed and executed; and a copy thereof shall be filed by the Agent with the Local Union affiliated with the Federation in whose territorial jurisdiction the services are to be performed.

(b) **Members must receive applicable minimum wage scale:** All such engagement contracts shall provide for retention by Members in gross monies, and/or other consideration, an amount not less than the applicable minimum wage scale (including Pension and Health and Welfare Fund contributions, if applicable) of the Federation and/or of any Local Union affiliated with the Federation in whose territorial Jurisdiction the services are to be performed. (See, also, paragraph (B) of Schedule 1 attached hereto).

8. **Federation Unfair List:** Agent shall not solicit or require members to perform services for, or on the premises of, any non-neutral purchaser of music who is listed on the Federation's Unfair List, provided that such listing is legal in accordance with the provisions of the Settlement Agreement, dated April 30, 1979.

9. **AFM Seal/Contract Forms and Non-Members:** Neither an officially approved contract form of the Federation nor the Trademark of the Federation shall be utilized by the Agent, in any manner whatsoever, in the Agent's representation of, or dealing with or for, non-members of the Federation. The Agent shall exercise reasonable care in carrying out the provisions of this paragraph.

10. **Agreement Non-Transferable:** This Agreement shall be personal to the Agent and the rights and privileges of the Agent

hereunder shall not be transferable or assignable by operation of law or otherwise without the prior consent, in writing, of the Federation. Such consent shall not be unreasonably withheld and if the consent is not granted the Federation shall furnish written reasons therefore.

(a) **Arbitration of disputes:** Except as provided in (b) or (i) below, any default, dispute, controversy, claim or difference arising between the agent and the Federation, a Local Union affiliated with the Federation, or any member of the Federation, or between the Agent and any other agent franchised by the Federation shall be submitted for a final and binding determination by the International Executive Board of the Federation (hereinunder called "IEB"), in accordance with the Rules of Practice and Procedures of the IEB, which shall contain a procedure for summary judgment with respect to allegations by the Agent that a member owes the Agent commissions. A copy of said Rules of Practice and Procedure may be obtained by written request to the Secretary- Treasurer of the Federation. The determination of the IEB shall be conclusive, final and binding on all parties; provided, however, that the termination of this Agreement, either by the Agent or the Federation, as provided in this agreement, shall not be deemed a default, dispute, controversy, claim or difference hereunder. The President of the Federation may, upon agreement of the parties render such conclusive, final and binding determination whenever, in the discretion of the President, the IEB will be unable to act with sufficient promptness under the circumstances.

(b) **Agent's claim against member:** When the Agent has a claim for commissions against a Member of the Local Union of the Federation in the territorial jurisdiction within which the Agent maintains his or her principal office, the Agent shall have the choice of either filing the claim with that Local Union or the IEB. Any such claim filed with said Local Union shall be initially adjudicated by the person, persons or body specified by the rules, Bylaws or practices of said Local Union. Any party to such Local Union adjudication may appeal from the adjudication thereof to the IEB within thirty (30) days from the date on which such party is notified of such Local Union decision or within such additional time as the President of the Federation or the IEB may specify. On such appeal, the IEB acting under its Rules of Practice and Procedure, may receive additional evidence from any party. Pending such appeal, the President of the Federation may stay the award on such terms and conditions as he or she may deem proper, including but not limited to the deposit of adequate security with the Federation. The determination of the IEB on appeal from the adjudication of such person, or persons or body shall be final and binding upon all parties. The adjudication from which an appeal is not taken to the IEB, as provided above, shall be final and binding upon all parties.

(c) **Timeliness:** No default, dispute, controversy, claim or difference shall be determined by the IEB and no claim shall be adjudicated by the Local Union, unless filed with the IEB or the Local Union within one (1) year following the occurrences of the event upon which the claim is based, except as provided in (d) or (e) below.

(d) **Acknowledgment/extension:** A written acknowledgment of any claim, dated and signed by the Member or Agent against whom such claim is asserted, shall extend the time in which such claim may be submitted for determination for a period of one (1) year following the date of such acknowledgment.

(e) **Extensions:** The delivery by the Agent of a statement of account to the Member and the failure of the Member to object thereto within the time therein prescribed, as provided in 12(a) below, shall extend the time in which any claim specified in such statement of account may be submitted for determination for a period of one (1) year following the date of mailing of such statement of account.

(f) **Penalties:** In the event that an award for money is made by either the IEB or the Local Union in accordance with the provision of this Section 10 and said money is not paid within twenty-one (21) days from the date the parties are notified of said award, six percent (6%) interest per annum shall be added to the amount of money awarded, provided that such interest shall be added only for the period of one (1) year from the date of such notification of the award or until the money is paid, whichever is shorter.

(g) **Court of appropriate jurisdiction:** The prevailing party in an arbitration case may enforce said award by bringing an action for judgment in confirmation thereof together with costs and reasonable attorneys fees incurred in enforcing the award. The action to confirm or enforce an arbitration award may be brought in courts located in New York County, New York, or in a court of appropriate jurisdiction in another State of the United States.

(h) **Direct payments/waiver:** If the agent elects to receive payment of commissions directly from a purchaser of the services of a Member, rather than from the Member, the Agent waives all right to file a claim for said commissions under the foregoing provisions of this Section 10.

(i) **American Arbitration Association:** Notwithstanding the foregoing provisions of Section 10: Should an Agent file a claim for arbitration in accordance with the Commercial Arbitration Rules of the American Arbitration Association, judgment upon an arbitration award rendered on any claim may be entered in any court having jurisdiction thereof. The Agent shall pay the full cost of such arbitration proceeding, except any costs personally incurred by a Member for himself or herself, his or her attorney or his or her own witnesses. In the event the Agent chooses to submit his or her claim under the procedures outlined in Section 10(a) through (h) above, rather than to initially submit his or her claim in accordance wit the provisions of this Subsection(i), the Agent may not thereafter proceed under this Subsection(i). Conversely, when the Agent submits a claim for arbitration in accordance with the provisions of this Subsection(i), he or she may not thereafter submit the claim under Section 10(a) through (h) above.

11. **Statement of Account Requirements:** The statement of account referred to in Section 10(e) above must comply with all of the following requirements:

(a) Such statement of account shall be rendered by the Agent to the Member at least once in each twelve (12) months' period during the term of the agreement between the Agent and the Member.

(b) Such statement of account shall be in reasonable form and detailed sufficiently to inform the recipient of (I) each receipt by the Agent in connection with performances by the Member since the date of the last such statement and the places and dates of such performances; (II) each disbursement made by the Agent to or on behalf of the Member as of date of the last such statement; and (III) the net amount owed by the Agent to the Member or by the Member to the Agent as of the date of such statement.

(c) Such statement of account shall be deemed to have been duly delivered, if mailed by certified or registered mail, return receipt requested, addressed to the Member at the address last filed by such Member with the Agent.

(d) Such statement of account shall state prominently that objection to any item therein contained shall be made, in writing, within a stated time which, in no event, shall be less than sixty (60) days following the date of the mailing of such statement; and if said objection is not made as provided in this Subsection(d), such failure to object will be deemed to be prima facie evidence that the statement of account is correct.

12. Rebooking of Steady Engagements

(a) Provided that the contract for a steady engagement indicates clearly which personnel performing said engagement are "key personnel," in the event a "Signatory Musician" to that contract or "key personnel" designated in that contract (as signed or initiated by said "key personnel") are rebooked for a steady engagement in the same location, as defined in Schedule 1(A)(i) of this Agreement, regardless of who rebooks them, within sixty (60) days (which period may be extended up to no more than one hundred and eighty (180) days if agreed in writing) of the completion of their previous engagement at that location; said "Signatory Musician" and/or "key personnel" who are rebooked shall be liable to Agent who originally booked them, for the commission on the subsequent contract in accordance with the provisions of Schedule 1 of this Agreement. The date of the rebooking is the date of signing of the subsequent contract for the engagement and the provisions of this Section 12(a) shall apply only to the first rebooking within the period set forth above.

(b) **Fees:** The Federation shall furnish to the Agent, for a fee of $100.00 per annum, a copy of each issue of the Federation's "International Musician" and a copy of the Federation's list of affiliated Local Unions, which are printed while this Agreement is in effect; and the Federation shall furnish to Agent, the certificate designating the Agent as a franchised Agent, which certificate shall be returned to the Federation in the event this Agreement and Agent's franchise are terminated in accordance with the provisions of Section 13 below.

13. Term of Agreement:

(a) This agreement shall be in full force and effect for one (1) year following the date set forth below, provided however, that Agent may terminate or cancel this Agreement, at his or her sole discretion, at any time during said one (1) year period, or during any successive one (1) year period of renewal, as set forth in (b) below, by at least thirty (30) days written notice served upon the Office of the President of the Federation by certified or registered mail, return receipt requested; and provided further, that the Federation may terminate or cancel this Agreement and its franchise to the Agent as qualified to act as an agent for its Members during said one (1) year period, or during any successive one (1) year period of renewal, as set forth in (b) below, by written notice to Agent, only when Agent, either willfully or through gross negligence, has caused any Member to suffer a monetary loss and it is reasonably foreseeable that Members who use the services of Agent may suffer a monetary loss. In the event the Federation terminates this Agreement and cancels Agent's franchise, as provided above, there shall be no requirement for the Federation to refranchise Agent at any time thereafter and if, in its sole discretion, Federation decides to refranchise Agent upon his or her reapplication, Federation may provide whatever reasonable conditions it desires upon said refranchising. Prior to the Federation terminating this Agreement and revoking its franchise with respect to an Agent, as provided above, the President of the Federation shall furnish, in writing, to said Agent notice of the Federation's intent to terminate the Agreement and revoke its franchise at least thirty (30) days in advance of said termination and revocation; and upon written request therefor furnished to the President by said Agent within ten (10) days after receipt of said notice by this Agent, the Agent shall be granted a hearing by the President, or his or her designee(s), at a date, time and place to be determined by the President in his or her sole discretion. If such hearing is requested, the Agent may be represented at said hearing by an attorney and, subsequent to said hearing, the President, or his or her designee(s), shall serve written notice upon the Agent with respect to the disposition of the matter.

(b) **Termination:** This Agreement shall automatically terminate, and Agent's franchise as qualified to act as an agent for Members of the Federation shall be automatically canceled, one (1) year from the date of this Agreement set forth below, or on any succeeding anniversary date of this Agreement unless said Agent furnishes to the Office of the President of the Federation a written request for renewal prior to the end of the first year of this Agreement and prior to the end of each one year period thereafter. The Federation shall furnish to the Agent written notice of the said termination date at least thirty (30) days prior to the said termination date. In addition, by notice, in writing, to Agent at least thirty (30) days prior to any anniversary date of this Agreement, the Federation may modify or amend this Agreement, as it deems necessary, to carry out the policy and objectives of the Federation as set forth in (A) above, and any such modification or amendments shall take effect on said anniversary date.

(c) **Failure to Renew:** If Agent fails to renew this agreement and his or her franchise, in accordance with (b) above, the Federation shall be under no requirement to refranchise the Agent or renew this agreement at any time thereafter, and if the Federation decides, in its sole discretion, to refranchise Agent and renew this Agreement upon application by Agent, the Federation may impose any reasonable conditions upon said refranchising and renewal as it deems necessary.

(d) **Termination—Agent's Loss of Rights and Privileges:** Upon termination of this Agreement and Agent's franchise, as provided above , the Agent's right, privilege and authority to represent Members shall terminate and the Agent and each and every Member shall thereby and thereupon be deemed released and discharged of and from any and all agreements, contracts and arrangements with Agent covered by this Agreement; and of and from any and all claims by Agent which relate to continuing representation of such Members by Agent following such termination; but such termination shall not affect any contracts then existing between any Member and purchaser of the services of such Member or the right of the Agent to commissions earned from services previously rendered but not yet paid at the time of such termination.

14. Court of Jurisdiction:
This Agreement has been made in the Borough of Manhattan, City of New York, New York, and shall be construed, interpreted and applied according to the laws of the State of New York. Any claim, action or cause of action arising under this agreement and brought against the Federation shall be brought only in courts located in New York County, New York.

IN WITNESS THEREOF, the parties hereto have hereunto set the hands and seals:

AGENT:

BY:

American Federation of Musicians

BY:

Date:

APPENDIX 2

AF of M Performance Contract (Local Engagements)

Whenever The Term "The Local Union" Is Used In This Contract, It Shall Mean Local Union No. _____ Of The Federation.

THIS CONTRACT for the personal services of musicians on the engagement described below is made this _____ day of _____, 19 _____, between the undersigned purchaser of music (herein called "Purchaser") and the undersigned musician or musicians.

1. Name and Address of Place of Engagement: _____

Name of Band or Group: _____

Number of Musicians: _____ Number of Vocalists: _____

2. Date (s) of Engagement; daily or weekly schedule and daily clock hours:

3. Type of Engagement (specify whether dance, stage show, banquet, etc.): _____

4. Compensation Agreed Upon: $_____
(Amount and Terms)

5. Purchaser Will Make Payments As Follows: _____
(Specify when payments are to be made)

_____ (Continued on reverse side) _____

IN WITNESS WHEREOF, the parties hereto have hereunto set their names and seals on the day and year first above written.

X	X
Print Purchaser's Full and Correct Name (If Purchaser is Corporation, Full and Correct Corporate Name)	Print Name of Signatory Musician Home Local Union No.
Signature of Purchaser (or Agent thereof)	Signature of Signatory Musician
Street Address	Musician's Home Address
City State Zip Code	City State Zip Code
Telephone	Telephone

Booking Agent   Agreement No.   Address

Names of All Musicians	Local Union No.	U.S. Social Security Nos.	Direct Pay
			$

6. No performance or rehearsal shall be recorded, reproduced or transmitted from the place of performance, in any manner or by any means whatsoever, in the absence of a specific written agreement with or approved in writing by the American Federation of Musicians ("Federation") relating to and permitting such recording, reproduction or transmission. This prohibition shall not be subject to any procedure of arbitration and the American Federation of Musicians ("Federation") may enforce this prohibition in any court of competent jurisdiction.

7. This contract, and the terms and conditions contained herein, may be enforced by the Purchaser, and its agents, and by each musician who is a party to this contract or whose name appears on the contract or who has, in fact, performed the engagement contracted for (herein called "participating musician(s)"), and by the agent or agent(s) of each participating musician, including the Local Union. It is expressly understood by the Purchaser and the musician(s) who are parties to this contract that neither the Federation nor the Local Union are parties to this contract in any capacity except as expressly provided in 6 above and, therefore, that neither the Federation nor the Local Union shall be liable for the performance or breach of any provision hereof.

8. A representative of the Local Union shall have access to the place of engagement covered by this contract for purposes of communicating with the musician (s) performing the engagement and the Purchaser.

9. ADDITIONAL PROVISIONS: _____

APPENDIX 3

AF of M Performance Contract (Touring)

Whenever The Term "The Local Union" Is Used In This Contract, It Shall Mean Local Union No. _____ Of The Federation With Jurisdiction Over The Territory In Which The Engagement Covered Is To Be Performed.

THIS CONTRACT for the personal services of musicians on the engagement described below is made this _____ day of _____, 19 _____, between the undersigned purchaser of music (herein called "Purchaser") and the undersigned musician or musicians.

1. Name and Address of Place of Engagement: _____

   Name of Band or Group: _____

   Number of Musicians: _____ Number of Vocalists: _____

2. Date (s) of Engagement; daily or weekly schedule and daily clock hours:

3. Type of Engagement (specify whether dance, stage show, banquet, etc.): _____

4. Compensation Agreed Upon: $ _____
   (Amount and Terms)

5. Purchaser Will Make Payments As Follows: _____
   (Specify when payments are to be made)

_____ *(Continued on reverse side)* _____

IN WITNESS WHEREOF, the parties hereto have hereunto set their names and seals on the day and year first above written.

Print Purchaser's Full and Correct Name
(If Purchaser is Corporation, Full and Correct Corporate Name)

Print Name of Signatory Musician   Home Local Union No.

X _____   X _____
Signature of Purchaser (or Agent thereof)   Signature of Signatory Musician

Street Address   Musician's Home Address

City   State   Zip Code   City   State   Zip Code

Telephone   Telephone

Booking Agent   Agreement No.   Address to Which Official Communications
Should Be Sent to Signatory Musician

Address

Names of All Musicians	Local Union No.	U.S. Social Security Nos.	Direct Pay
			$

6. No performance on the engagement shall be recorded, reproduced or transmitted from the place of performance, in any manner or by any means whatsoever, in the absence of a specific written agreement with the Federation relating to and permitting such recording, reproduction or transmission.

7. It is expressly understood by the Purchaser and the musician(s) who are parties to this contract that neither the Federation nor the Local Union are parties to this contract in any capacity except as expressly provided in 6 above and, therefore, that neither the Federation nor the Local Union shall be liable for the performance or breach of any provision hereof.

8. A representative of the Local Union, or the Federation, shall have access to the place of engagement covered by this contract for purposes of communicating with the musician (s) performing the engagement and the Purchaser.

9. The agreement of the musicians to perform is subject to proven detention by sickness, accidents, riots, strikes, epidemics, acts of God, or any other legitimate conditions beyond their control.

10. ADDITIONAL PROVISIONS: _____

APPENDIX 4

Broadcast Music, Inc. (BMI) Writer Agreement

BMI

BMI • *320 West 57th Street, New York, NY 10019-3790 • 212-586-2000 • FAX 212-245-8986*

Date

Dear

The following shall constitute the agreement between us:

1. As used in this agreement:

(a) The word "Period" shall mean the term from   to   ,
and continuing thereafter for additional terms of two years each unless terminated by either party at the end of said initial term or any additional term, upon notice by registered or certified mail not more than six (6) months or less than three (3) months prior to the end of any such term.

(b) The words "Work" or "Works" shall mean:

(i) All musical compositions (including the musical segments and individual compositions written for a dramatic or dramatico-musical work) composed by you alone or with one or more co-writers during the Period; and

(ii) All musical compositions (including the musical segments and individual compositions written for a dramatic or dramatico-musical work) composed by you alone or with one or more co-writers prior to the Period, except those in which there is an outstanding grant of the right of public performance to a person other than a publisher affiliated with BMI.

2. You agree that:

(a) Within ten (10) days after the execution of this agreement you will furnish to us a completed clearance form available in blank from us with respect to each Work heretofore composed by you which has been published in printed copies or recorded commercially or synchronized commercially with film or tape or which is being currently performed or which you consider as likely to be performed.

(b) In each instance that a Work for which a clearance form has not been submitted to us pursuant to sub-paragraph 2(a) is published in printed copies or recorded commercially or in synchronization with film or tape or is considered by you as likely to be performed, whether such Work is composed prior to the execution of this agreement or hereafter during the Period, you will promptly furnish to us a completed clearance form with respect to each such Work.

(c) If requested by us in writing, you will promptly furnish to us a legible lead sheet or other written or printed copy of a Work.

3. The submission of each clearance form pursuant to paragraph 2 shall constitute a warranty and representation by you that all of the information contained thereon is true and correct and that no performing rights in such Work have been granted to or reserved by others except as specifically set forth therein in connection with Works heretofore written or co-written by you.

4. Except as otherwise provided herein, you hereby grant to us for the Period:

(a) All the rights that you own or acquire publicly to perform, and to license others to perform, anywhere in the world, any part or all of the Works.

(b) The non-exclusive right to record, and to license others to record, any part or all of any of the Works on electrical transcriptions, wire, tape, film or otherwise, but only for the purpose of performing such Work publicly by means of radio and television or for archive or audition purposes. This right does not include recording for the purpose of sale to the public or for the purpose of synchronization (i) with motion pictures intended primarily for theatrical exhibition or (ii) with programs distributed by means of syndication to broadcasting stations, cable systems or other similar distribution outlets.

(c) The non-exclusive right to adapt or arrange any part or all of any of the Works for performance purposes, and to license others to do so.

5. Notwithstanding the provisions of sub-paragraph 4(a):

(a) The rights granted to us by sub-paragraph 4(a) shall not include the right to perform or license the performance of more than one song or aria from a dramatic or dramatico-musical work which is an opera, operetta or musical show or more than five (5) minutes from a dramatic or dramatico-musical work which is a ballet, if such performance is accompanied by the dramatic action, costumes or scenery of that dramatic or dramatico-musical work.

(b) You, together with all the publishers and your co-writers, if any, shall have the right jointly, by written notice to us, to exclude from the grant made by sub-paragraph 4(a) performances of Works comprising more than thirty (30) minutes of a dramatic or dramatico-musical work, but this right shall not apply to such performances from (i) a score originally written for or performed as part of a theatrical or television film, (ii) a score originally written for or performed as part of a radio or television program, or (iii) the original cast, sound track or similar album of a dramatic or dramatico-musical work.

(c) You, the publishers and/or your co-writers, if any, retain the right to issue non-exclusive licenses for performances of a Work or Works in the United States, its territories and possessions (other than to another performing rights licensing organization), provided that within ten (10) days of the issuance of such license we are given written notice thereof and a copy of the license is supplied to us.

6.   (a) As full consideration for all rights granted to us hereunder and as security therefor, we agree to pay to you, with respect to each of the Works in which we obtain and retain performing rights during the Period:

(i) For radio and television performances of a Work in the United States, its territories and possessions, amounts calculated pursuant to our then current standard practices upon the basis of the then current performance rates generally paid by us to our affiliated writers for similar performances of similar compositions. The number of performances for which you shall be entitled to payment shall be estimated by us in accordance with our then current system of computing the number of such performances.

You acknowledge that we license performances of the Works of our affiliates by means other than on radio and television, but that unless and until such time as methods are adopted for tabulation of such performances, payment will be based solely on performances in those media and locations then currently surveyed. In the event that during the Period we shall establish a system of separate payment for performances by means other than radio and television, we shall pay you upon the basis of the then current performance rates generally paid by us to our other affiliated writers for similar performances of similar compositions.

(ii) In the case of a Work composed by you with one or more co-writers, the sum payable to you hereunder shall be a pro rata share, determined on the basis of the number of co-writers, unless you shall have transmitted to us a copy of an agreement between you and your co-writers providing for a different division of payment.

(iii) Monies received by us from any performing rights licensing organization outside of the United States, its territories and possessions, which are designated by such performing rights licensing organization as the author's share of foreign performance royalties earned by your Works after the deduction of our then current handling charge applicable to our affiliated writers and in accordance with our then current standard practices of payment for such performances.

(b) Notwithstanding the provisions of sub-paragraph 6(a), we shall have no obligation to make payment hereunder with respect to (i) any performance of a Work which occurs prior to the date on which we have received from you all of the information and material with respect to such Work which is referred to in paragraphs 2 and 3, or (ii) any performance of a Work as to which a direct license as described in sub-paragraph 5(c) has been granted by you, your co-writers, if any, or the publishers, or (iii) any performance for which no license fee shall be collected by us, or (iv) any performance of a Work which you claim was either omitted from or miscalculated on a royalty statement and for which we shall not have received written notice from you of such claimed omission or miscalculation within nine (9) months of the date of such statement.

7. In accordance with our then current standard practices, we will furnish periodic statements to you during each year of the Period showing the monies due pursuant to sub-paragraph 6(a). Each such statement shall be accompanied by payment of the sum thereby shown to be due you, subject to all proper deductions, if any, for taxes, advances or amounts due BMI from you.

8.   (a) Nothing in this agreement requires us to continue to license the Works subsequent to the termination of this agreement. In the event that we continue to license your interest in any Work, however, we shall continue to make payments to you for such Work for so long as you do not make or purport to make directly or indirectly any grant of performing rights in such Work to any other licensing organization. The amounts of such payments shall be calculated pursuant to our then current standard practices upon the basis of the then current performance rates generally paid by us to our affiliated writers for similar performances of similar compositions. You agree to notify us by registered or certified mail of any grant or purported grant by you directly or indirectly of performing rights to any other performing rights organization within ten (10) days from the making of such grant or purported grant and if you fail so to inform us thereof and we make payments to you for any period after the making of any such grant or purported grant, you agree to repay to us all amounts so paid by us promptly with or without demand by us. In addition, if we inquire of you by registered or certified mail, addressed to your last known address, whether you have made any such grant or purported grant and you fail to confirm to us by registered or certified mail within thirty (30) days of the mailing of such inquiry that you have not made any such grant or purported grant, we may, from and after such date, discontinue making any payments to you.

(b) Our obligation to continue payment to you after the termination of this agreement for performances outside of the United States, its territories and possessions, of Works which BMI continues to license after such termination shall be dependent upon our receipt in the United States of payments designated by foreign performing rights organizations as the author's share of foreign performance royalties earned by your Works. Payment of such foreign royalties shall be subject to deduction of our then current handling charge applicable to our affiliated writers and shall be in accordance with our then current standard practices of payment for such performances.

(c) In the event that we have reason to believe that you will receive, are entitled to receive, or are receiving payment from a performing rights licensing organization other than BMI for or based on United States performances of one or more of your Works during a period when such Works were licensed by us pursuant to this agreement, we shall have the right to withhold payment for such performances from you until receipt of evidence satisfactory to us that you were not or will not be so paid by such other organization. In the event that you were or will be so paid or do not supply such evidence within eighteen (18) months from the date of our request therefor, we shall be under no obligation to make any payment to you for performances of such Works during such period.

9. In the event that this agreement shall terminate at a time when, after crediting all earnings reflected by statements rendered to you prior to the effective date of such termination, there remains an unearned balance of advances paid to you by us, such termination shall not be effective until the close of the calendar quarterly period during which (a) you shall repay such unearned balance of advances, or (b) you shall notify us by registered or certified mail that you have received a statement rendered by us at our normal accounting time showing that such unearned balance of advances has been fully recouped by us.

10. You warrant and represent that you have the right to enter into this agreement; that you are not bound by any prior commitments which conflict with your commitments hereunder; that each of the Works, composed by you alone or with one or more co-writers, is original; and that exercise of the rights granted by you herein will not constitute an infringement of copyright or violation of any other right of, or unfair competition with, any person, firm or corporation. You agree to indemnify and hold harmless us, our licensees, the advertisers of our licensees and their respective agents, servants and employees from and against any and all loss or damage resulting from any claim of whatever nature arising from or in connection with the exercise of any of the rights granted by you in this agreement. Upon notification to us or any of the other parties herein indemnified of a claim with respect to any of the Works, we shall have the right to exclude such Work from this agreement and/or to withhold payment of all sums which become due pursuant to this agreement or any modification thereof until receipt of satisfactory written evidence that such claim has been withdrawn, settled or adjudicated.

11. (a) We shall have the right, upon written notice to you, to exclude from this agreement, at any time, any Work which in our opinion is similar to a previously existing composition and might constitute a copyright infringement, or has a title or music or lyric similar to that of a previously existing composition and might lead to a claim of unfair competition.

(b) In the case of Works which in our opinion are based on compositions in the public domain, we shall have the right, upon written notice to you, either (i) to exclude any such Work from this agreement, or (ii) to classify any such Work as entitled to receive only a fraction of the full credit that would otherwise be given for performances thereof.

(c) In the event that any Work is excluded from this agreement pursuant to paragraph 10 or sub-paragraph 11(a) or (b), all rights in such Work shall automatically revert to you ten (10) days after the date of our notice to you of such exclusion. In the event that a Work is classified for less than full credit under sub-paragraph 11(b)(ii), you shall have the right, by giving notice to us, within ten (10) days after the date of our notice advising you of the credit allocated to the Work, to terminate our rights therein, and all rights in such Work shall thereupon revert to you.

12. In each instance that you write, or are employed or commissioned by a motion picture producer to write, during the Period, all or part of the score of a motion picture intended primarily for exhibition in theaters, or by the producer of a musical show or revue for the legitimate stage to write, during the Period, all or part of the musical compositions contained therein, we agree, on request, to advise the producer of the film that such part of the score as is written by you may be performed as part of the exhibition of said film in theaters in the United States, its territories and possessions, without compensation to us, or to the producer of the musical show or revue that your compositions embodied therein may be performed on the stage with living artists as part of such musical show or revue, without compensation to us. In the event that we notify you that we have established a system for the collection of royalties for performance of the scores of motion picture films in theaters in the United States, its territories and possessions, we shall no longer be obligated to take such action with respect to motion picture scores.

13. You make, constitute and appoint us, or our nominee, your true and lawful attorney, irrevocably during the Period, in our name or that of our nominee, or in your name, or otherwise, in our sole judgment, to do all acts, take all proceedings, execute, acknowledge and deliver any and all instruments, papers, documents, process or pleadings that, in our sole judgment, may be necessary, proper or expedient to restrain infringement of and/or to enforce and protect the rights granted by you hereunder, and to recover damages in respect to or for the infringement or other violation of said rights, and in our sole judgment to join you and/or others in whose names the copyrights to any of the Works may stand; to discontinue, compromise or refer to arbitration, any such actions or proceedings or to make any other disposition of the disputes in relation to the Works, provided that any action or proceeding commenced by us pursuant to the provisions of this paragraph shall be at our sole expense and for our sole benefit. Notwithstanding the foregoing, nothing in this paragraph 13 requires us to take any proceeding or other action against any person, firm, partnership or other entity or any writer or publisher, whether or not affiliated with us, who you claim may be infringing your Works or otherwise violating the rights granted by you hereunder. In addition, you understand and agree that the licensing by us of any musical compositions which you claim may be infringing your Works or otherwise violating the rights granted by you hereunder, shall not constitute an infringement of your Works on our part.

14. BMI shall have the right, in its sole discretion, to terminate this agreement on at least thirty (30) days' notice by registered or certified mail if you, your agents, employees or representatives, directly or indirectly, solicit or accept payment from writers for composing music for lyrics or writing lyrics to music or for reviewing, publishing, promoting, recording or rendering other services connected with the exploitation of any composition, or permit use of your name or your affiliation with us in connection with any of the foregoing. In the event of such termination no payments shall be due to you pursuant to paragraph 8.

15. No monies due or to become due to you shall be assignable, whether by way of assignment, sale or power granted to an attorney-in-fact, without our prior written consent. If any assignment of such monies is made by you without such prior written consent, no rights of any kind against us will be acquired by the assignee, purchaser or attorney-in-fact.

16. In the event that during the Period (a) mail addressed to you at the last address furnished by you pursuant to paragraph 20 shall be returned by the post office, or (b) monies shall not have been earned by you pursuant to paragraph 6 for a period of two consecutive years or more, or (c) you shall die, BMI shall have the right to terminate this agreement on at least thirty (30) days' notice by registered or certified mail addressed to the last address furnished by you pursuant to paragraph 20 and, in the case of your death, to the representative of your estate, if known to BMI. In the event of such termination no payments shall be due to you pursuant to paragraph 8.

17. You acknowledge that the rights obtained by you pursuant to this agreement constitute rights to payment of money and that during the Period we shall hold title to the performing rights granted to us hereunder. In the event that during the Period you shall file a petition in bankruptcy, such a petition shall be filed against you, you shall make an assignment for the benefit of creditors, you shall consent to the appointment of a receiver or trustee for all or part of your property, or you shall institute or shall have instituted against you any other insolvency proceeding under the United States bankruptcy laws or any other applicable law, we shall retain title to the performing rights in all Works the rights to which are granted to us hereunder and shall subrogate your trustee in bankruptcy or receiver and any subsequent purchasers from them to your right to payment of money for said Works in accordance with the terms and conditions of this agreement.

18. (a) You hereby authorize us to negotiate for and collect royalties or monies to which you may become entitled as a writer pursuant to the Audio Home Recording Act of 1992 and/or any amendments thereto or substitutions therefor and, to the extent possible, collect for and distribute to you royalties arising from or as compensation for home recording in countries outside the United States, its territories and possessions. This authorization with respect to royalties and monies under the Audio Home Recording Act of 1992 may be revoked by you at the end of any calendar year on prior written notice by you to us by registered or certified mail. Such revocation shall be effective beginning with the calendar year subsequent to the time of notice and shall in no way affect the Period of this agreement with respect to any of the other rights granted to BMI by you hereunder.

(b) We agree to distribute to you royalties and monies collected by us pursuant to the authorization granted in sub-paragraph 18(a), pursuant to our then prevailing practices, including deduction of our expenses therefor.

19. All disputes of any kind, nature or description arising in connection with the terms and conditions of this agreement shall be submitted to the American Arbitration Association in New York, New York, for arbitration under its then prevailing rules, the arbitrator(s) to be selected as follows: Each of us shall, by written notice to the other, have the right to appoint one arbitrator. If, within ten (10) days following the giving of such notice by one of us, the other shall not, by written notice, appoint another arbitrator, the first arbitrator shall be the sole arbitrator. If two arbitrators are so appointed, they shall appoint a third arbitrator. If ten (10) days elapse after the appointment of the second arbitrator and the two arbitrators are unable to agree upon the third arbitrator, then either of us may, in writing, request the American Arbitration Association to appoint the third arbitrator. The award made in the arbitration shall be binding and conclusive on both of us and shall include the fixing of the costs, expenses and reasonable attorneys' fees of arbitration, which shall be borne by the unsuccessful party. Judgment may be entered in New York State Supreme Court or any other court having jurisdiction.

20. You agree to notify our Department of Writer/Publisher Administration promptly in writing of any change in your address. Any notice sent to you pursuant to the terms of this agreement shall be valid if addressed to you at the last address so furnished by you.

21. This agreement constitutes the entire agreement between you and us, cannot be changed except in a writing signed by you and us and shall be governed and construed pursuant to the laws of the State of New York.

22. In the event that any part or parts of this agreement are found to be void by a court of competent jurisdiction, the remaining part or parts shall nevertheless be binding with the same force and effect as if the void part or parts were deleted from this agreement.

Very truly yours,

BROADCAST MUSIC, INC.

ACCEPTED AND AGREED TO:

By...

Vice President

....

APPENDIX 5

Songwriters Guild of America Writer-Publisher Contract

NOTE TO SONGWRITERS: (A) DO NOT SIGN THIS CONTRACT IF IT HAS ANY CHANGES UNLESS YOU HAVE FIRST DISCUSSED SUCH CHANGES WITH THE GUILD; (B) FOR YOUR PROTECTION PLEASE SEND A FULLY EXECUTED COPY OF THIS CONTRACT TO THE GUILD.

POPULAR SONGWRITERS CONTRACT
© Copyright 1978 AGAC

AGREEMENT made this .... day of .... , 19 .... , between

....

(hereinafter called "Publisher") and ....

....

(Jointly and/or severally hereinafter collectively called "Writer"):

WITNESSETH:

Composition
(Insert title
of composition→
here)
1. The Writer hereby assigns, transfers and delivers to the Publisher a certain heretofore unpublished original musical composition, written and/or composed by the above-named Writer now entitled .... (hereinafter referred to as "the composition"), including the title, words and music thereof, and the right to secure copyright therein throughout the entire world, and to have and to hold the said copyright and all rights of whatsoever nature thereunder existing, for

(Insert number
of years here)
.... years from the date of this contract or 35 years from the date of the first release of a *not more than 40* commercial sound recording of the composition, whichever term ends earlier, unless this contract is sooner terminated in accordance with the provisions hereof.

Performing
Rights Affiliation
(Delete Two) —→
2. In all respects this contract shall be subject to any existing agreements between the parties hereto and the following small performing rights licensing organization with which Writer and Publisher are affiliated: (ASCAP, BMI, SESAC). Nothing contained herein shall, or shall be deemed to, alter, vary or modify the rights of Writer and Publisher to share in, receive and retain the proceeds distributed to them by such small performing rights licensing organization pursuant to their respective agreement with it.

Warranty
3. The Writer hereby warrants that the composition is his sole, exclusive and original work, that he has full right and power to make this contract, and that there exists no adverse claim to or in the composition, except as aforesaid in Paragraph 2 hereof and except such rights as are specifically set forth in Paragraph 23 hereof.

Royalties
4. In consideration of this contract, the Publisher agrees to pay the Writer as follows:

(Insert amount
of advance here) ——→
(a) $..................... as an advance against royalties, receipt of which is hereby acknowledged, which sum shall remain the property of the Writer and shall be deductible only from payments hereafter becoming due the Writer under this contract.

Piano Copies
(b) In respect of regular piano copies sold and paid for in the United States and Canada, the following royalties per copy:

Sliding Scale
(Insert percentage here)
..........% (in no case, however, less than 10%) of the wholesale selling price of the first 200,000 copies or less; plus
..........% (in no case, however, less than 12%) of the wholesale selling price of copies in excess of 200,000 and not exceeding 500,000; plus
..........% (in no case, however, less than 15%) of the wholesale selling price of copies in excess of 500,000.

Foreign Royalties
(Insert percentage here)
(c) ....% (in no case, however, less than 50%) of all net sums received by the Publisher in respect of regular piano copies, orchestrations, band arrangements, octavos, quartets, arrangements for combinations of voices and/or instruments, and/or other copies of the composition sold in any country other than the United States and Canada, provided, however, that if the Publisher should sell such copies through, or cause them to be sold by, a subsidiary or affiliate which is actually doing business in a foreign country, then in respect of such sales, the Publisher shall pay to the Writer not less than 5% of the marked retail selling price in respect of each such copy sold and paid for.

Orchestrations and
Other Arrangements,
etc.

(Insert percentage here) ——→
(d) In respect of each copy sold and paid for in the United States and Canada, or for export from the United States, of orchestrations, band arrangements, octavos, quartets, arrangements for combinations of voices and/or instruments, and/or other copies of the composition (other than regular piano copies) the following royalties on the wholesale selling price (after trade discounts, if any):
..........% (in no case, however, less than 10%) on the first 200,000 copies or less; plus
..........% (in no case, however, less than 12%) on all copies in excess of 200,000 and not exceeding 500,000; plus
..........% (in no case, however, less than 15%) on all copies in excess of 500,000.

Publisher's
Song Book,
Folio, etc.
(e) (i) If the composition, or any part thereof, is included in any song book, folio or similar publication issued by the Publisher containing at least four, but not more than twenty-five musical compositions, the royalty to be paid by the Publisher to the Writer shall be an amount determined by dividing 10% of the wholesale selling price (after trade discounts, if any) of the copies sold, among the total number of the Publisher's copyrighted musical compositions included in such publication. If such publication contains more than twenty-five musical compositions, the said 10% shall be increased by an additional ½% for each additional musical composition.

Licensee's
Song Book,
Folio, etc.
(ii) If, pursuant to a license granted by the Publisher to a licensee not controlled by or affiliated with it, the composition, or any part thereof, is included in any song book, folio or similar publication, containing at least four musical compositions, the royalty to be paid by the Publisher to the Writer shall be that proportion of 50% of the gross amount received by it from the licensee, as the number of uses of the composition under the license and during the license period, bears to the total number of uses of the Publisher's copyrighted musical compositions under the license and during the license period.

(iii) In computing the number of the Publisher's copyrighted musical compositions under subdivisions (i) and (ii) hereof, there shall be excluded musical compositions in the public domain and arrangements thereof and those with respect to which the Publisher does not currently publish and offer for sale regular piano copies.

(iv) Royalties on publications containing less than four musical compositions shall be payable at regular piano copy rates.

Professional
Material and
Free Copies
(f) As to "professional material" not sold or resold, no royalty shall be payable. Free copies of the lyrics of the composition shall not be distributed except under the following conditions: (i) with the Writer's written consent; or (ii) when printed without music in limited numbers for charitable, religious or governmental purposes, if no profit is derived, directly or indirectly; or (iii) when authorized for printing in a book, magazine or periodical, where such use is incidental to a novel or story (as distinguished from use in a book of lyrics or a lyric magazine or folio), provided that any such use shall bear the Writer's name and the proper copyright notice; or (iv) when distributed solely for the purpose of exploiting the composition, provided, that such exploitation is restricted to the distribution of limited numbers of such copies for the purpose of influencing the sale of the composition, that the distribution is independent of the sale of any other musical compositions, services, goods, wares or merchandise, and that no profit is made, directly or indirectly, in connection therewith.

Mechanicals, (g) ....% (in no case, however, less than 50%) of:
Electrical **(Insert** All gross receipts of the Publisher in respect of any licenses (including statutory royalties) authorizing the manufac-
Transcription, **percentage** ture of parts of instruments serving to mechanically reproduce the composition, or to use the composition in synchroni-
Synchronization, **here)** zation with sound motion pictures, or to reproduce it upon electrical transcription for broadcasting purposes; and of any
All Other Rights and all gross receipts of the Publisher from any other source or right now known or which may hereafter come into
existence, except as provided in paragraph 2.

Licensing (h) If the Publisher administers licenses authorizing the manufacture of parts of instruments serving to mechanically
Agent's reproduce said composition, or the use of said composition in synchronization or in timed relation with sound motion
Charges pictures or its reproduction upon electrical transcriptions, or any of them, through an agent, trustee or other administrator acting for a substantial part of the industry and not under the exclusive control of the Publisher (hereinafter
sometimes referred to as licensing agent), the Publisher, in determining his receipts, shall be entitled to deduct from
gross license fees paid by the Licensees, a sum equal to the charges paid by the Publisher to said licensing agent,
provided, however, that in respect to synchronization or timed relation with sound motion pictures, said deduction shall
in no event exceed $150.00 or 10% of said gross license fee, whichever is less; in connection with the manufacture of
parts of instruments serving to mechanically reproduce said composition, said deductions shall not exceed 5% of said
gross license fee; and in connection with electrical transcriptions, said deduction shall not exceed 10% of said gross
license fee.

Block Licenses (i) The Publisher agrees that the use of the composition will not be included in any bulk or block license heretofore or
hereafter granted, and that it will not grant any bulk or block license to include the same, without the written consent of
the Writer in each instance, except (i) that the Publisher may grant such licenses with respect to electrical transcription
for broadcasting purposes, but in such event, the Publisher shall pay to the Writer that proportion of 50% of the gross
amount received by it under each such license as the number of uses of the composition under each such license period
bears to the total number of uses of the Publisher's copyrighted musical compositions under
each such license during each such license period; in computing the number of the Publisher's copyrighted musical
compositions for this purpose, there shall be excluded musical compositions in the public domain and arrangements
thereof and those with respect to which the Publisher does not currently publish and offer for sale regular piano copies;
(ii) that the Publisher may appoint agents or representatives in countries outside of the United States and Canada to use
and to grant licenses for the use of the composition on the customary royalty fee basis under which the Publisher shall
receive not less than 10% of the marked retail selling price in respect of regular piano copies, and 50% of all other
revenue; if, in connection with any such bulk or block license, the Publisher shall have received any advance, the Writer
shall not be entitled to share therein, but no part of said advance shall be deducted in computing the composition's
earnings under said bulk or block license. A bulk or block license shall be deemed to mean any license or agreement,
domestic or foreign, whereby rights are granted in respect of two or more musical compositions.

Television and New Uses (j) Except to the extent that the Publisher and Writer have heretofore or may hereafter assign to or vest in the small
performing rights licensing organization with which Writer and Publisher are affiliated, the said rights or the right to
grant licenses therefor, it is agreed that no licenses shall be granted without the written consent, in each instance, of the
Writer for the use of the composition by means of television, or by any means, or for any purposes not commercially
established, or for which licenses were not granted by the Publisher on musical compositions prior to June 1, 1937.

Writer's Consent (k) The Publisher shall not, without the written consent of the Writer in each case, give or grant any right or license (i) to use
to Licenses the title of the composition, or (ii) for the exclusive use of the composition in any form or for any purpose, or for any
period of time, or for any territory, other than its customary arrangements with foreign publishers, or (iii) to give a
dramatic representation of the composition or to dramatize the plot or story thereof, or (iv) for a vocal rendition of the
composition in synchronization with sound motion pictures, or (v) for any synchronization use thereof, or (vi) for the use
of the composition or a quotation or excerpt therefrom in any article, book, periodical, advertisement or other similar
publication. If, however, the Publisher shall give to the Writer written notice by certified mail, return receipt requested,
or telegram, specifying the right or license to be given or granted, the name of the licensee and the terms and conditions
thereof, including the price or other compensation to be received therefor, then, unless the Writer (or any one or more of
them) shall, within five business days after the delivery of such notice to the address of the Writer hereinafter designated,
object thereto, the Publisher may grant such right or license in accordance with the said notice without first obtaining the
consent of the Writer. Such notice shall be deemed sufficient if sent to the Writer at the address or addresses hereinafter
designated or at the address or addresses last furnished to the Publisher in writing by the Writer.

Trust for Writer (l) Any portion of the receipts which may become due to the Writer from license fees (in excess of offsets), whether
received directly from the licensee or from any licensing agent of the Publisher, shall, if not paid immediately on the
receipt thereof by the Publisher, belong to the Writer and shall be held in trust for the Writer until payment is made; the
ownership of said trust fund by the Writer shall not be questioned whether the monies are physically segregated or not.

Writer (m) The Publisher agrees that it will not issue any license as a result of which it will receive any financial benefit in which the
Participation Writer does not participate.

Writer (n) On all regular piano copies, orchestrations, band or other arrangements, octavos, quartets, commercial sound recordings
Credit and other reproductions of the composition or parts thereof, in whatever form and however produced, Publisher shall
include or cause to be included, in addition to the copyright notice, the name of the Writer, and Publisher shall include a
similar requirement in every license or authorization issued by it with respect to the composition.

Writers' 5. Whenever the term "Writer" is used herein, it shall be deemed to mean all of the persons herein defined as "Writer" and any
Respective and all royalties herein provided to be paid to the Writer shall be paid equally to such persons if there be more than one, unless
Shares otherwise provided in Paragraph 23.

Release of 6. (a) (i) The Publisher shall, within....................months from the date of this contract (the "initial period"), cause a
Commercial Sound commercial sound recording of the composition to be made and released in the customary form and through the customary commercial
Recording channels. If at the end of such initial period a sound recording has not been made and released, as above provided, then, subject to the
(Insert period not provisions of the next succeeding subdivision, this contract shall terminate.
exceeding 12 months)

(Insert amount to be not (ii) If, prior to the expiration of the initial period, Publisher pays the Writer the sum of $........(which shall not be charged
less than $250) against or recoupable out of any advances, royalties or other monies theretofor paid, then due, or which thereafter may become due the
(Insert period not Writer from the Publisher pursuant to this contract or otherwise), Publisher shall have an additional............months (the "additional
exceeding six months) period") commencing with the end of the initial period, within which to cause such commercial sound recording to be made and
released as provided in subdivision (i) above. If at the end of the additional period a commercial sound recording has not been made and
released, as above provided, then this contract shall terminate.

(iii) Upon termination pursuant to this Paragraph 6(a), all rights of any and every nature in and to the composition and in
and to any and all copyrights secured thereon in the United States and throughout the world shall automatically re-vest in and become
the property of the Writer and shall be reassigned to him by the Publisher. The Writer shall not be obligated to return or pay to the
Publisher any advance or indebtedness as a condition of such re-assignment; the said re-assignment shall be in accordance with and
subject to the provisions of Paragraph 8 hereof, and, in addition, the Publisher shall pay to the Writer all gross sums which it has
theretofore or may thereafter receive in respect of the composition.

Writer's Copies (b) The Publisher shall furnish, or cause to be furnished, to the Writer six copies of the commercial sound recording referred to in Paragraph 6(a).

Piano Copies, Piano Arrangement or Lead Sheet (Select (i) or (ii)) (c) The Publisher shall

□ (i) within 30 days after the initial release of a commercial sound recording of the composition, make, publish and offer for sale regular piano copies of the composition in the form and through the channels customarily employed by it for that purpose;

□ (ii) within 30 days after execution of this contract make a piano arrangement or lead sheet of the composition and furnish six copies thereof to the Writer.

In the event neither subdivision (i) nor (ii) of this subparagraph (c) is selected, the provisions of subdivision (ii) shall be automatically deemed to have been selected by the parties.

Foreign Copyright 7. (a) Each copyright on the composition in countries other than the United States shall be secured only in the name of the Publisher, and the Publisher shall not at any time divest itself of said foreign copyright directly or indirectly.

Foreign Publication (b) No rights shall be granted by the Publisher in the composition to any foreign publisher or licensee inconsistent with the terms hereof, nor shall any foreign publication rights in the composition be given to a foreign publisher or licensee unless and until the Publisher shall have complied with the provisions of Paragraph 6 hereof.

Foreign Advance (c) If foreign rights in the composition are separately conveyed, otherwise than as a part of the Publisher's current and/or future catalog, not less than 50% of any advance received in respect thereof shall be credited to the account of and paid to the Writer.

Foreign Percentage (d) The percentage of the Writer on monies received from foreign sources shall be computed on the Publisher's net receipts, provided, however, that no deductions shall be made for offsets of monies due from the Publisher to said foreign sources; or for advances made by such foreign sources to the Publisher, unless the Writer shall have received at least 50% of said advances.

No Foreign Allocations (e) In computing the receipts of the Publisher from licenses granted in respect of synchronization with sound motion pictures, or in respect of any world-wide licenses, or in respect of licenses granted by the Publisher for use of the composition in countries other than the United States, no amount shall be deducted for payments or allocations to publishers or licensees in such countries.

Termination or Expiration of Contract 8. Upon the termination or expiration of this contract, all rights of any and every nature in and to the composition and in and to any and all copyrights secured thereon in the United States and throughout the world, shall re-vest in and become the property of the Writer, and shall be re-assigned to the Writer by the Publisher free of any and all encumbrances of any nature whatsoever, provided that:

(a) If the Publisher, prior to such termination or expiration, shall have granted a domestic license for the use of the composition, not inconsistent with the terms and provisions of this contract, the re-assignment may be subject to the terms of such license.

(b) Publisher shall assign to the Writer all rights which it may have under any such agreement or license referred to in subdivision (a) in respect of the composition, including, but not limited to, the right to receive all royalties or other monies earned by the composition thereunder after the date of termination or expiration of this contract. Should the Publisher thereafter receive or be credited with any royalties or other monies so earned, it shall pay the same to the Writer.

(c) The Writer shall not be obligated to return or pay to the Publisher any advance or indebtedness as a condition of the re-assignment provided for in this Paragraph 8, and shall be entitled to receive the plates and copies of the composition in the possession of the Publisher.

(d) Publisher shall pay any and all royalties which may have accrued to the Writer prior to such termination or expiration.

(e) The Publisher shall execute any and all documents and do any and all acts or things necessary to effect any and all re-assignments to the Writer herein provided for.

Negotiations for New or Unspecified Uses 9. If the Publisher desires to exercise a right in and to the composition now known or which may hereafter become known, but for which no specific provision has been made herein, the Publisher shall give written notice to the Writer thereof. Negotiations respecting all the terms and conditions of any such disposition shall thereupon be entered into between the Publisher and the Writer and no such right shall be exercised until specific agreement has been made.

Royalty Statements and Payments 10. The Publisher shall render to the Writer, hereafter, royalty statements accompanied by remittance of the amount due at the times such statements and remittances are customarily rendered by the Publisher, provided, however, that such statements and remittances shall be rendered either semi-annually or quarterly and not more than forty-five days after the end of each such semi-annual or quarterly period, as the case may be. The Writer may at any time, or from time to time, make written request for a detailed royalty statement, and the Publisher shall, within sixty days, comply therewith. Such royalty statements shall set forth in detail the various items, foreign and domestic, for which royalties are payable thereunder and the amounts thereof, including, but not limited to, the number of copies sold and the number of uses made in each royalty category. If a use is made in a publication of the character provided in Paragraph 4, subdivision (e) hereof, there shall be included in said royalty statement the title of said publication, the publisher or issuer thereof, the date of and number of uses, the gross license fee received in connection with each publication, the share thereto of all the writers under contract with the Publisher, and the Writer's share thereof. There shall likewise be included in said statement a description of every other use of the composition, and if by a licensee or licensees their name or names, and if said use is upon a part of an instrument serving to reproduce the composition mechanically, the type of mechanical reproduction, the title of the label thereon, the name or names of the artists performing the same, together with the gross license fees received, and the Writer's share thereof.

Examination of Books 11. (a) The Publisher shall from time to time, upon written demand of the Writer or his representative, permit the Writer or his representative to inspect at the place of business of the Publisher, all books, records and documents relating to the composition and all licenses granted, uses had and payments made therefor, such right of inspection to include, but not by way of limitation, the right to examine all original accountings and records relating to uses and payments by manufacturers of commercial sound recordings and music rolls; and the Writer or his representative may appoint an accountant who shall at any time during usual business hours have access to all records of the Publisher relating to the composition for the purpose of verifying royalty statements rendered or which are delinquent under the terms hereof.

(b) The Publisher shall, upon written demand of the Writer or his representative, cause any licensing agent in the United States and Canada to furnish to the Writer or his representative, statements showing in detail all licenses granted, uses had and payments made in connection with the composition, which licenses or permits were granted, or payments were received, by or through said licensing agent, and to permit the Writer or his representative to inspect at the place of business of such licensing agent, all books, records and documents of such licensing agent, relating thereto. Any and all agreements made by the Publisher with any such licensing agent shall provide that any such licensing agent will comply with the terms and provisions hereof. In the event that the Publisher shall instruct such licensing agent to furnish to the Writer or his representative statements as provided for herein, and to permit the inspection of the books, records and documents as herein provided, then if such licensing agent should refuse to comply with the said instructions, or any of them, the Publisher agrees to institute and prosecute diligently and in good faith such action or proceedings as may be necessary to compel compliance with the said instructions.

(c) With respect to foreign licensing agents, the Publisher shall make available the books or records of said licensing agents in countries outside of the United States and Canada to the extent such books or records are available to the Publisher, except that the Publisher may in lieu thereof make available any accountants' reports and audits which the Publisher is able to obtain.

(d) If as a result of any examination of books, records or documents pursuant to Paragraphs 11(a), 11(b) or 11(c) hereof, it is determined that, with respect to any royalty statement rendered by or on behalf of the Publisher to the Writer, the Writer is owed a sum equal to or greater than five percent of the sum shown on that royalty statement as being due to the Writer, then the Publisher shall pay to the Writer the entire cost of such examination, not to exceed 50% of the amount shown to be due the Writer.

(e) (i) In the event the Publisher administers its own licenses for the manufacture of parts of instruments serving to mechanically reproduce the composition rather than employing a licensing agent for that purpose, the Publisher shall include in each license agreement a provision permitting the Publisher, the Writer or their respective representatives to inspect, at the place of business of such licensee, all books, records and documents of such licensee relating to such license. Within 30 days after written demand by the Writer, the Publisher shall commence to inspect such licensee's books, records and documents and shall furnish a written report of such inspection to the Writer within 90 days following such demand. If the Publisher fails, after written demand by the Writer, to so inspect the licensee's books, records and documents, or fails to furnish such report, the Writer or his representative may inspect such licensee's books, records and documents at his own expense.

(ii) In the further event that the Publisher and the licensee referred to in subdivision (i) above are subsidiaries or affiliates of the same entity or one is a subsidiary or affiliate of the other, then, unless the Publisher employs a licensing agent to administer the licenses referred to in subdivision (i) above, the Writer shall have the right to make the inspection referred to in subdivision (i) above without the necessity of making written demand on the Publisher as provided in subdivision (i) above.

(iii) If as a result of any inspection by the Writer pursuant to subdivisions (i) and (ii) of this subparagraph (e) the Writer recovers additional monies from the licensee, the Publisher and the Writer shall share equally in the cost of such inspection.

Default in Payment or Prevention of Examination

12. If the Publisher shall fail or refuse, within sixty days after written demand, to furnish or cause to be furnished, such statements, books, records or documents, or to permit inspection thereof, as provided for in Paragraphs 10 and 11 hereof, or within thirty days after written demand, to make the payment of any royalties due under this contract, then the Writer shall be entitled, upon ten days' written notice, to terminate this contract. However if the Publisher shall:

(a) Within the said ten-day period serve upon the Writer a written notice demanding arbitration; and

(b) Submit to arbitration its claim that it has complied with its obligation to furnish statements, books, records or documents, or permitted inspection thereof or to pay royalties, as the case may be, or both, and thereafter comply with any award of the arbitrator within ten days after such award or within such time as the arbitrator may specify;

then this contract shall continue in full force and effect as if the Writer had not sent such notice of termination. If the Publisher shall fail to comply with the foregoing provisions, then this contract shall be deemed to have been terminated as of the date of the Writer's written notice of termination.

Derivative Works

13. No derivative work prepared under authority of Publisher during the term of this contract may be utilized by Publisher or any other party after termination or expiration of this contract.

Notices

14. All written demands and notices provided for herein shall be sent by certified mail, return receipt requested.

Suits for Infringement

15. Any legal action brought by the Publisher against any alleged infringer of the composition shall be initiated and prosecuted at its sole cost and expense, but if the Publisher should fail, within thirty days after written demand, to institute such action, the Writer shall be entitled to institute such suit at his cost and expense. All sums recovered as a result of any such action shall, after the deduction of the reasonable expense thereof, be divided equally between the Publisher and the Writer. No settlement of any such action may be made by either party without first notifying the other; in the event that either party should object to such settlement, then such settlement shall not be made if the party objecting assumes the prosecution of the action and all expenses thereof, except that any sums thereafter recovered shall be divided equally between the Publisher and the Writer after the deduction of the reasonable expenses thereof.

Infringement Claims

16. (a) If a claim is presented against the Publisher alleging that the composition is an infringement upon some other work or a violation of any other right of another, and because therof the Publisher is jeopardized, it shall forthwith serve a written notice upon the Writer setting forth the full details of such claim. The pendency of said claim shall not relieve the Publisher of the obligation to make payment of the royalties to the Writer hereunder, unless the Publisher shall deposit said royalties as and when they would otherwise be payable, in an account in the joint names of the Publisher and the Writer in a bank or trust company in New York, New York, if the Writer on the date of execution of this contract resides East of the Mississippi River, or in Los Angeles, California, if the Writer on the date of execution of this contract resides West of the Mississippi River. If no suit be filed within nine months after said written notice from the Publisher to the Writer, all monies deposited in said joint account shall be paid over to the Writer plus any interest which may have been earned thereon.

(b) Should an action be instituted against the Publisher claiming that the composition is an infringement upon some other work or a violation of any other right of another, the Publisher shall forthwith serve written notice upon the Writer containing the full details of such claim. Notwithstanding the commencement of such action, the Publisher shall continue to pay the royalties hereunder to the Writer unless it shall, from and after the date of the service of the summons, deposit said royalties as and when they would otherwise be payable, in an account in the joint names of the Publisher and the Writer in a bank or trust company in New York, New York, if the Writer on the date of execution of this contract resides East of the Mississippi River, or in Los Angeles, California, if the Writer on the date of execution of this contract resides West of the Mississippi River. If the said suit shall be finally adjudicated in favor of the Publisher or shall be settled, there shall be released and paid to the Writer all of such sums held in escrow less any amount paid out of the Writer's share with the Writer's written consent in settlement of said action. Should the said suit finally result adversely to the Publisher, the said amount on deposit shall be released to the Publisher to the extent of any expense or damage it incurs and the balance shall be paid over to the Writer.

(c) In any of the foregoing events, however, the Writer shall be entitled to payment of said royalties or the money so deposited at and after such time as he files with the Publisher a surety company bond, or a bond in other form acceptable to the Publisher, in the sum of such payments to secure the return thereof to the extent that the Publisher may be entitled to such return. The foregoing payments or deposits or the filing of a bond shall be without prejudice to the rights of the Publisher or Writer in the premises.

Arbitration

17. Any and all differences, disputes or controversies arising out of or in connection with this contract shall be submitted to arbitration before a sole arbitrator under the then prevailing rules of the American Arbitration Association. The location of the arbitration shall be New York, New York, if the Writer on the date of execution of this contract resides East of the Mississippi River, or Los Angeles, California, if the Writer on the date of execution of this contract resides West of the Mississippi River. The parties hereby individually and jointly agree to abide by and perform any award rendered in such arbitration. Judgment upon any such award rendered may be entered in any court having jurisdiction thereof.

Assignment

18. Except to the extent herein otherwise expressly provided, the Publisher shall not sell, transfer, assign, convey, encumber or otherwise dispose of the composition or the copyright or copyrights secured thereon without the prior written consent of the Writer. The Writer has been induced to enter into this contract in reliance upon the value to him of the personal service and ability of the Publisher in the exploitation of the composition, and by reason thereof it is the intention of the parties and the essence of the relationship between them that the rights herein granted to the Publisher shall remain with the Publisher and that the same shall not pass to any other person, including, without limitations, successors to or receivers or trustees of the property of the Publisher, either by act or deed of the Publisher or by operation of law, and in the event of the voluntary or involuntary bankruptcy of the Publisher, this contract shall terminate, provided, however, that the composition may be included by the Publisher in a bona fide voluntary sale of its music business or its entire catalog of musical compositions, or in a merger or consolidation of the Publisher with another corporation, in which event the Publisher shall immediately give written notice thereof to the Writer; and provided further that the composition and the copyright therein may be assigned by the Publisher to a subsidiary or affiliated company generally engaged in the music publishing business. If the Publisher is an individual, the composition may pass to a legatee or distributee as part of the inheritance of the Publisher's music business and entire catalog of musical compositions. Any such transfer or assignment shall, however, be conditioned upon the execution and delivery by the transferee or assignee to the Writer of an agreement to be bound by and to perform all of the terms and conditions of this contract to be performed on the part of the Publisher.

Subsidiary Defined

19. A subsidiary, affiliate, or any person, firm or corporation controlled by the Publisher or by such subsidiary or affiliate, as used in this contract, shall be deemed to include any person, firm or corporation, under common control with, or the majority of whose stock or capital contribution is owned or controlled by the Publisher or by any of its officers, directors, partners or associates, or whose policies and actions are subject to domination or control by the Publisher or any of its officers, directors, partners or associates.

Amounts

20. The amounts and percentages specified in this contract shall be deemed to be the amounts and percentages agreed upon by the parties hereto, unless other amounts or percentages are inserted in the blank spaces provided therefor.

Modifications

21. This contract is binding upon and shall enure to the benefit of the parties hereto and their respective successors in interest (as hereinbefore limited). If the Writer (or one or more of them) shall not be living, any notices may be given to, or consents given by, his or their successors in interest. No change or modification of this contract shall be effective unless reduced to writing and signed by the parties hereto.

The words in this contract shall be so construed that the singular shall include the plural and the plural shall include the singular where the context so requires and the masculine shall include the feminine and the feminine shall include the masculine where the context so requires.

Paragraph Headings

22. The paragraph headings are inserted only as a matter of convenience and for reference, and in no way define, limit or describe the scope or intent of this contract nor in any way affect this contract.

Special Provisions

23.

Witness: ....   Publisher ....

....   By ....

Witness: ....   Address ....

....   Writer ....(L.S.)

Witness: ....   Address ....

....   Soc. Sec. # ....

Witness: ....   Writer ....(L.S.)

....   Address ....

Soc. Sec. # ....

Writer ....(L.S.)

Address ....

Soc. Sec. # ....

FOR YOUR PROTECTION,
SEND A COPY OF THE FULLY SIGNED CONTRACT TO THE GUILD.

* * * * *

Special Exceptions to apply only if filled in and initialed by the parties.

☐ The composition is part of an original score (not an interpolation) of

  ☐ Living Stage Production   ☐ Motion Picture   ☐ Night Club Revue
  ☐ Televised Musical Production

which is the subject of an agreement between the parties dated   , a copy of which is hereto annexed. Unless said agreement requires compliance with Paragraph 6 in respect of a greater number of musical compositions, the Publisher shall be deemed to have complied with said Paragraph 6 with respect to the composition if it fully performs the terms of said Paragraph 6 in respect of any one musical composition included in said score.

APPENDIX 6
Popular Songwriters Contract

AGREEMENT made this   day of   ,19   .between

(hereinafter called "Publisher") and

jointly and/or severally, (hereinafter called "Writer(s)"):

WITNESSETH:

(1) The Writer(s) hereby sells, assigns, transfers and delivers to the Publisher, its successors and assigns, a certain heretofore unpublished original musical composition, written and/or composed by the Writer(s) now entitled:

Title   Year in which creation was completed

including the title, copyrights and/or words and music thereof, all of the rights therein, as well as the entire exclusive right to publicly perform and televise the same, the right to secure copyright therein, and renewals and extensions thereof, throughout the world, in its own name as proprietor or otherwise, and such copyrights, renewals and extensions; TO HAVE AND TO HOLD the said musical composition, all the rights therein, the copyrights therein, and renewals and extensions thereof for the full terms thereof. The Writer(s) hereby conveys an irrevocable power of attorney, authorizing the Publisher, its successors and assigns, to file applications for renewal and renew and extend the copyrights in his name, and upon the issuance of such renewals, to execute proper and formal assignments thereof in his name, so as to secure to the Publisher, its successors and assigns, the renewal copyrights and extensions thereof.

(2) In all respects this contract shall be subject to any existing agreements between all of the parties hereto and the American Society of Composers, Authors and Publishers.

(3) The Writer(s) hereby warrants that the said composition is his sole, exclusive and original work, and that he has full right and power to make the within agreement, and that there exists no adverse claim to or in the said composition, except as set forth in Clause 2 hereof.

(4) In consideration of this agreement, the Publisher agrees to pay the Writer(s) as follows:

(a) In respect of regular piano copies sold and paid for in the United States of America, a royalty of   cents per copy.

(b) A royalty of   % of all net sums received by the Publisher in respect of regular piano copies and/or orchestrations thereof sold and paid for in any foreign country, or sold and paid for in the United States pursuant to a print right granted by the Publisher.

(c) A royalty of   cents per copy of orchestrations thereof in any form sold and paid for in the United States of America.

(d) A royalty equal to that proportion of twelve and one-half (12½%) per cent of the wholesale selling price of each folio or book issued by the Publisher, and sold and paid for and not returned as the said composition bears to the total number of musical compositions in such folio or book.

(e) As to "professional material" — not sold or resold, no royalty shall be payable.

(f) An amount equal to   % of:

All receipts of the Publisher in respect of any licenses issued authorizing the manufacture and distribution of phono-records embodying in said composition, or the use of the said composition in synchronization with sound motion pictures, or the reproduction thereof upon so-called electrical transcription for broadcasting purposes; and of any and all receipts of the Publisher from any other source or right now known or which may hereafter come into existence, all such sums to be divided amongst the Writer(s) of said composition as provided in Paragraph 5 hereof; provided, however, that if the Publisher administers the said licenses, or any of them, through the agent, trustee or other administrator acting for a substantial part of the industry and not in the exclusive employ of the Publisher, the Publisher, in determining his receipts, shall be entitled to deduct from gross license fees paid by the licensees a sum equal to the charges paid by the said Publisher to said agent, trustee or administrator.

(g) The percentage of the Writer(s) on monies received from foreign sources shall be computed on the Publisher's net receipts in U.S. Dollar currency, and at the same rate of exchange as that received by the Publisher.

(h) The Writer(s) shall not be entitled to any share of the monies distributed to the Publisher by the American Society of Composers, Authors and Publishers or any other performing rights society throughout the world which makes a distribution to writers either directly or through the American Society of Composers, Authors and Publishers of an amount which, in the aggregate, is at least equal to the aggregate amount distributed to Publishers.

(5) It is understood and agreed by and between all of the parties hereto that all sums hereunder payable jointly to the Writer(s) shall be divided amongst them respectively as follows:

NAME   SHARE

_____   _____

_____   _____

_____   _____

(6) The Publisher shall render the Writer(s), as above, on or about each August 15th and February 15th covering the six months ending June 30th and December 31st hereafter, so long as he shall continue publication or the licensing of any rights in the said composition, royalty statements accompanied by remittance of the amount due.

(7) The Publisher shall have the right to alter, change, edit or translate the composition or any part thereof, in any way it may be necessary. In the event it be necessary for the Publisher to cause lyrics to be written in other languages for and as part of the composition, the Publisher shall in such event have the right to deduct from the heretofore agreed royalties payable to the Writer(s), the cost or obligation thereof, but in no event more than a sum equal to one-half.

(8) The Writer(s) hereby agrees to indemnify and save harmless the Publisher against any loss, expense or damage by reason of any adverse claims made by others with respect to the composition and agreed that all expenses incurred in defense of any such claims, including counsel fees, as well as any and all sums paid by the Publisher, pursuant to a judgment, arbitration or any settlement or adjustment which may be made in the discretion of the Publisher, or otherwise, shall at all times be borne by the Writer(s), and may be deducted by the Publisher from any money accruing to the Writer(s) under this agreement or otherwise.

(9) This agreement is binding upon the parties hereto and their respective successors in interest.

If work has been recorded and released fill in:

Date and Place of First release: _____

Record Company: _____

Record Number: _____

SS #

Date of Birth:

Witness: Writer: _____ (L.S.)

_____   Address: _____

                                  Publisher: _____

Witness: By: _____

_____   Address: _____

APPENDIX 7

Exclusive Songwriter Contract

AGREEMENT made this   day of   , 19   between,

hereinafter designated as Publisher and

.... of ....

hereinafter designated as Writer.

WITNESSETH:

For and in consideration of the mutual covenants and agreements hereinafter contained, and the further sum of One Dollar by each of the parties in hand paid to the other, receipt whereof is hereby acknowledged, it is mutually agreed as follows:

(1)   The Writer agrees to compose and write music and/or lyrics exclusively for and during the period of this agreement and/or extension thereof, for and on behalf of the Publisher and/or any of its related or associated companies. The Writer agrees that he will not, as an author and/or composer of musical compositions, render his services for any other person, firm or corporation during the term of this agreement or any extension thereof, unless he first obtains the written consent of the Publisher.

(2)   The term of this agreement shall be for a period of .... year(s) commencing .... and terminating ....

(3)   The Writer agrees to, and by these presents does hereby sell, assign, transfer and deliver to the Publisher, its successors and assigns, all rights whatsoever, including public performance, for the entire world, in and to all and every work that he has at any time heretofore written and now owns, as well as all and every work that he shall write, compose or create during the full term and/or extension hereof, either alone or in collaboration with others; together with the copyrights and/or the right to copyright the same as proprietor in its own name, or otherwise, as it may elect in all countries, and to obtain renewals of each and every such copyright, to the fullest extent. The Writer herein conveys an irrevocable power of attorney authorizing and empowering the Publisher, its successors and assigns, to file application and renew the copyrights in the name of the Writer, and upon such renewals to execute proper and formal assignments thereof, so as to secure to the Publisher, its successors and assigns, the renewal terms of, in and to the said copyrights, works and/or compositions.

(4)   The Writer warrants that all of said compositions are and/or will be original works; that he has the right to make the within agreement, and that there exists and/or will exist no adverse claim to or in the said compositions, and that the Writer will indemnify and hold the Publisher harmless.

(5)   The Publisher covenants that it is engaged in the music publishing industry and as such will make reasonable efforts to publish or exploit certain of the musical compositions composed and written by the Writer, wherein title has been vested unto the Publisher, as copyright owner, by virtue of the terms of this agreement.

(6)   In consideration of this agreement, the Publisher agrees to pay to the Writer, jointly, only the following royalties:

(a)   ...... ¢ per copy, in respect of regular piano copies and/or orchestrations, sold in the United States and for which the Publisher received payment; a royalty equal to that proportion of twelve and one-half (12½%) per cent of the wholesale selling price of each folio or book issued by the Publisher, and sold and paid for and not returned as the said composition bears to the total number of musical compositions in such folio or book.

(b)   ...... % of the net amount received by the Publisher, in respect of regular piano copies and/or orchestrations sold and paid for in any foreign country, or sold and paid for in the United States pursuant to a print right granted by the Publisher.

(c)   ...... % of the net amount received by the Publisher, in respect of any licenses issued authorizing the manufacture and distribution of phonorecords and/or electrical transcriptions embodying said work, or the use of said work in synchronization with sound motion pictures.

(d)   The share of performing fees allocated to the Writer and designated as the Writer Share, if and when such Writer Share is received by the Publisher.

In the event that a composition has not been wholly written by the Writer, the above royalties shall be paid jointly and in equal shares to all writers, and in the event lyrics are written for a composition, other than in the original language, the Publisher shall have the right to deduct from the above royalties, the cost or obligation therefore, but in no event more than a sum equal to one-half (½) thereof. The Publisher shall have the right to alter, change, edit or translate the work(s) or any part thereof, in any way it may be necessary, and to cause new lyrics to be written in other languages.

(7)   Heretofore agreed royalties shall be payable to the Writer with respect to net amounts received by the Publisher from foreign countries, only when such net amounts are received by the Publisher in United States dollar currency; and at the same rate of exchange as that received by the Publisher.

(8)   Statements shall be rendered on February 15th and August 15th of each year, or as soon as possible thereafter, for the periods ending December 31st and June 30th of each year.

(9)   In addition hereto, the Writer sells, assigns, transfers and delivers to the Publisher, its successors and assigns, any and all works acquired and to be acquired hereunder, all of the rights therein, the right to secure copyrights, renewals and extensions thereof throughout the world, and the copyrights, renewals and extensions thereof; TO HAVE AND TO HOLD the said works, copyrights, renewals and extensions thereof and all rights of whatsoever nature thereunder existing, for the full terms thereof. The Writer hereby conveys an irrevocable power of attorney, authorizing the Publisher, its successors and

assigns, to file applications for renewal and renew and extend the copyrights in his name, and upon the issuance of such renewals, to execute proper and formal assignments thereof in his name, so as to secure to the Publisher, its successors and assigns, the renewal copyrights and extensions thereof. The Writer hereby also conveys an irrevocable power of attorney authorizing the Publisher, its successors and assigns to execute proper and separate assignments in his name, in favor of the Publisher, its successors and assigns so as to secure to it the said copyrights, and all the rights therein throughout the world for the full life of such copyrights.

(10) It is agreed between the parties that the Publisher shall have the option and right to renew and extend this agreement upon the same terms for an additional period of   year(s) by giving written notice by registered mail to the Writer not later than Thirty (30) days prior to the termination.

(11) This agreement is to be construed and its validity determined according to the laws of the State of New York, and shall apply to, bind and be for the benefit of the heirs, executors, administrators, successors and assigns of the parties hereto.

IN WITNESS WHEREOF the parties hereto have hereunto set their hands and affixed their seals the day and year first above written.

WITNESS: SS #
                                  Date of Birth_____
                                             WRITER

WITNESS: PUBLISHER:

                                  By_____

Management Agreement

MANAGEMENT AGREEMENT

THIS AGREEMENT is made and entered into as of this __ day of _____, 199_, by and between **MANAGER'S NAME, INC.,** a Name of state corporation, whose address is _____ hereinafter referred to as "Manager," and **ARTIST NAME** whose address is 215 Anywhere Street, Hitsville, State 0U812, hereinafter referred to as "Artist."

W I T N E S S E T H:

WHEREAS, Artist wishes to obtain advice, guidance, counsel and direction in the development and furtherance of Artist's career as a musician, composer, arranger, publisher and performing Artist, and in such new and different areas as Artist's artistic talents can be developed and exploited, and

WHEREAS, Manager, by reason of Manager's contacts, experience and background, is qualified to render such advice, guidance, counsel and direction to Artist;

NOW THEREFORE, in consideration of the mutual promises herein contained, it is agreed and understood as follows:

1.   <u>Engagement</u>.   Manager agrees to render such advice, guidance, counsel and other services as Artist may reasonably require to further Artist's career as a musician, composer, arranger, publisher, actor, writer and performing Artist, and to develop new and different areas within which Artist's artistic talents can be developed and exploited, including but not limited to the following services:

a.   to represent Artist and act as Artist's negotiator, to fix the terms governing all manner of disposition, use, employment or exploitation of Artist's talents and the products thereof; and

b.   to supervise Artist's professional employment and, on Artist's behalf, to consult with employers and prospective employers so as to assure the proper use and continued demand for Artist's services; and

c.   to be available at reasonable times and places to confer with Artist in connection with all matters concerning Artist's professional career, business interests, employment and publicity; and

d.   to exploit Artist's personality in all media and, in connection therewith to approve and permit, for the purpose of trade, advertising and publicity, the use, dissemination, reproduction or publication of Artist's name, photographic likeness, voice and artistic and musical materials;

e.   to engage, discharge and/or direct such theatrical agents, booking agencies, and employment agencies as well as other firms, persons or corporations who may be retained for the purpose of securing contracts, engagements or employment for Artist. It is understood, however, that Manager is not a booking agent but rather shall represent Artist with all such agencies. Manager is not obligated to and shall not render any services or advice which would require Manager to be licensed as an employment agency in any jurisdiction;

f.   to represent Artist in all dealings with any union; and

g.   to exercise all powers granted to Manager pursuant to paragraph "4" hereof.

2.   **Exclusivity of Manager**.   Manager is not required to render exclusive services to Artist, or to devote the entire time of Manager or the entire time of any of Manager's employees to Artist's affairs. Nothing herein shall be construed as limiting Manager's rights to represent other persons whose talents may be similar to or who may be in competition with Artist, or to have and pursue business interests which may be similar to or may compete with those of Artist.

3.   **Exclusivity of Artist**.   Artist hereby appoints Manager as Artist's sole and exclusive personal manager in all matters usually and normally within the jurisdiction and authority of personal managers, including but not limited to the advice, guidance, counsel and direction specifically referred to in paragraph "1" hereof. Artist agrees to seek such advice, guidance, counsel and direction from Manager solely and exclusively, and agrees that Artist will not engage any other agent, representative or manager to render similar services, and that Artist will not negotiate, accept or execute any agreement, understanding or undertaking concerning Artist's career without prior consultation with Manager. Nothing herein shall be construed to prevent Artist from consulting with Artist's attorney, business manager, or tax advisor.

4.   **Power of Attorney**. a.   Artist hereby irrevocably appoints Manager for the term of this Agreement and any extensions hereof as Artist's true and lawful attorney-in-fact to sign, make, execute and deliver any and all contracts in Artist's name; to make, execute, endorse, accept, collect and deliver any and all bills of exchange, checks and notes as Artist's said attorney; to demand, sue for, collect, recover and receive goods, claims, money, interest or other items that may be due to Artist or belong to Artist; and to make, execute and deliver receipts, releases or other discharges therefor under sale or otherwise; and to defend, settle, adjust, compound, submit to arbitration and compromise, all actions, suits, accounts, reckonings, claims and demands whatsoever that are or shall be pending in such manner and in all respects as Manager in Manager's sole discretion shall deem advisable; and without in any way limiting the foregoing, generally to do, execute and perform any other act, deed or thing whatsoever that reasonably ought to be done, executed and performed of any and every nature and kind as fully and effectively as Artist could do if personally present; and Artist hereby ratifies and affirms all acts performed by Manager by virtue of this power of attorney.

b.   Artist and Manager agree that any funds received by either of them as a result of Artist's entertainment activities shall be immediately transmitted to a mutually selected accountant or business manager who shall be instructed by Artist to deduct therefrom any commissions or expense reimbursement due to Manager hereunder and to pay such commissions or reimbursements to Manager within three (3) business days thereafter and the balance of such funds as the Artist directs. Such accountant or business manager shall be instructed by Artist and Manager to produce statements accounting to both Artist and Manager for all revenue, expenses and disbursements received, incurred or made respectively not less often than monthly. Manager and Artist agree to make a copy of this Agreement available to such accountant or business manager upon execution. The cost of such accountant's or business manager's services shall be paid by Artist.

c.   Notwithstanding the foregoing, Manager agrees that Manager shall not exercise the powers-of attorney described in this paragraph 4, without first disclosing to Artist the material terms of the transaction in which Manager plans to act on behalf of Artist, and after such disclosure Manager obtains Artist's consent. In the event Artist is not available to Manager to discuss the material terms of the transaction and to provide Artist's consent, and the exigent circumstances and the best interests of the Artist demand that Manager act immediately by exercising said powers, Manager agrees to notify Artist as soon as possible as to the action taken by Manager and all material terms of the transaction. In so acting, Manager agrees to act as a reasonably prudent person under similar circumstances, and Manager agrees to be diligent in communicating promptly with the Artist as to the action taken.

d.   It is expressly understood that the foregoing power of attorney is limited to matters reasonably related to Artist's career as musician, composer, arranger, publisher and performing artist and such new and different areas within which Artist's artistic talents can be developed and exploited. Notwithstanding the foregoing, it is expressly agreed by Artist and Manager that such power of attorney granted herein shall not include the right for Manager to bind Artist to any agreement whose term is longer than two (2) weeks, or any exclusive songwriting or recording agreements.

e.   Artist agrees and understands that the grant of power of attorney to Manager is coupled with an interest, which Artist irrevocably grants to Manager, in Artist's career, artistic talents and the products of said career and talents, and in Artist's earnings arising by reason of such career, talents and products.

5.   <u>Compensation</u>.   a.   As compensation for services to be rendered hereunder, Manager shall receive from Artist (or shall retain from Artist's gross monthly earnings) at the end of each calendar month during the term hereof, a sum of money equal to twenty percent (20%) of Artist's gross monthly earnings from personal appearance income and fifteen percent (15%) from Artist's all other entertainment industry sources only as provided herein. Artist hereby assigns to Manager an interest in such earnings to the extent of twenty percent (20%) and fifteen percent (15%) respectively thereof. Said assignment is intended by Artist to create an assignment coupled with an interest.

b.   The term "gross monthly earnings" as used herein, refers to the total of all earnings, which shall not be accumulated or averaged (whether in the form of salary, bonuses, royalties (or advances against royalties), interests, percentages, shares of profits, merchandise, shares in ventures, products, properties, or any other kind or type of income which is reasonably related to Artist's career in the entertainment, amusement, music, recording, motion picture, television, radio, literary, theatrical and advertising fields and all similar areas whether now known or hereafter devised, in which Artist's artistic talents are developed and exploited), received during any calendar month by Artist or by any of Artist's heirs, executors, administrators, assigns, or by any person, firm or corporation (including Manager) on Artist's behalf. It is understood that, for the purpose hereof, no expense, cost or disbursement incurred by Artist in connection with the receipt of "gross monthly earnings" shall be deducted therefrom prior to the calculation of Manager's compensation hereunder. The term "personal appearance income" shall be deemed by the parties hereto to refer to Artist's engagement as a musical artist at various venues, such as fairs, concerts, nightclubs, television and similar appearances where Artist performs before an audience and as such term is generally understood in the U.S. music industry.

c.   Notwithstanding anything to the contrary stated herein, with respect to merchandising income of the Artist only, for the purpose of computing Manager's commission hereunder only, such commission shall be computed as follows:

i.   If Artist sells Artist merchandise on a "in-house" basis, Manager shall be paid a commission on the basis of multiplying twenty-five percent (25%) times the total revenue from all merchandise sales, less the following: costs of goods sold, venue fees (if any), taxes, commission paid to crew members employed by Artist for the purpose of selling merchandise. "In-house" sales shall be deemed by the parties to mean that Artist is handling merchandise directly through Artist's own direct employees to design, purchase raw goods, cause such goods to be imprinted with Artist's identification, warehouse and sell such merchandise directly at Artist's personal appearances, through Artist's fan club, direct mail or similar distribution channels.

ii.   If Artist enters into a merchandising agreement with a third party, the effect of which is that Artist is paid an advance or any license fee, Manager's commission shall be computed by multiplying fifteen percent (15%) times Artist's gross income under such merchandising agreement including any and all advances with no reductions therefrom. For purposes of this paragraph a "third party" shall be deemed by the parties to mean outside companies, including but not limited to companies like

Brockam, Niceman, and Winterland, whose primary business is the production, manufacture and sales of artist merchandise for which artists are paid a license fee only.

     d.   The compensation agreed to be paid to Manager shall be based upon gross monthly earnings (as herein defined) of Artist accruing to or received by Artist during the term of this Agreement or subsequent to the termination of this Agreement as a result of: (i) any services performed by Artist during or prior to the term hereof, or (ii) any contract negotiated during or prior to the term hereof and any renewal, extension or modification of such contract, or (iii) any product of Artist's services or talents or of any property created by Artist in whole or in part during or prior to the term hereof. Artist's obligation to pay commission to Manager beyond the term of this Agreement shall be subject to Manager's rights as defined by this Paragraph 5(c) hereof, and in no event shall Artist have any obligation to pay commission to Manager on any income received by Artist after the expiration of forty-eight (48) months following the expiration or termination of this Agreement, except as provided below, or unless otherwise agreed by Artist in a written agreement. Notwithstanding anything to the contrary stated herein, Manager's rate of commission payable under this Agreement for contracts entered into during the term of this Agreement, but performed after the expiration or termination of the term of this Agreement shall be payable as follows: (i) in the first year following the expiration or termination of the term, 20% with respect to personal appearances and 15% with respect to all other entertainment industry income; (ii) in the second year following the expiration or termination of the term, 15% with respect to personal appearances and 10% with respect to all other entertainment industry income; (iii) in the third year following the expiration or termination of the term, 10% with respect to personal appearances and 5% with respect to all other entertainment industry income; and (iv) in the fourth year following the expiration or termination of the term, 5%. In any event, Manager shall be entitled to be paid commissions on any record albums or master recordings recorded during the term of this Agreement as long as Artist receives income therefrom at the full rate of commission, i.e. 15%. Manager shall not be entitled to receive any commission on records recorded or musical compositions written after the term of this Agreement.

     e.   In the event that Artist forms a corporation during the term hereof for the purpose of furnishing and exploiting Artist's artistic talents, Artist agrees that the commissions payable by Artist to Manager hereunder shall not be diminished from what said commissions would have been had such corporation not been formed.

     f.   Artist agrees that all gross monthly earnings as herein defined shall be paid directly to the accountant or business manager selected by Artist and Manager by all persons, firms or corporations, and shall not be paid by such persons, firms or corporations to Artist.

     g.   Notwithstanding the foregoing, however, Artist shall pay no commission to Manager for Artist's income from the following:

     (i) music publishing as a songwriter or music publisher, with respect to such income which Artist receives under any exclusive songwriter agreement with Manager's Music, a division of Manager's Corp, Inc., or in any other agreement through which any division of Manager's Corp, Inc. receives a portion of the publishing ownership of musical compositions created by Artist during the term hereof.

     (ii) any monies which Artist receives to reimburse or pay record or video production costs;

     (iii) any monies which Artist receives to reimburse sound and light expenses or as an "opening act" as that term is understood in the music industry;

     (iv) and/or any monies which Artist receives in the form of advances from any record company for tour support or independent record promotion.

6.   Reimbursement of Expenses.   Artist shall be solely responsible for payment of all booking agency fees, union dues, publicity costs, promotional or exploitation costs, traveling expenses and/or wardrobe expenses and all other expenses, fees and costs incurred by Artist. In the event that Manager advances any of the foregoing fees, costs or expenses on behalf of Artist, or incurs any other reasonable costs, fees or expenses in direct connection with Artist's professional career or with the performance of Manager's services hereunder, Artist shall promptly reimburse Manager for such fees, costs and expenses. Without limiting the foregoing, such direct expenses, costs or fees incurred by Manager shall include direct long distance phone calls, promotion and publicity expenses and travel and living expenses and costs whenever Manager, in Manager's opinion, shall deem it advisable to accompany Artist. No legal fees, accounting fees or bookkeeping fees of Manager shall be reimbursable by Artist, unless Artist expressly approves such expenses in advance. None of Manager's general overhead expenses shall be reimbursed by Artist hereunder. Notwithstanding the foregoing, in order for Manager to be reimbursed by Artist for expenses, Manager agrees to adhere to the following requirements:

a.   Manager will not travel at a higher class than Artist or stay at more expensive accommodations than Artist.

b.   If Manager travels on behalf of more than one client including Artist, expenses will be fairly prorated between (among) the clients.

c.   In order to be reimbursed, Manager must present valid receipts or other evidence of expenditures incurred.

7.   Warranties.   a.   Artist warrants that Artist is under no disability, restriction or prohibition with respect to Artist's right to execute this Agreement and perform its terms and conditions. Artist warrants and represents that no act or omission by Artist hereunder will violate any right or interest of any person or firm or will subject Manager to any liability, or claim of liability to any person. Artist agrees to indemnify Manager and to hold Manager harmless against any damages, costs, expenses, fees (including attorneys' fees) incurred by Manager in any claim, suit or proceeding instituted by or against Manager in which any assertion is made which is inconsistent with any warranty, representation or covenant of Artist.

b.   Manager warrants that Manager is under no disability, restriction or prohibition with respect to Manager's right to execute this agreement and perform its terms and conditions. Manager warrants and represents that no act or omission by Manager hereunder will violate any right or interest of any person or firm or will subject Artist to any liability, or claim of liability to any person. Manager agrees to indemnify Artist and to hold Artist harmless against any damages, costs, expenses, fees (including attorneys' fees) incurred by Artist in any claim, suit or proceeding instituted by or against Artist in which any assertion is made which is made which is inconsistent with any warranty, representation or covenant of Manager.

8.   Term. a.   The initial term of this Agreement shall be for a period of three (3) years from the date Artist's first single record is released for sale to the public.

b.   Manager shall have one (1) irrevocable option to renew this Agreement for an additional period of two (2) years which option shall be deemed by the parties to be automatically exercised, unless written notice is mailed to Artist by Manager no less than thirty (30) days prior to the expiration of the initial term or subsequent option period, provided Artist has grossed at least Blank Dollars ($0,000,000.00) in commissionable earnings from entertainment industry sources during the previous three (3) years.

c.   In the event that Artist shall fail for any reason to fulfill any obligation assumed by Artist hereunder (all of which obligations are agreed to be "of the essence" and material), Manager shall be entitled (by written notice mailed to Artist at any time) to extend the duration of the initial term (or of the option period in the event that such notice is mailed by Manager during the option period) for a period of time equal to the duration of such failure by Artist and until Artist shall fully cure any such failure. It is understood that no failure or delay of Manager to enforce the rights of Manager under this subparagraph shall be deemed a waiver of Manager's subsequent right to exert the rights granted to Manager hereunder.

9.   Amendments.   There shall be no change, amendment or modification of this Agreement unless it is reduced to writing and signed by all parties hereto. No waiver of any breach of this Agreement shall be construed as a continuing waiver or consent to any subsequent breach hereof.

10.   Breach.   It is agreed that as a condition precedent to any assertion by either party that the other party is in default in performing any obligation contained herein, the party claiming such default must advise the other party in writing of the specific facts upon which it is claimed that such party is in default and of the specific obligation which it is claimed has been breached, and the breaching party shall be allowed a period of thirty (30) days after receipt of such written notice, within which to cure such default. It is agreed that in the event that the alleged breach is cured within such thirty (30) day period, that the alleged breach shall then be deemed to have never occurred.

11.   Equitable Remedies.   Artist acknowledges and agrees that Manager's right to represent Artist, as Artist's sole and exclusive personal Manager, and Artist's obligation to solely and exclusively use Manager in such capacity, are unique, irreplaceable and extraordinary rights and obligations, and that any breach or threatened breach by Artist thereof shall be material and shall cause Manager immediate and irreparable damages which cannot be adequately compensated for by money judgment. Accordingly, Artist agrees that, in addition to all other forms of relief and all other remedies which may be available to Manager in the event of any such breach or threatened breach by Artist, Manager shall be entitled to seek and obtain injunctive relief against Artist, and Artist agrees that in seeking such injunctive relief, Manager shall not be obligated to secure any bond or relief.

12.   Relationship of Parties.   This Agreement does not and shall not be construed to create a partnership or joint venture between the parties hereto.

13.   Venue.   This Agreement and all amendments or modifications hereof shall be governed by and interpreted in accordance with the laws of the State of Confusion governing contracts wholly executed and performed therein, and shall be binding upon and inure to the benefit of the parties, their respective heirs, executors, administrators and successors. Jurisdiction for any suit filed to enforce the provisions of this Agreement by either party shall be filed in the federal or state courts of Mostfavorable District of Confusion in Hitsville, Confusion or Miracle County, Confusion.

14.   Notices.   All written correspondence and notification shall be sent by Certified Mail, Return Receipt Requested, to the respective addresses set forth above, and shall be considered received by said other party upon deposit in the United States Mail.

15.   Personal Services.   Manager shall furnish the personal services of one of the following persons to be personally available to Artist at reasonable times to provide the management services contemplated by the Management Agreement: U. Betcha Will, I. M. Manager, or Hugh Donit. Manager hereby agrees that in the event that either of I. M. Manager, or Hugh Donit is not personally available to render the services of Manager as described herein (except for limited periods of time not to exceed ninety (90) days because of illness), then Artist shall have the option to terminate the Management Agreement upon thirty (30) days notice to Manager.

16.   Legal Counsel.   Artist hereby acknowledges that Artist has been afforded an opportunity to consult with an attorney of Artist's own choosing who is

knowledgeable regarding entertainment industry contracts, and that Artist has either consulted with such attorney or has knowingly waived such right to consult with counsel prior to entering into this Agreement.

17.   Miscellaneous.   This Agreement embodies all the representations, terms and conditions of the parties' agreement, and there is no other collateral agreement, oral or written, between the parties in any manner relating to the subject matter hereof. All references herein to the singular may also be deemed to include the plural and vice versa, and any references to one gender may be deemed to include other genders as the context requires. No alteration, amendment or modification hereof shall be binding unless set forth in a writing signed by all of the parties hereto. No waiver of any breach of this Agreement shall be construed as a continuing waiver or consent to any subsequent breach hereof. The invalidity of any clause, part or provision of this Agreement shall be restrictive in effect to said clause, part or provision, and shall not be deemed to affect the validity of the entire Agreement. This Agreement shall not take effect until fully executed by all of the parties hereto. This Agreement may be executed in any number of counterparts, each of which shall be deemed an original, but all of which together shall constitute one and the same instrument. The headings contained herein are purely for the convenience of the parties and have no other meaning or effect. In the event of litigation, the prevailing party shall be entitled to recover any and all reasonable costs including attorneys' fees incurred in the enforcement of the terms of this Agreement, or any breach thereof. Nothing in this Agreement shall be construed as requiring the commission of any act contrary to law or contrary to any regulation of any applicable union or guild. Wherever there is any conflict between the provisions of this Agreement, and any present or future statute, law, ordinance or regulation, the latter shall prevail but in such event, the provision of this Agreement shall be curtailed or limited to the extent necessary to bring it within the requirements of said law or regulation.

IN WITNESS WHEREOF, the parties have caused this Agreement to be executed as of the day and year first indicated above.

Manager:

_____

By: an authorized signatory

APPENDIX 9

Recording Contract (excerpt)

AGREEMENT made as of the _____ day of _____, 19_____ by and between ARISTA RECORDS, INC., 6 West 57th Street, New York, New York 10019 ("Company") and _____, f/s/o _____.
                                                   ("Producer")   ("Artist")

In consideration of the representations and warranties and the mutual promises hereinafter set forth, it is agreed as follows:

1. For the purposes of this agreement, the following terms shall have the following meanings:

   (a) "Master" means a recording of one (1) Composition embodying the recorded performances of Artist.

   (b) (i) "Seven-inch Single" means a phonograph record embodying thereon one (1) or two (2) Masters; "Twelve-inch Single" means a phonograph record embodying thereon not less than one (1) Master and not more than four (4) Masters; Seven-inch Singles and Twelve-inch Singles are herein sometimes collectively referred to as "Singles."

   (ii) "EP" means a phonograph record embodying thereon not less than five (5) Masters and not more than seven (7) Masters.

   (iii) "LP" means a phonograph record embodying thereon not less than eight (8) Masters and not more than ten (10) Masters, containing a minimum of thirty-six (36) minutes of Artist's performances.

   (c) Notwithstanding paragraph 1(b) above, if a particular record is marketed by Company or its Licensees as a particular configuration of record (e.g., Seven-inch Single, Twelve-inch Single, EP, etc.), then such record shall be deemed to be such form of configuration.

   (d) "Records" and "phonograph records", mean all forms of reproductions, now or hereafter known, including new technologies, embodying audio alone, and/or audio coupled with visual images.

   (e) "Retail list price" means the suggested retail list price in, at Company's election, the country of manufacture or sale of records sold in the United States and in any other country where Company manufactures and sells records for its own account as opposed to licensing such rights to third parties and, for records sold elsewhere, the suggested retail list price, or a constructed price, whichever is the basis used by a particular Licensee of Company to report to Company. Notwithstanding anything to the contrary contained in this agreement, Company may change the method by which it computes royalties (for some or all of the Territory) from one of the above methods to some other method (the "New Method"). If Company adopts a New Method, such New Method shall be deemed incorporated herein in lieu of the present method of computing royalties with respect to all records derived from the Masters thereafter sold, an appropriate reference in respect of the New Method shall replace the current references to the retail list price, and the royalty rates provided for herein shall be adjusted to the appropriate royalty which would be applied to the New Method so that upon the first change to the New Method, the dollars-and-cents royalty amounts payable with respect to the top-line LPs in any configuration being sold by Company would be identical to that which was payable immediately prior to such change. All other royalty rates shall be proportionately adjusted. The royalty adjustments to be made pursuant to this paragraph shall be based on net dollars-and-cents royalty amounts and shall take into account any factors (including, without limitation, Company's regular "free goods" policies before and after Company's adoption of the New Method) affecting such net royalty amounts.

   (f) "Composition" means a musical composition or medley consisting of music with or without words.

   (g) "Recording Costs" means all costs incurred with respect to the production of Masters embodying Artist's performances. Recording Costs include, without limitation, union scale, the costs of all instruments, musicians, vocalists, conductors, arrangers, orchestrators, copyists, etc., payments to a trustee or fund based on wages to the extent required by any agreement between Company and any labor organization or trustee, all studio costs, tape, editing, mixing, mastering to tape, engineering, the costs of cutting references, travel, per diems, production fees and/or advances, rehearsal halls, costs of non-studio facilities and equipment, dubbing, transportation of instruments and other costs and expenses incurred in producing the Masters hereunder, which are customarily recognized as Recording Costs in the phonograph record industry.

   (h) "Territory" means the world.

   (i) "Deliver" or "Delivery" or "Delivered" (or any of said terms in lower case) when used with Masters means Company's receipt of newly-recorded satisfactory Masters to constitute the LP concerned (two-track stereo tapes, fully edited, mixed, leadered and equalized), together with one (1) reference master and all necessary licenses, approvals, consents and permissions, in accordance with the terms of this agreement.

   (j) "Licensee" or "licensee" includes, without limitation, sublicensees, affiliates, subsidiaries, wholly or partly owned, and other divisions of Company.

   (k) "Books and Records" or "books and records" means that portion of Company's books and records which specifically reports sales of records embodying the Masters produced hereunder and/or specifically reports net royalty receipts or the net amount received from any other exploitation of such Masters; provided that such defined term shall not be deemed to include any manufacturing records (e.g., inventory and/or production records) or any other of Company's records.

   (l) "Initially released in the United States" means the initial date customarily used by Company as the release date for any configuration of a particular LP.

2. (a) Producer shall produce and deliver Masters embodying the performances of Artist exclusively to Company for a term consisting of an Initial Period and the Option Periods hereinafter set forth if Company exercises any one or more of its options. The Initial Period as the same may be extended is hereinafter called the "Term". Producer hereby irrevocably grants to Company the option to extend the Initial Period for four (4) further consecutive renewal periods ("Option Periods"). Each option shall be exercised, if at all, by written notice to Producer prior to or on the date that the Term would otherwise expire. Each period of the Term is sometimes hereinafter referred to as a "Contract Period".

   (b) The first Contract Period shall commence on the date hereof and shall continue until the end of the ninth full month after the month in which there occurs the completion of Delivery of the recording obligation for the first Contract Period. Each Option Period shall commence upon the date following the last day of the immediately preceding Contract Period and shall continue until the end of the ninth full month after the month in which there occurs the completion of Delivery of the recording obligation for the Option Period concerned. Notwithstanding the two preceding sentences, if

Company exercises its Overcall Right for any Contract Period, then such Contract Period shall instead continue until the end of the ninth full month after the month in which there occurs the completion of Delivery of the Overcall LP for the Contract Period concerned.

3. (a) Producer warrants that, during the Term, Artist will record Masters exclusively for Producer and Company, in an approved recording studio, embodying Compositions not theretofore recorded by Artist, and Producer shall deliver to Company the number of Masters embodying the performances of Artist as herein provided. Company shall have the right and opportunity to have a representative attend each recording session.

(b) During each Contract Period, Producer shall produce and deliver to Company Masters to constitute one (1) LP embodying Artist's performances in accordance with the provisions of this agreement. The aforesaid Masters to be recorded during each Contract Period are herein sometimes referred to as the "recording obligation" or the "committed LPs" for the Contract Period concerned. Company shall have the right and option to require Producer to produce and deliver to Company Masters to constitute one (1) additional LP during each Contract Period. Said option is referred to herein as the "Overcall Right" and said additional Masters to be recorded during each Contract Period are herein referred to as the "Overcall LP." Company can exercise the Overcall Right at any time prior to or on the date the particular Contract Period would otherwise expire. The Overcall LP shall be subject to the terms and conditions of this agreement.

(c) Company and Producer shall jointly select the Compositions to be recorded and each Master shall be subject to Company's approval as satisfactory for the manufacture and sale of phonograph records. Upon Company's request, Producer shall cause Artist to record additional Compositions and/or re-record any Composition recorded hereunder, as necessary, until a Master which in Company's sole judgment is satisfactory for the manufacture and sale of phonograph records shall have been obtained.

(d) Company can release so-called "Greatest Hits" or "Best Of" LPs without Producer's consent, and no such LP shall be deemed to be in partial or complete fulfillment of any of Producer's obligations hereunder. Producer shall not deliver Masters to constitute two or more LPs intended to be marketed as a single package ("Multiple Record Set") to satisfy Producer's obligation to deliver Masters to constitute one (1) LP without Company's prior written consent, which consent may be withheld for any reason. If Producer delivers and Company accepts Masters to constitute a Multiple Record Set, it shall be deemed to be a single LP for the purposes of this agreement. No Masters consisting of "live" or instrumental recordings shall be delivered or shall be deemed to be in partial or complete fulfillment of any of Producer's obligations hereunder.

(e) Producer's submission of Masters to Company shall constitute Producer's representation that it has obtained all necessary licenses, approvals, consents and permissions. Company's payment of any monies due in respect of the delivery of Masters hereunder shall not be deemed to be a waiver of Producer's obligation to obtain and furnish all such licenses, approvals, consents and permissions and shall not be deemed to be a waiver of Producer's obligation to make delivery.

4. (a) Producer warrants that, during the Term, Artist will not perform or authorize or knowingly permit to be recorded any performance, for or by anyone other than Company, without in each case taking measures to prevent the exploitation of phonograph records embodying such performances. Producer further warrants that, during the Term, Producer and Artist will not license or consent to the use of Artist's name, likeness, voice, biographical material or other identification ("Artist's Identification"), in connection with the recording or exploitation of phonograph records by anyone other than Company.

(b) Producer warrants that neither it nor Artist will produce or perform in connection with the production of any record embodying any Composition recorded by Artist under this agreement prior to the later of five (5) years subsequent to the date of Delivery to Company of a Master embodying that Composition or two (2) years subsequent to the expiration of the Term of this agreement. Should Producer or Artist so produce or perform in connection with any such Composition during the period referred to above, then, without limiting any of Company's other rights or remedies, Company shall have no further obligation to pay royalties to Producer which otherwise would accrue to Producer hereunder on records which contain Artist's performance of such Composition.

5. Each Master produced during the Term shall, from the inception of its creation, be considered a "work made for hire" for Company within the meaning of the U.S. Copyright Law. If it is determined that a Master does not so qualify, then such Master, together with all rights in it, shall be deemed transferred to Company by this agreement. All such Masters shall be recorded by Producer and performed by Artist on Company's behalf and all records made therefrom, together with the performances embodied therein, shall, from the inception of their creation, be entirely the property of Company in perpetuity, throughout the Territory, free of any claim whatsoever by Producer or by Artist, or by any persons deriving any rights or interests therefrom; and Company shall have the right to secure the sound recording (P) copyright in and to the Masters in Company's name as the owner and author thereof and to secure any and all renewals of such copyright. Producer and Artist shall execute and deliver to Company such instruments of transfer and other documents regarding the rights of Company in the Masters as Company may reasonably request to carry out the purposes of this agreement, and Company may sign such documents in Producer's or Artist's name and make appropriate disposition of them. Company (and its Licensees) shall have the exclusive right to use the Masters in perpetuity and throughout the Territory or any part thereof in any manner it sees fit, including, without limitation, the exclusive right:

(a) To manufacture, distribute and exploit the Masters and records embodying the Masters, in any or all fields of use, by any method now or hereafter known, upon such terms and conditions as Company (and its Licensees) may elect or, in its sole discretion, to refrain therefrom;

(b) To release records embodying the Masters under any name, and trademark or label which Company (and its Licensees) may from time to time elect;

(c) To use (including publish) the names (including all professional, group and assumed or fictitious names), likenesses, photographs and biographical material of any party, including Artist, rendering services in connection with the Masters for the purpose of publicizing or exploiting the rights granted hereunder; and

(d) To publicly perform or to permit the public performance of the Masters by means of radio broadcast, television broadcast or any other method now or hereafter known including new technologies.

6. Company shall pay to Producer the following royalties for the use by Company or its Licensees of the Masters against which all advances paid to or on behalf of Producer, including, without limitation, the sums referred to in paragraphs 8 and 9 shall be chargeable:

(a) (i) A royalty of the following percent of the retail list price for the following records derived from the Masters recorded during the following Contract Periods and sold by Company for distribution in the United States and not returned (the "basic royalty rate" for the United States):

TYPE OF RECORD	CONTRACT PERIOD	RATE
(A) LPs	1st	_____
(B) LPs	2nd	_____

(C) LPs	3rd, 4th and 5th	_____
(D) Seven-inch Singles	1st and 2nd	_____
(E) Seven-inch Singles	3rd, 4th and 5th	_____
(F) Twelve-inch Singles	1st and 2nd	_____
(G) Twelve-inch Singles	3rd, 4th and 5th	_____

(ii) As to EPs derived from the Masters, sold by Company for distribution in the United States and not returned, the royalty rate shall be two-thirds (2/3) of the otherwise applicable LP royalty rate provided for above.

(iii) As to Multiple Record Sets derived from the Masters, sold by Company for distribution in the United States and not returned, the royalty rate shall be one-half (1/2) of the otherwise applicable LP royalty rate provided for above.

(iv) Notwithstanding the royalty rates contained in subparagraph 6(a) (i) above, with respect to net sales of a particular LP through normal retail channels in the United States, for which royalties are payable pursuant to such subparagraph, in excess of the following number of units, the applicable royalty rate for such excess sales shall be the applicable rate set forth below:

LP	UNITS	RATES
First or second LP	250,000	_____
in first Contract Period:	500,000	_____
First or Second LP	250,000	_____
in second Contract Period:	500,000	_____

(b) (i) A royalty of the following percent of the retail list price for all LPs derived from the Masters recorded during the following Contract Periods and sold by Company or its regular foreign distributors for distribution outside of the United States, as to which Company receives payment (the "basic royalty rate" for outside of the United States):

Territory	Contract Period	Rate

(ii) As to EPs, Singles and Multiple Record Sets derived from the Masters sold by Company or its regular foreign distributors for distribution outside of the United States, as to which Company receives payment, the royalty rate shall be one-half (1/2) of the otherwise applicable LP royalty rate provided for in this paragraph 6(b).

(iii) As to sales of such records released by Company's Licensees (other than its regular foreign distributors), Company shall credit Producer's royalty account with fifty (50%) percent of Company's net royalty receipts from such sales.

(c) Notwithstanding anything to the contrary contained in paragraphs 6(a) and 6(b) above:

(i) As to records derived from the Masters and sold by Company or its regular foreign distributors in the "compact disc" format or the digital audio format (or any other format not specifically provided for in this paragraph 6), the retail list price of the record shall be deemed to be no greater than the retail list price for Company's or Company's regular foreign distributors' (as applicable) then-current similar vinyl disc record or analog tape equivalent (whichever is lower).

(ii) Notwithstanding anything to the contrary contained in subparagraph 6(c) (i) above, for the purpose of calculating the royalty payable for sales in the "compact disc" format in the United States of the _____ LP for the _____ Contract Period and such sales of each subsequent LP Delivered hereunder in such format(s), the retail list price for the particular LPs concerned shall be deemed to be eighty (80%) percent of the actual retail list price for the particular record concerned.

(d) As to sales of records not consisting entirely of Masters delivered hereunder, Producer's royalties otherwise payable hereunder shall be prorated based upon the number of such Masters which are on such records compared to the total number of recordings on such records.

(e) Royalties shall be calculated based upon the retail list price after deducting all taxes and duties and Company's customary container charges. At the present time, Company's customary container charges are as follows for the following records: ten (10%) percent of the retail list price for disc records (other than Seven-inch Singles released in standard generic sleeves and other than those LPs listed below); twelve and one-half (12-1/2%) percent of the retail list price for a single disc LP released in a double-fold album jacket or in an album jacket which contains an insert; twenty (20%) percent of the retail list price for a non-disc record for Multiple Record Sets, for audio-visual records and for a double-disc LP released in a double-fold album jacket; twenty-five (25%) percent of the retail list price for a record accounted for pursuant to subparagraph 6(c) (ii) above; and five (5%) percent of the retail list price in addition to the container charges set forth in this paragraph for records in oversized cardboard containers (e.g., 3" × 12", 4" × 12" cardboard containers).

(f) As to LPs derived from the Masters, which have a retail list price that is at least Two ($2.00) Dollars (or its foreign equivalent) less than the retail list price used for top line phonograph records released by Company or its regular foreign distributors in the particular country, the royalty rate shall be one-half (1/2) of the otherwise applicable basic royalty rate provided for in paragraphs 6(a) and 6(b) above. As to such records released by Company's Licensees (other than its regular foreign distributors), Company shall credit Producer's royalty account with fifty (50%) percent of Company's net royalty receipts from such sales.

(g) As to records derived from the Masters sold through record clubs or similar sales plans or devices by Company's Licensees, Company shall credit Producer's royalty account with fifty (50%) percent of Company's net royalty receipts from such sales.

(h) In computing the number of records sold hereunder, Company shall have the right to deduct returns and credits of any nature. Company shall have the right to withhold a portion of Producer's royalties as a reserve in accordance with normal company policies, which for LPs in any configuration are as follows:

(i) Thirty (30%) percent of the royalties otherwise earned during a given accounting period, except that, if an LP is released during the last sixty (60) days of an accounting period, then the reserve for such accounting period shall be forty (40%) percent.

(ii) Over each of the four (4) accounting periods immediately following the accounting period in which the applicable reserve was established,

Company shall credit Producer's royalty account with one-fourth of the royalty reserve amount originally withheld with respect to a given accounting period.

(i)   No royalties shall be payable for promotional records designed for distribution without charge or for sale at a substantially lower price than the regular price of Company's equivalent records.

(j)   As to flat fee licenses of the Masters to third parties for phonograph records use and all other types of use, Company shall credit Producer's royalty account with fifty (50%) percent of the net amount received by Company and attributable to the Masters under each such license.

(k)   For each eighty-five (85) disc LPs or tapes (or EPs) that Company ships to its distributors for which royalties shall be payable hereunder, Company shall have the right to ship to its distributors on a no-charge basis or at a cost which is fifty (50%) percent or less of Company's regular wholesale price fifteen (15) disc LPs or tapes (or EPs) for which royalties shall not be payable; for each eighty (80) compact disc records that Company ships to its distributors for which royalties shall be payable hereunder, Company shall have the right to ship to its distributors on a no charge basis or at a cost which is fifty (50%) percent or less of Company's regular wholesale price twenty (20) compact disc records for which royalties shall not be payable; and for each one hundred (100) Singles that Company ships to its distributors for which royalties shall be payable hereunder, Company shall have the right to ship to its distributors on a no-charge basis or at a cost which is fifty (50%) percent or less of Company's regular wholesale price thirty (30) Singles for which royalties shall not be payable. No royalties shall be payable for records used for the purpose of publicity or advertising, for records distributed to radio stations, television stations, motion picture companies, publishers or others, for records used on transportation facilities or as in-store play samplers, for records sold as cutouts or overstock, or for records sold as scrap. Notwithstanding anything to the contrary hereinabove set forth, if Company changes its overall policy with respect to records shipped to distributors on a no-charge basis or at a cost which is fifty (50%) percent or less of Company's regular wholesale price on which royalties are not payable, then Company shall have the right to change the limitations hereinabove set forth in accordance with such new policy. If records derived from the Masters are sold to distributors or others for less than Company's regular wholesale price, or at a discount therefrom, but for more than fifty (50%) percent of such regular wholesale price, then, for purposes of this paragraph, a percentage of such records shall be deemed non-royalty bearing records, which percentage shall be an amount equal to the percentage amount of the applicable discount; provided, however, that the aggregate number of records deemed to have been shipped on a non-royalty bearing basis pursuant to this sentence and the number of records so shipped pursuant to the preceding sentences of this paragraph 6(k), shall be subject to the limitations set forth above in this paragraph 6(k) or otherwise herein. Company shall have the right to exceed any of the limitations described in this paragraph for promotions, including short term and catalog programs, without Producer's consent. Records returned shall be prorated between royalty free records and records on which royalties are payable in the same proportion as such returned records are credited to distributors.

(l)   For the sale by Company's Licensees of records which include Masters delivered hereunder through "key outlet marketing" and/or direct mail or mail order, and/or audiophile or other specialty markets, and for the sale by Company's Licensees of records not consisting entirely of Masters delivered hereunder through normal retail channels, Company shall credit Producer's royalty account with fifty (50%) percent of Company's net royalty receipts attributable to the Masters from such sales.

(m)   The royalty rate for records derived from the Masters and sold for sale in Armed Forces Post Exchanges shall be one-half (1/2) of the otherwise applicable basic royalty rate provided for in paragraphs 6(a) and 6(b) above.

(n)   The royalty rate payable hereunder for records derived from the Masters and sold by Company as "premiums", and for records derived from the Masters and sold by Company or its Licensees in conjunction with a major television or radio promotion campaign, shall be one-half (1/2) of the otherwise applicable basic royalty rate provided for in paragraphs 6(a) and 6(b) above and the retail list price for such records shall be deemed to be Company's or its Licensees' actual sales price. As to such records sold as "premiums" by Company's Licensees, Company shall credit Producer's royalty account with fifty (50%) percent of Company's net royalty receipts from such sales. Company shall be entitled to use and publish, and to license or permit others to use and publish, Artist's Identification with respect to the products or services in connection with which such "premium" records are sold or distributed.

(o)   With respect to any Master embodying Artist's performances hereunder together with the performance of another artist or artists to whom Company is or becomes obligated to pay royalties in respect of phonograph records embodying the joint performances contained on such Master: (i) the royalty rate to be used in determining the royalties payable to Producer in respect of such Master shall be computed by multiplying the royalty rate otherwise applicable thereto by a fraction, the numerator of which shall be one and the denominator of which shall be the total number of royalty artists whose performances are embodied on such Master; and (ii) in determining the portion of Recording Costs applicable to such Master which shall be charged against Producer's royalties, such proportion shall be computed by multiplying the aggregate amount of such Recording Costs by the same fraction used in determining the royalties payable to Producer in respect of such Master. No such joint recording shall be counted toward the fulfillment of the recording obligation hereunder unless Company shall specifically consent, in writing, to count such joint recording toward the fulfillment of such recording obligation.

(p)   Royalties for phonograph records derived from the Masters and sold for distribution outside of the United States shall be paid at the same rate of exchange as Company is paid, provided, however, that such royalties shall not be payable until payment has been received by Company in the United States in United States Dollars. If Company shall not receive payment in the United States or in United States Dollars and shall elect to accept payment in a foreign currency or in a foreign country, Company may deposit to the credit of Producer (and at the expense of Producer) in such country in a depository selected by Company payments so received applicable to royalties hereunder, and shall notify Producer promptly thereof. Deposit as aforesaid shall fulfill the obligations of Company as to phonograph record sales to which such royalty payments are applicable.

7.   (a)   Company shall account to Producer on or before the first day of October for the period ending the preceding June 30th, and on or before the first day of April for the period ending the preceding December 31st, together with the payment of any royalties accrued during such preceding half-year. Royalties payable or credited to Producer hereunder shall be less whatever taxes the laws of any applicable jurisdiction require be withheld in connection with such royalties. All statements shall be binding upon Producer unless specific written objection, stating the basis thereof, is given to Company within one (1) year from the date rendered. Producer shall be foreclosed from maintaining any action, claim or proceeding against Company in any forum or tribunal with respect to any statement or accounting due hereunder unless Producer commences such action, claim or proceeding in a court of competent jurisdiction within two (2) years after the date such statement or accounting is rendered. Producer shall have the right to appoint a Certified Public Accountant, who is not then currently engaged in an outstanding audit of Company, to examine Company's books and records insofar as they pertain to this agreement provided such examination shall take place at Company's offices during normal business hours, on reasonable written notice, not more than once in any calendar year during which Producer receives a statement and at Producer's sole expense. Such examination shall be conditioned upon the accountant's agreement to Company that he is not being compensated on a contingent fee basis. Producer acknowledges that Company's books and records contain confidential trade information and warrants and represents that neither Producer nor Artist nor their representatives will communicate to others or use on behalf of any other person any facts or information obtained as a result of such examination of Company's books and records.

(b) If Producer claims that additional monies are payable to Producer, Company shall not be deemed in material breach of this agreement unless such claim shall have been reduced to a final judgment by a court of competent jurisdiction and Company shall have failed to pay Producer the amount thereof within thirty (30) days after Company shall have received notice of the entry of such judgment.

8. (a) Company shall advance all Recording Costs incurred in connection with the production of the Masters in accordance with a written budget submitted by Producer and approved by Company prior to the recording session for such Masters. Company shall not withhold approval of a budget for the production of Masters to constitute an LP if the total recording budget submitted for the production of such Masters does not include any fees in excess of union scale or any other unusual expense and if the total recording budget for the production of such LP, including any fees to be paid to the individual producer, does not exceed ninety (90%) percent of the applicable minimum Recording Fund fixed in paragraph 9 below (as same may be reduced pursuant to the provisions of this agreement).

(b) If Recording Costs for the production of the Masters exceed the applicable approved budget, then Producer shall be solely responsible for and shall pay such excess costs, provided, however, that Company shall have the right to pay such excess and, without limiting its rights, to deduct the amount of such excess from any sums that may be payable to Producer hereunder.

9. Company shall advance to Producer the following sums to be charged against and recouped from royalties payable by Company to Producer:

10. In addition to delivering the Masters hereunder, Producer shall deliver to Company or, at Company's option, shall keep available for Company and subject to Company's control at the recording studios the following: each and every original session tape, each multi-track master, a non-equalized copy of the Masters and each and every mother, Master, acetate copy or other derivative of the Masters.

11. Company shall be responsible for the payment of mechanical copyright royalties directly to the copyright proprietors. Producer warrants that the Compositions embodied on the Masters shall be available for mechanical licensing and Producer shall assist Company in entering into mechanical licenses, which licenses (subject to the provisions outlined herein) shall be in the general form utilized by The Harry Fox Agency, Inc., or in a form that is otherwise acceptable to Company. The mechanical licenses for Compositions recorded pursuant to this agreement which are written, in whole or in part, by Artist or by an individual producer of Masters, or owned or controlled directly or indirectly, by Producer, Artist or such individual producer or by any party associated or affiliated with Producer, Artist or such individual producer ("Controlled Composition") shall be licensed to Company, for the Territory excluding the United States, at the rates set forth below and such mechanical licenses shall also provide that mechanical royalties shall only be payable on records for which royalties are payable pursuant to paragraph 6 hereof. In addition, each Controlled Composition is hereby licensed to Company, for the United States, at the rates set forth below and mechanical royalties for such uses of such Compositions shall only be payable on records for which royalties are payable pursuant to paragraph 6 hereof.

(a) Three-fourths (3/4) of the then-current minimum fixed statutory copyright royalty rate under the U.S. Copyright Law per Controlled Composition for the United States, determined as of the date the Masters embodying Controlled Compositions were initially recorded or the last date by which the Masters embodying such Controlled Compositions were originally scheduled to be recorded pursuant to paragraph 24(b), whichever is earlier; Two (2¢) cents per Controlled Composition for Canada; and the minimum statutory rate or, if there is no such minimum statutory rate, the standard industry rate per Controlled Composition for each other country in the Territory;

(b) Notwithstanding the rates specified in paragraph 11(a) above, it is specifically understood and agreed that the maximum copyright royalty rate which Company will be required to pay in respect of a record released hereunder in any configuration shall be equal to the number of Masters contained on such record times the applicable rate provided for in paragraph 11(a) (the "maximum mechanical rate"), but in no event shall the maximum mechanical rate for an LP in any configuration exceed ten times such applicable rate nor shall the maximum mechanical rate for a Single exceed two times such applicable rate. Notwithstanding the immediately preceding sentence, if the same version (i.e., the same mix) of a Master embodying a particular Composition is contained on both sides of a cassette tape, then Company shall be obligated to pay a mechanical royalty in respect of only one use of such Composition in connection with the particular tape concerned. If Company or any of its Licensees releases a Multiple Record Set, the maximum mechanical rate otherwise applicable by a fraction, the numerator of which is the retail list price for the Multiple Record Set in the configuration concerned and the denominator of which is the retail list price used for top line phonograph records in such configuration released by Company. Without limiting Company's rights pursuant to the foregoing, in the event the aggregate copyright royalty rate for a record shall exceed the maximum mechanical rate, it is specifically understood and agreed that such excess may be deducted from any and all sums due Producer hereunder including without limitation royalties payable for Controlled Compositions.

(c) Notwithstanding anything to the contrary contained in paragraph 11(b) hereof, Producer shall not be responsible for mechanical copyright royalty payments in excess of the maximum mechanical rate, which excess is due solely to the inclusion on an LP of a Composition which is not a Controlled Composition for which Company becomes obligated to pay a mechanical royalty at a rate in excess of the applicable rate set forth in paragraph 11(a) above, provided: (i) such Composition was initially submitted to Producer by Company; or (ii) Producer uses its reasonable efforts to obtain a license from the copyright proprietor at the rate set forth in paragraph 11(a) above, Producer notifies Company in writing prior to the recording of such Composition that it is unable to obtain such a rate, and Company nevertheless approves the recording of such Composition.

(d) Notwithstanding the rates specified in paragraph 11(a) above, the mechanical royalty rates for Controlled Compositions embodied on LPs sold with a reduced retail list price pursuant to paragraph 6(f) hereof shall be one-half (1/2) of the otherwise applicable rate set forth in paragraph 11(a) above.

(e) No mechanical copyright royalties shall be payable in respect of Controlled Compositions which are arrangements of selections in the public domain or in respect of any other instrumentations, orchestrations and arrangements owned or controlled, directly or indirectly, by Producer or by Artist or by an individual producer of Masters. Notwithstanding the foregoing, if any arrangement of a selection in the public domain is credited by ASCAP or BMI and Producer furnishes to Company a copy of the letter from ASCAP or BMI setting forth the percentage of credit which the publisher will receive for such public performances, then Company shall license such arrangement at a mechanical copyright royalty rate equal to the relevant rate specified in paragraph 11(a) above multiplied by the percentage utilized by ASCAP or BMI.

(f) With respect to Controlled Compositions licensed hereunder for the United States, Company shall render to Producer quarterly statements, and payments therefor, of all royalties payable hereunder, within sixty (60) days after March 31, June 30, September 30 and December 31, for each quarter for which any such royalties accrue pursuant to the terms hereof. Company shall have the right to withhold a portion of such royalties as a reserve in accordance with normal company policies. The provisions of paragraph 7 hereof (other than the first sentence of said paragraph) shall be applicable to accountings rendered by Company pursuant to this paragraph 11.

(g) The provisions of this paragraph 11 shall constitute and are accepted by Producer, on Producer's and Artist's behalf and on behalf of any other owner of any Controlled Compositions or any rights therein, as full compliance by Company with all of its obligations, under the compulsory license provisions of the Copyright Law, as the same may be amended, or otherwise, arising from or connected with Company's use of said Controlled Compositions.

12. Artist shall be available, from time to time during the Term, at Company's request and expense, whenever the same will not unreasonably interfere with other professional activities of Artist, to appear for photo sessions and interviews and to perform other reasonable promotional services.

13. Producer warrants and represents the following:

(a) Producer has the right to enter into this agreement and to grant to Company the rights granted hereunder. If Producer is a corporation, then Producer is and shall be a corporation in good standing in the jurisdiction of its incorporation.

(b) Producer has a valid and enforceable agreement with Artist under which Artist is required to perform exclusively for Producer as a recording artist during the Term of this agreement. During the Term of this agreement, Producer will take all steps necessary or desirable to keep the same in full force and effect so that Company shall have the benefits of Artist's services hereunder as if Artist had contracted directly with Company.

(c) During the Term, Producer and Artist shall not be bound by any agreement which will interfere in any manner with the complete performance of this agreement by Producer and by Artist. Producer and Artist are and shall be under no disability, restriction or prohibition with respect to their rights to sign and perform under this agreement, including without limitation, restrictions regarding Compositions Artist may record for Company.

(d) As of the date hereof, there are no prior recorded performances by Artist unreleased within the United States.

(e) The Masters and Videos shall be produced in accordance with the rules and regulations of the American Federation of Musicians, the American Federation of Television and Radio Artists and all other unions having jurisdiction, including without limitation paragraph 31 of the 1987 - 1990 AFTRA Code of Fair Practice for Phonograph Recordings (or the comparable provision of any successor agreement) and all persons rendering services in connection with the Masters shall fully comply with the provisions of the Immigration Reform Control Act of 1986.

(f) The Materials, as hereinafter defined, or any use thereof will not violate or infringe upon the rights of any third party. "Materials", as used in this paragraph, means (i) all Controlled Compositions, (ii) each name used by Producer, Artist and/or any individual producer in connection with the Masters delivered hereunder, and (iii) all other musical, dramatic, artistic, and literary materials, ideas and other intellectual properties (including, without limitation, publicity material), furnished or selected by Producer, Artist and/or any individual producer and contained in or used in connection with any Masters delivered hereunder or the packaging, sale, distribution, advertising, publicizing, or any other exploitation thereof. Company's acceptance and/or utilization of Masters or Materials hereunder shall not constitute a waiver of any of Producer's and/or Artist's representations, warranties or agreements in respect thereof.

(g) Producer shall be solely responsible for and shall pay all sums due Artist, the individual producer of the Masters (subject to paragraph 15 herein), and all other parties entitled to receive royalties in connection with the use of the Masters. The sums set forth in paragraphs 6 and 28 include all royalties due such parties and Company shall not be obligated to pay any advances or royalties in excess of those expressly provided herein.

(h) Producer does hereby indemnify, save and hold Company harmless of and from any and all loss and damage (including reasonable attorneys' fees) arising out of or connected with any claim by any third party or any act by Producer or Artist which is inconsistent with any of the warranties, representations or agreements made by Producer in this agreement, and agrees to reimburse Company on demand for any payment made or loss suffered with respect to any claim or act to which the foregoing indemnity applies. If the amount of any such claim or loss has not been determined, Company may withhold sums due Producer hereunder in an amount consistent with such claim or loss pending such determination. Company shall notify Producer in writing of any claim and Producer shall have the right to participate in the defense of any claim with counsel of Producer's own choice and at Producer's own expense; provided Company shall have the right at all times, in its sole discretion, to retain or resume control of the conduct thereof. Notwithstanding anything to the contrary contained in paragraph 25 hereof, solely for the purpose of enforcing the provisions of the foregoing indemnification, Producer and Artist shall submit to the personal jurisdiction of any court, tribunal or forum in which an action or proceeding is brought against Company involving a claim to which the foregoing indemnification applies.

14. (a) By notice to Producer, Company may suspend its obligations and/or extend the expiration date of the then-current Contract Period hereunder for the duration of any default or breach by Producer or Artist in the performance of any of Producer's or Artist's obligations, warranties or representations hereunder, or any labor disagreement, fire, catastrophe, shortage of materials or other event beyond Company's control that materially hampers or makes commercially impracticable Company's normal business operations. In addition, in the event of any breach or default by Producer or Artist in the performance of any obligations, warranties or representations hereunder, Company may terminate the Term by notice to Producer. Company may elect to exercise any or all of its rights pursuant to this paragraph in addition to any other rights or remedies it may have at law or otherwise.

(b) If, at any time during the Term hereof, Artist fails for a continuous period of 180 days or more to perform actively before audiences or on live television presentations, Company, by written notice to Producer, in addition to any other rights or remedies which it may have at law or otherwise, may terminate the Term hereof.

(c) Notwithstanding anything to the contrary contained herein, if Company advances any monies hereunder to Producer or on Producer's behalf with respect to Masters to constitute any LP to be produced hereunder and thereafter Producer fails to deliver such Masters in accordance with the terms of this agreement, then, in addition to any other rights or remedies which Company may have as a result thereof and upon Company's written demand therefor, Producer shall promptly repay to Company such theretofore paid monies.

15. (a) Company and Producer shall mutually select the individual producer of the Masters embodying Artist's performances. If the individual producer approved to produce Masters hereunder is not then on Company's staff, Producer, shall engage and pay for the services rendered by such individual producer, and Company shall be under no obligation in connection therewith. If the individual producer approved to produce Masters hereunder is then on Company's staff, Company shall furnish and pay for the services rendered by such individual producer, and in respect of records derived from Masters produced by such individual producer, four (4%) percent shall be deducted from the otherwise applicable royalty rate provided for in paragraph 6(a) hereof, plus appropriate deductions and apportionments for Singles, foreign, club and other ancillary sales, etc. Notwithstanding the above, Company may engage the approved individual producer directly; in such event, Producer hereby directs Company to deduct, from all monies payable or becoming payable to Producer, the royalties that Company is obligated to pay such individual producer in respect of records derived from Masters produced by such individual producer. If the individual producer is on Company's staff or is engaged directly by Company, all sums to be recouped by Company from royalties due Producer pursuant to the provisions of this agreement shall be recouped from royalties due Producer after deducting the royalties due such individual producer.

(b) All monies paid by Company or its Licensees for independent promotion for records derived from any of the Masters shall be charged against and recouped from royalties due Producer hereunder.

16. Company may require Producer to formally give or withhold any approval or consent hereunder by notifying Producer in writing requesting the same and furnishing Producer with the information or material in respect of which such approval or consent is sought. Producer shall notify Company in writing of approval or disapproval within three (3) business days after such notice is received by Producer. _____ shall be deemed an authorized agent of Producer to give such approval or disapproval. In the event of disapproval or no consent, the reasons therefor shall be stated. Failure to so notify Company within the aforesaid period shall be deemed to be consent or approval.

17. During the Term, neither Producer nor Artist shall endorse any blank tape or other blank recording media (except professional tape and professional recording equipment) or otherwise permit Artist's Identification to be used in connection with such products.

18. (a) Producer agrees that, in all of Artist's endeavors in the entertainment field, Producer and Artist will exert best efforts to cause Artist to be billed as an "Arista Records Exclusive Recording Artist".

(b) Producer agrees to furnish Company at no cost twenty (20) tickets for each of Artist's concert performances during the Term hereof.

19. This agreement has been entered into in the State of New York, and the validity, interpretation and legal effect of this agreement shall be governed by the laws of the State of New York applicable to contracts entered into and performed entirely within the State of New York, with respect to the determination of any claim, dispute or disagreement which may arise out of the interpretation, performance, or breach of this agreement. All claims, disputes or disagreements which may arise out of the interpretation, performance or breach of this agreement shall be submitted exclusively to the jurisdiction of the state courts of the State of New York or the Federal District courts located in New York City. Any process in any such action or proceeding may among other methods be served upon Producer by delivering or mailing the same pursuant to paragraph 23 hereof. Any such delivery or mail service shall be deemed to have the same force and effect as personal service within the State of New York. Producer hereby submits to the jurisdiction of the aforesaid courts.

20. This writing sets forth the entire understanding between the parties with respect to the subject matter hereof. No modification or waiver of any provision of or of any default under this agreement shall be binding upon Company or Producer unless confirmed in writing by an authorized officer of Company and Producer. No such waiver shall constitute a waiver by Company of compliance thereafter with the same or any other provision or of its right to enforce the same or any other provision thereafter.

21. (a) The term "Artist" or "Group" as used in this agreement, shall be deemed to refer jointly and severally to the individuals first mentioned herein as comprising Artist and to such other individual(s) who during the Term shall then comprise the Group. The substitution of any individuals in the Group and the adding to or subtracting from the individuals comprising the Group shall be done only with the written approval of Company. Any such substituted or added individual shall be deemed to have agreed to be bound by all of the terms and conditions of this agreement. Producer shall notify Company immediately in writing if any member of the Group leaves the Group or if any individual is added to the Group or if the Group disbands; in such case, Company shall have the right, to be exercised within ninety (90) days after Company's receipt of such written notice, to terminate the Term of this agreement by notifying Producer in writing. If Company so requests within said ninety (90) day period, Producer shall deliver to Company a "demo" tape embodying the performances of the members of the Group at that time or, at Company's election, shall hold a live audition by such members, and the ninety (90) day period in which Company may elect to terminate the Term of this agreement shall be deemed to commence upon the date of the delivery to Company of the demo tape or upon the date of the live audition, as the case may be.

(b) Each of the individuals comprising the Group agree that, if any of them leave the Group or if the Group disbands, Company shall have the irrevocable option to be exercised within ninety (90) days after Company receives written notice that an individual has left the Group (or, if within such ninety (90) day period Company so requests a demo tape or live audition by such leaving member, within ninety (90) days following the date of delivery to Company of the demo tape or of the live audition) to enter into an exclusive individual recording agreement with any one or more of such individuals (including for a Term equal to the initial Contract Period and any and all Option Periods provided for herein), except that: the royalties payable to such individual shall be two-thirds of the royalties provided for herein; the amount to be paid for Recording Costs shall be the amount provided for in the first sentence of paragraph 8(a); and there shall be no payments made pursuant to paragraph 9. If the Group has an unearned balance (i.e., unrecouped advances or other outstanding offsets against Producer's royalties hereunder), then Company shall have the right to apply sums payable to each such leaving member pursuant to any such exclusive individual recording agreement against the Group's unearned balance; provided, however, if the Group has not disbanded, Company shall not be entitled to recoup more than a prorata share of the Group's unearned balance (i.e., a ratio based on the number one (1) compared to the total number of Group members as of the date the leaving member concerned enters into an exclusive individual recording agreement with Company) from sums payable to such leaving member. Each such individual recording agreement shall remain in full force and effect whether or not Company exercises its right to any or all Option Periods with respect to the Group, or with respect to any of the other individuals comprising the Group.

22. (a) Company shall have the right, but not the obligation, to produce one (1) or more film(s) or videotape(s) ("Video(s)") based upon Artist's performance(s). Producer warrants and represents that Artist shall be available to perform for the production of each Video and that Producer and Artist shall fully cooperate with the producer, director and all other production personnel in the production of each Video. For each Video that Company so produces, Company will bear all of the production costs contained within a budget described in paragraph 28(b) below.

(b) Each such Video shall be produced in accordance with a written budget approved by Company prior to its production. If production costs for the production of a particular Video exceed those contained in the applicable approved budget, then Producer shall be solely responsible for and shall pay such excess costs if such excess costs are incurred as a result of Producer's and/or Artist's acts or omissions, provided, however, that Company shall have the right to pay such excess and, without limiting its rights, to deduct the amount of such excess from any sums which may be payable to Producer under this agreement. Each Video shall be shot on a date or dates and at a location to be approved by Company. Company and Producer shall mutually approve the Composition which is to be the subject of the Video, the concept and storyboard of the Video, the director and any other creative participants of the Video. A Composition embodied on a Single is hereby deemed approved by Producer.

(c) Company shall pay to Producer the following royalties for the sale by Company or its Licensees of Videos, against which all amounts incurred and/or paid by Company in respect of the production costs of Videos and all other advances paid to or on behalf of Producer shall be chargeable:

(i) A royalty of ten (10%) percent of the retail list price for all Videos sold by Company for distribution in the United States and not returned (rather than the royalty under paragraph 6(a) hereof).

(ii) A royalty of seven and one-half (7-1/2%) percent of the retail list price for all Videos sold by Company or its regular foreign distributors for distribution outside of the United States, as to which Company receives payment (rather than the royalty under paragraph 6(b) hereof).

(iii) A royalty of fifty (50%) percent of Company's net receipts for all other commercial exploitations of Videos.

(iv) The above amounts shall be inclusive of any payments required to be made to any third parties.

(v) Except as otherwise provided herein, the provisions of paragraphs 6 and 7 concerning the computation and payment of record royalties shall be applicable to the payment of Video royalties.

(d) With respect to records containing separate portions of audio alone and audio coupled with visual images (e.g., CDVs), Company shall pay to Producer the royalties set forth in paragraph 6 hereof, rather than the royalties set forth in paragraph 28(c) above; provided, however, Company shall be entitled to charge fifty (50%) percent of the royalties payable to Producer in respect of such records against the production costs of Videos.

(e) Company shall be entitled to recoup fifty (50%) percent of the production costs of Videos from the royalties payable to Producer under paragraph 6 hereof.

(f) Producer shall issue (or shall cause the music publishing companies having the right to do so to issue) (i) worldwide, perpetual synchronization licenses, and (ii) perpetual licenses for public performance in the United States (to the extent that ASCAP and BMI are unable to issue same) to Company at no cost for the promotional use and commercial exploitation of all Controlled Compositions in Videos effective as of the commencement of production of the applicable Video (and Producer's execution of this agreement shall constitute the issuance of such licenses by any music publishing company which is owned or controlled directly or indirectly by Producer, Artist or the individual producer of a Master embodied in a particular Video or by any party associated or affiliated with Producer, Artist or such individual producer). If Producer fails to cause any such music publishing company to issue any such license to Company, and if Company thereafter pays any fee to such music publishing company in order to obtain any such license, then Company shall have the right, without limiting its rights, to deduct the amount of such license fee from any sums payable to Producer under this agreement.

(g) Each Video shall be Company's exclusive property throughout the Territory and Company shall have the right to exploit each Video for promotional and commercial purposes in perpetuity throughout the Territory. Company shall have no obligation to pay Producer or Artist in connection with Company's distribution, exhibition and broadcast of each Video for promotional purposes throughout the Territory.

IN WITNESS WHEREOF, the parties hereto have executed this agreement the day and year hereinabove first written.

ARISTA RECORDS, INC.

By _____

_____

By _____

Federal Tax Identification Number

_____

APPENDIX 10

Organizations, Unions, and Guilds

American Federation of Musicians (AF of M), 1501 Broadway, Suite 600, New York, NY 10036. (212) 869-1330

American Federation of Television and Radio Artists (AFTRA), 260 Madison Ave., New York, NY 10016. (212) 532-0800

American Guild of Musical Artists (AGMA), 1727 Broadway, New York, NY 10019-5284. (212) 265-3687

American Guild of Variety Artists (AGVA), 184 Fifth Ave., New York, NY 10010. (212) 675-1003

American Society of Composers, Authors and Publishers (ASCAP), One Lincoln Plaza, New York, NY 10023. (212) 595-3050

Broadcast Music, Inc. (BMI), 320 West 57th St., New York, NY 10019. (212) 586-2000

In Los Angeles: 8730 Sunset Boulevard, 3rd Floor West, Los Angeles, CA 90069. (310) 659-9109

In Nashville: 10 Music Square East, Nashville, TN 37203. (615) 401-2000

Conference of Personal Managers, East, 1650 Broadway, Suite 705, New York, NY 10019. (212) 265-3366

Conference of Personal Managers, West, 10231 Riverside Drive, Suite 303, Toluca Lake, CA 91602. (818) 762-6276

Country Music Association (CMA), 1 Music Circle South, Nashville, TN 37203. (615) 244-2840

Gospel Music Association, 1205 Division Street, Nashville, TN 37203. (615) 242-0303

The Harry Fox Agency, Inc., 711 Third Ave., 8th Floor, New York, NY 10017. (212) 370-5330

Music Performance Trust Funds, 1501 Broadway, Suite 202, New York, NY 10036-5503. (212) 391-3950

National Academy of Recording Arts and Sciences (NARAS), 3402 Pico Blvd., Santa Monica, CA 90405 (310) 392-3777

In New York: 156 West 56th St., Suite 1701, New York, NY 10019. (212) 245-5440

National Music Publishers Association, 711 Third Ave., 8th Floor, New York, NY 10017. (212) 370-5330

Recording Industry Association of America, Inc. (RIAA), 1330 Connecticut Ave. NW, Suite 300, Washington, DC 20036. (202) 775-0101

SESAC, 55 Music Square East, Nashville, TN 37203. (615) 320-0055

The Songwriters Guild of America, 1560 Broadway, Suite 1306, New York, NY 10036. (212) 768-7902

In Los Angeles: 6430 Sunset Boulevard, #1002, Hollywood, CA 90028. (213) 462-1108

In Nashville: 1222 16th Ave. South, #25, Nashville, TN 37212. (615) 329-1782

Index

Access, 107–108
Accounting, 59, 77, 80–82, 141, 216, 252–253
Adaptations, foreign, 200–201
Advances, 138–139
Advertising, 218
Advisability, of representation, 35
Appointment designation, 48
Appointments, securing of, 26–28
Arrangements, foreign, 200–201
Artist(s): and conference, 35–40, 44; evaluation of, 83–88; finding of manager by, 20–30; finding of, 31–33
Artist and Repertoire (A&R), 216–217
Artistic control, 141
Artist management. *See* Management
Artist-manager relationship, 1–61, 238–239
Artist relations, 218
Artist's development team, 114–121
At-source payments, 199–200
Attitude, 233–234
Attorneys, 77, 78–80, 81–82
Authority, appointment of, 48–50

Banking, 70
Belief, 13–14
Blackout period, 57
Booking agency, 181–182, 237–238
Bookkeeping, 73–74
Breaks, 105–113
Budgeting, 74–75, 252–253
Business, form of, 64–69
Business advisers, 81–82
Business affairs, company, 216
Business managers, 77, 81–82
Business review, 234–235

Career(s): building blocks of, 110–113; expectations for, 37; launching of, 13–19; maintenance and control of, 203–239; management, three truths of, 11–12; planning of, 63–104; review and evaluation of, 233–239; right manager for, 37–38; taking charge of, 19
Career development, company, 218–219
Charisma, 92–93
Clients, attracting of, 32; *See also* Artist(s)
Clubs, 172–176
Collaboration, in planning, 99–100
College concerts, 177
Commercials, 183, 186–188, 192–193
Commissions, 38, 57–58, 182. *See also* Management compensation
Commitment, career, 16
Concerts, 177–180
Conflicts of interest, 39–40
Contacts, industry, 109–110
Contract(s): live performance, 180–181; management, 45–61; merchandising, commercial, and endorsement, 191–192; recording, *see* Record deals
Controlled compositions, 141–142

Corporate sponsorships, 183–184, 189–191, 193
Corporation, of artist, 66–67
Costs: music video, 160–161; recording, 138
Creative inventory, 83–96
Creative review, 235–236
Credit, use of, 253
Cross-collateralization, 139

Decision time, 44
Definitions, contract, 60
Demo, 123, 124–125
Desire, for a career, 15
Developmental deal, 125
Development department, 218–219
Development team, 114–121
Disputes, 58
Distribution, 217
Do-it-yourself promotion campaigns, 96

Earning pattern, of artist, 248
Education, of manager, 108–109
Employment agency disclaimer, 49–50
Endorsements, 183–184, 188–191, 193
Equipment insurance, 72–73
Estate planning, 255
Excise taxes, 136–137
Exclusive personal services agreement, 126–127
Exclusivity, 52–54
Exposure, 87–88
Extensions, of contract, 55–56

Fairs, 177, 178
Feel for business, 110
Fees. *See* Commissions
Festivals, 177–178
Film, 150, 158, 169–170
Finished master recording, 123–124
First impression, 28–30
Flexibility, 112
Follow-through, 111
Foreign music publishing, 198–201
Foreign record sales, 195–198
Free goods, 137

Global issues, 194–202
Goals, 100–104

Historical profile, 87
Hotels, 176

Image, 85–87, 88–94, 101–102; projecting and marketing of, 94–96
Income, music publishing, 148–151
Indemnification clauses, 58–59
Insurance, 71–73
Investments, 254
Involvement, reasons for, 35

Knowledge of industry, 108, 109–110

Legal issues, 60, 76, 168, 216
Liability insurance, 72
Life insurance, 73
Limited liability company, 67

Limited management, 18–19
Listening rooms, 174–175
Live performance contracts, 180–181
Lounges, 173
Luck, 112–113

Management: alternatives of, 16–19; nature of, 6–7; and record deals, 7–12, 122–142
Management compensation, 38–49, 50–52. *See also* Commissions
Management contract, 45–61
Manager(s): assets of, 108–110; background and track record of, 37–38; and conference, 40–44; day in life of, 204–213, 243–247; death or disability of, 57–58; duties of, in contract, 48–49; finding of artist by, 30–33; finding of, 20–30; nonresponsibilities of, 10–11; product, 219; qualifications of, 8–10; reasons for involvement with, 35–36; right, 37–38; role of, 6–7; *See also* Artist-manager relationship; Business managers
Manager's checklist, 42–44
Marketing, 94–96, 217
Mechanical royalties, 149
Merchandising, 183–185, 193
Money: managing, 251–256. *See also* Management compensation
Motion pictures, 150, 158, 169–170
Multitrack demo, 123, 124–125
Music publishing, 143–157, 198–201
Music videos, 158, 159–161

Name, choice of, 93
National club chains, 176
Negotiating record contract, 134–142
"No commercials" policy, 192–193

Packaging deduction, 136
Parties, private, 177
Partnership, 66
Percentage base, 50–51
Performance theaters, 175–176
Performing exposure, 87–88
Performing rights, 149–150
Persistence, 30, 111
Personal appearances, 95–96, 171–182, 201–202
Personnel, 69, 127, 128, 129
Physical appearance, 84–85
Planner, vision of, 98–99
Planning, 63–104
Poise and presence, 85–86
Power of attorney, 49
Preliminary exploratory conference, 35–44
Preparation, and career, 110–111
Press, 218
Press kit, 95
Printed music, sale of, 150
Private parties, 177
Producer, 125–127, 236
Producer's royalty, 139–140
Product managers, 219
Promotion(s), 140, 178–180, 217–218. *See also* Marketing
Protective functions, 229–230
Publicity, 218
Public relations, 228–229

Publishing, music, 143–157

Quality recording, 123–125
Questions, right, 34–44

Radio, 158, 165–169
Realism, 112
Record company: approaching of, 132–134; evaluation by, 130–132; evaluation of, 237; helping of, 214–222
Record deals, 7–12, 122–142
Recording, quality, 123–125
Recording and release requirements, 140
Recording exposure, 88
Record sales, foreign, 195–198
Rehearsals, 129
Reimbursement of expenses, 52
Renewals, of contract, 55–56
Retirement, 255
Returns, reserves for, 137
Road. *See* Touring
Rock clubs, 173–174
Royalties, 135–136, 137–140, 141, 149, 198, 199

Sales department, company, 217
Sales kit, 28–30
Self-image, and goals, 101–102
Self-management, 17–18, 100
Self-publishing, 153–154
Service mark, 69–70
Showcase, artist-sponsored, 175
Showcase clubs, 174–175
Show rooms, 173–174
Skills, 93–94
Sole proprietorship, 65–66
Songwriters' issues, 84, 199, 235–236
Stardom, achieving, 257–261
Studio, finding of, 127–128
Subpublishing, 198–201
Success, 120–121, 241–250
Synchronization fees, 150
Syndication, 168

Tactics, developing of, 103–104
Taking charge of career, 19
Talent(s), 14–15, 93–94
Taxes, 73–74, 136–137, 254–255
Team, development, 114–121
Technology, and radio, 168–169
Television, 158–159, 161–165
Termination, of contract, 56–57
Term(s): basic, in contracts, 47–60, 135–142; of contracts, 54–58, 140
Timelines, goal, 101
Time of payment, 51–52
Total management, 19
Touring, 141, 185, 189–191, 223–232
Translations, 200–201
Travel arrangements, 228
Trusts, 59–60

Unique sound, 84
Updating, of plan, 104

Vehicle insurance, 72

Warranties, 58–59

BillboardBooks

IF YOU ENJOYED THIS TITLE, YOU MIGHT
WANT OTHER BOOKS IN OUR CATALOG.

THE REAL DEAL:
How to Get Signed to a Record Label From A to Z
by Daylle Deanna Schwartz
Crucial information and advice that any musician desiring a record deal needs. Explains the roles of agent, attorney, A&R person, producer, and manager; copyright and music publishing; the importance of live performance; ways to build a following; using networking; the pros and cons of releasing an independent recording. With advice from top creative and business pros and a resource section. 256 pages. Paperback. $16.95. 0-8230-7611-3.

THIS BUSINESS OF MUSIC,
Seventh Edition by M. William Krasilovsky and Sidney Shemel
The bible of the music business, with over 250,000 copies sold. A practical guide to the music industry for publishers, writers, record companies, producers, artists, and agents. Provides detailed information on virtually every economic, legal, and financial aspect of the complex business of music. 736 pages. Hardcover. $29.95. 0-8230-7755-1.

THE BILLBOARD GUIDE TO MUSIC PUBLICITY,
Revised Edition by Jim Pettigrew, Jr.
Provides career-minded musicians and their representatives with key information about getting media exposure, preparing effective publicity materials, and developing short-term and long-range publicity. Discusses desktop publishing, compact disks, copy-editing, and includes a recommended reading list. 176 pages. 16 illustrations. Paperback. $18.95. 0-8230-7626-1.

The above titles should all be available from your neighborhood bookseller. If you don't find a copy on the shelf, books can also be ordered either through the store or directly from Watson-Guptill Publications. To order copies by phone or to request information on any of these titles, please call our toll-free number: 1-800-278-8477. To order copies by mail, send a check or money order for the cost of the book, with $2.00 postage and handling for one book and $.50 for each additional book, plus applicable sales tax in the states of CA, DC, IL, OH, MA, NJ, NY, PA, TN, and VA, to:

Watson-Guptill Publications
PO Box 2013
Lakewood, NJ 08701-9913